CW00394834

GIRLVERT

A Barnacle Book
Los Angeles | New York

A PORNO MEMOIR

ORIANA SMALL AKA ASHLEY BLUE

A Barnacle Book
453 South Spring Street, Suite 531
Los Angeles, CA 90013
abarnaclebook.com
davenaz.com/oriana
askori.com

Cover illustration by Corey Smith
B&W photos by Dennis McGrath

Design by Tamra Rolf

Second Printing

Library of Congress Cataloging-in-Print Data
Small, Oriana, 1981–
Girlvert: A Porno Memoir / by Oriana Small AKA Ashley Blue

1. Small, Oriana, 1981– 2. Porn actress—United States—Biography.
3. Ashley Blue (alias)

Includes Select Filmography (p. 306)

ISBN-13: 978-0982505632
ISBN-13: 978-0982505687 (ebook)
ISBN-13: 978-0982505694 (limited art edition—SOLD OUT)

The woman inspects her hand. She holds it away from her face and looks at it as if it does not quite belong to her, as if its history is something she has read. Thirty-two years before, the hand had gone into her mouth regularly.

—BEN GREENMAN, *"Her Hand (Atlanta, 2015)"*

TABLE OF CONTENTS

GIRLVERT

A PORNO MEMOIR

CHAPTER ONE

MODELING AND RECREATIONAL SEX

*"FIGURE MODELS NO EXPERIENCE NECESSARY
WORLD MODELING..."*

THIS was the ad. I was dissecting the classified section of the *Los Angeles Daily News*. The paper was spread out all over the carpet of my studio apartment. I was living in a raunchy part in Hollywood. Transvestite prostitutes worked the street outside my window. It was three in the afternoon. I read each of the ads twice, desperately searching for my next potential workplace failure and limiting my focus to any job not requiring previous experience. I kept coming back to this one: *World Modeling*. The word scared me though, *modeling*. Who exactly did I think I was, responding to a modeling ad?

I hung up on the guy who answered the first time I dialed this so-called World Modeling office. I gathered the guts to speak and tried again. I hadn't expected a guy to be answering the phone at a modeling agency. The smooth-operating actor's voice on the other end told me to come in for a consultation, if I was interested.

"Just like that?" I said. "Don't you want to know what I look like first? I could be five hundred pounds for all you know."

"It doesn't matter. Just come into our office, and we'll talk more about it. I can explain more when you get here." His voice was so overtly persuasive that it struck me as suspiciously sleazy.

I was nervous. This was a stupid idea. They're going to say no. Definitely. Maybe they will say something worse. I'll be a laughing stock. Long after I leave their offices, they'll still be joking about how *I* came in to apply. What if they told me I was too short? Or too fat! Not once in my life has anyone told me I could be a model. It was an entirely far-fetched dream for a girl as average as me, *medium* in every way. I was neither tall nor gorgeous, big-eyed nor buxom...I would call myself *cute*, at best.

As I drove down the 101, the thought occurred to me: Maybe I could just model my feet. My feet look pretty good. But then I remembered the hair on my toes. And my second toe is noticeably longer than my big toe. Models have to be perfect, right? No modeling agency would give me a shot in hell. It would end in disappointment.

On the Van Nuys exit, I began to brace myself for the blow. I rehearsed what I was going to say when these people told me, "Sorry, you just don't have the right requirements to be a model. Come back when you've grown about a foot taller, midget!"

But, oh, how I needed a job! I'd been fired, asked to quit, and just plain not shown up (my favorite technique) for my last four jobs, all in only five months time. I'd recently quit Moorpark Community College after already dropping out of art school in San Francisco, had moved out of my aunt and uncle's home in Thousand Oaks, and I was on my own. I hated Thousand Oaks. It was stale, and all of the people in it were stale. Going to class seemed like a waste. I wanted to figure out all the answers to life on my terms. I knew where I could find them. I moved to Hollywood. What can I say. I was young.

I fantasized about being a Hollywood burnout or a rock groupie, someone who eclipsed herself before the age of thirty. I was too young, perhaps too shallow, to understand anything beyond skin-deep attraction and barfly philosophies. Work was not my number one priority in life. Going out, partying, and having fun came before anything else. And my idea of having fun consisted of experimenting with drugs and having sex with older men. Even if they weren't conventionally handsome, I always found something appealing about the older guys I slept with. Anything from the way their musky armpits smelled to an out-of-state accent. There was no rhyme or reason to my selection. Most of them were one-night stands, unless they had a big dick. I liked that.

Ever since high school, I was really into one-night-only sexual encounters. It could be as little as a make-out session or a blow-job. I loved meeting new men and going off somewhere to have sex. I never thought of it as "giving it up." I got something out of it, too. Instead of orgasms, I received knowledge. I was learning about men's bodies, and I was learning about my own body. Sex gave me a feeling of power. Sex *is* power. Sex made me feel pretty, wanted, needed, and smart. I did all I could to make those feelings stronger.

I have never been good at hiding my feelings—or ignoring them—and one thing I felt for certain was that the traditional service industry—waitressing, secretarial work, even lobbying/political activism—was not for me.

The modeling agency was on Van Nuys Boulevard in Sherman Oaks. I'd envisioned a tall, professional building with sleek, tinted glass on the outside. Imagining it, I could almost smell the spacious, fashionably decorated lobby, the waiting area full of headshots and résumés. I parked on the street, looking for it. I was so full of nervous energy that I forgot to pay the meter.

The building—the building in my mind—was not there. Instead, the door to World Modeling led up some ratty carpeted stairs above a corridor between two other equally questionable businesses. I couldn't even ascertain what kind of establishments they were. The signs on the building's façade were too old and faded. I had noticed an adult video shop on the corner. Sherman Oaks *sounds* nice, but Van Nuys Boulevard is still Van Nuys Boulevard: a good place to disappear to if you want to run away from home and live a miserable life. Ride the bus and do heroin.

I was wearing a cute little lavender dress and heeled sandals. I felt pretty. My skin was clear. Twenty year old, fresh-faced Oriana Rene Small. I took a deep breath before I opened the door to the suite.

Instead of inhaling an atmosphere of professional paper scents—magazine proofs and photographers' contact sheets—I took in a breath of cigarette smoke mingled with layers of dust and grime. Meekly, I pushed the door all the way open and found myself wrong on all counts about absolutely everything I'd imagined this to be. Covering every inch of wall space were pictures of female porno stars. Porn movie posters proudly and loudly blanketed the entire office. Several of them blazoned "Nikita Denise." It wasn't a small place but was so full of tits, G-strings, made-up faces, and big flouncy hair that it seemed to be caving in. There was a disgusting, torn-up, shabby brown couch. Two people sat on it, young and immoral-looking. I wondered if this place also casted for *Cops*.

An oily, tan-faced man behind one of the many desks welcomed me. He was the one I talked to on the phone: Tyler. My boyfriend's name was Tyler. I cautiously sat down in a chair in front of his desk. If there was anything filthy or smelly on the seat, I didn't want it sticking to me. I wished I could hover.

"Oriana, a pleasure."

"What kind of modeling is this, Tyler?"

He looked at me in all seriousness. "Call me Ty. We do primarily adult casting."

"Is this PORN?" I wanted to be polite, but I was fucking freaking. The obvious was too strange here. My underarms soaked with sweat.

"Yes. This is porn. If you want to get started, let me have a form of picture ID so I can make a copy. I," he cleared his throat, "of course need to make sure that you're at least eighteen years of age. Then, fill this out, and when you're ready, we'll go into the next room and take some Polaroids."

"You want me to take my clothes off? Here? Are you serious?" I didn't like being naked in a doctor's office.

"Yeah, we'll just be in that room, right over there," he pointed. "We can shut the door, if you'd like."

There were two or three more men behind desks, carrying on with business calls. I shut my ears to what they were saying. Already, my conscience had to be cleared of this experience. I got up, clutching my purse and my stomach. I am abrupt by nature, but I didn't even try to be polite. I was dizzy and fumbling. My face was completely red. I didn't know what to say, how to react. All I could muster was the same awkward smile I always resort to in awkward situations. I felt shame just being in the presence of these people.

"I'm sorry, I have to go. I can't do this right now. I have to think about this. I...I have to talk about it with my boyfriend. I'm sorry, I didn't mean to waste your time. His name is Tyler. Um, like yours. His name. My boyfriend's name is Tyler. Ah, bye."

Guilt was leading into shock and my face burned with embarrassment. What have I done? I thought. This was wrong! Oh, I am such a bad person! *I should have never come here*, I repeated in my head over and over, hoping that would make the huge new

scarlet letter "P" on my chest disappear. P for PORNOGRAPHY.
However, it was not a simple guilt. I was ashamed partly because
porn was supposed to be an evil, vile thing, but moreover, I was
ashamed because deep down inside, it turned me on. Coincid-
ing with my shock and surprise, I was allured. I don't think I
realized it as I shot out the door, eyes averted to everyone else's
in the room, but I was not going to be able to put this newly
discovered world behind me.

I fled the building, hurrying down the dingy stairway. I
stepped out on the sidewalk, looking down and turning my head
away from the cars on the street. I didn't want anyone to see me
leaving that place. The guy—Ty—the way he said "This is porn" so
matter-of-factly, made me feel suddenly and completely ignorant.
Of course some open-call advertisement in the very back of a city
newspaper is not going to be for real models. "Figure modeling"—
come on! I was just some medium-sized idiot with an outlandish
hope that I could land a legitimate modeling job.

No, it had to be something else for me. For some rare, minor-
ity breed of women, it's the high fashion catwalk. For the rest of
us, it's porn.

My stomach was a wreck. The nervousness made me sweat;
my armpits were reeking over my Teen Spirit deodorant. I ran
the last yards to my car in horror. In addition to a spasm of diarrhea threatening my bowels, I now had a motherfucking parking
ticket. Tyler!—I frantically called my boyfriend while driving back
from the valley. I must have sounded like someone who had nar-
rowly escaped abduction.

I pulled my little white Toyota Corolla into the single parking
spot at our apartment. Tyler was waiting for me outside, his
big brown eyes wide with worry. The diarrhea was explosive.

Everything—body and mind—was shaken up. I told Tyler about stumbling upon the porno agency. My shock was at a crescendo, and was complicated by my compulsion to share with Tyler my brewing revelation that I had to go back. I was flustered and confused about it all the way home. A darker side of me wanted to know more, more, more. I couldn't understand exactly why at that time. All I knew was that I could not find out alone.

"My god, baby. What happened?"

Tyler was sweet, and I loved him more than I'd ever loved anyone before him. He loved me with the same intensity. He was for the most part a caring boyfriend, and he was sincerely alarmed at what appeared to be a serious trauma. How was I going to explain to him where I'd been without feeling stupid for thinking that it was a real modeling agency to begin with? Would he believe me? He might think I went on purpose!—and be disgusted, thinking I was a whore. I felt like I had auditioned to be a prostitute, just like the working girls outside our window. And how, above all else, could I explain the confusing and complex notion that the whole experience was turning me on? But I had to take that chance and tell him. This wouldn't be the first time I would be found guilty of possessing a wandering eye. I'd been told already once before, "No more lies."

I had once cheated on Tyler, and I didn't tell him or anyone else about it. I thought he would never know, and therefore it would never hurt him. We'd only been dating for about three months. He was so fucking sexy, slim, over six feet tall with a megawatt smile and big, pouty lips. He was the boy of my dreams. We moved in together only weeks after we first met at a gay club on Santa Monica Boulevard. It was love at first sight. I dumped the boyfriend I was with at the time over the phone the day after I met Tyler.

Still, I cheated on him. I loved him. He was romantic, hand-some, artistic, and charming. Before Tyler, I had never taken any relationship seriously. I was only twenty years old, and there were a lot of dudes around. My mom used to cheat on my dad, and she was a liar, too. It's just part of being a woman, I thought.

Tyler found out I fucked my ex because he read it in my diary. I didn't think he was sneaky enough to do something like read my private diary. He must have had his suspicions. I wrote all about it and how bad, guilty, and good it felt to secretly fuck this other guy. The other man, my ex, had a big dick, and he was thirty-six years old. He was a kind of father figure. He loaned me the money to get into my Hollywood apartment, but he wasn't a sugar daddy. He made me pay all of the money back in full. I'd promised Tyler I'd never cheat on or lie to him again. I had to tell him I was in Sherman Oaks talking to a porno agent, because the percolating excitement of it all made me feel as though I had cheated on him—the same mix of guilt and pleasure.

"I saw an ad for models wanted in the *Daily News*. So, I went to their office today. I just went to talk to them, for a meeting, and so, I go in...and, well, it was...*porn!*" My voice was shaky, barely audible. I didn't want to say it too loud. Someone in our building might hear.

"Are you serious? You're fucking kidding me! You swear?" He was smiling ear-to-ear and then busted out laughing. "No way!"

I grabbed onto him, and he hugged me. He didn't show disgust or call me a whore and he didn't even accuse or suspect me of doing anything with the guys that worked at the agency. He wasn't angry or condemning. He was happy. Thrilled. Ecstatic and excited, to be exact. He *did* think I went to audition for porn on purpose, and he was happy about it.

"That's so funny! Oh, you're upset. It's okay, don't worry. So what? Okay, I believe you, you didn't realize you were going to end up at a porn office. That's great!"

"Well, I don't know what to think. I was scared shitless, but I can't stop thinking about it. I mean, it's porno." After a lot of back and forth and false rationalizing of reasons why I would never do porn, I finally asked, "Do you think you would ever want to...do it? I wouldn't do it by myself, not without you." I looked down at the floor and fidgeted my foot from side to side. My eyes could barely meet his when I uttered the question. I was so embarrassed to ask this of Tyler, but my curiosity was mounting fast. I felt like I needed his permission, his approval. I always needed to bounce my ideas off of him, if only to gauge by his reaction if I was a bad person. Tyler had the truer heart of the two of us, and I felt a little inadequate with my own judgment.

"Yeah! Oh, my god, YES! Let's do it! Let's do porn!" It was as if I had just proposed marriage. And as with the quick and rash decisions of newlyweds, we just knew that everything was going to be awesome.

We were going to ruin our lives. Together.

The thing is, porno was not too far removed from what we'd already been doing sexually, and maybe that's why it seemed the next natural step—with no cause for debate—would be to video-tape it. Long before I'd ever seen it in a porno movie, group sex was introduced to me by Tyler and his Norwegian rocker buddy, Colby. They'd presented the concept of double penetration with cheerleaders' enthusiasm, and I'm a total pushover when it comes to a dare. I also didn't want to be uncool, so I jumped into the wonderful world of DP. Everybody wins with a DP. Two guys can fuck a girl at once, and it's virtually invented for girls who just can't get enough cock. It became a weekend goal of ours to find an orgy. I thought that everyone in Hollywood did coke and got double penetrated.

We would all take ecstasy and sniff lines of cocaine. I loved both of those drugs and was willing to do anything while I was on them. Getting fucked by Tyler and Colby at the same time was very cool—at the time. They both were good-natured, fun guys that everyone liked. They described themselves as erotic beings who knew everything about the makings of great sex. Tyler was beautiful, and Colby wasn't so bad. He was tall and had white-blonde hair. I couldn't say he was downright sexy, but he definitely had a look. His style was all about Von Dutch, and Tyler worshiped it. He was a former bass player in a number of local Hollywood bands, and he was obsessed with fucking lots of different women. Colby talked about the girls that he fucked all the time. He told us more than once that his record of girls fucked in one night was eleven.

What did I know about sexual confidence at twenty years old? Not a lot. I never thought I was hot enough or pretty enough for Tyler. I definitely didn't feel hip enough to be a chick that Colby would be interested in. They were charming and always bragged about the hot chicks that had all fallen victim to their love. I ate all this shit up. Every word from their lips might as well have come straight from the *Kama Sutra* itself. When they fucked me at the same time, in my ass and in my pussy, and when I sucked their cocks simultaneously, I felt special. They wanted to do all this crazy stuff with me, and I was the crazy girl that was down for it. I was the sexy little nymph who could turn them on. I felt important.

Yes, I felt important when Tyler and Colby double-penetrated me. Admitting it seems silly. This is the honest truth, though: I wanted to please them so badly. Validation from them was everything. All Tyler had to do was coax me a little, and I would have one cock in my mouth and get fucked by the other. Some nights there were more random guys that I really didn't know, but Colby said they were cool. I trusted him, his opinion. Colby was the friend that Tyler looked up to the most. He idolized Colby. The fact that he loved to party with us had deep meaning for Tyler.

They first introduced the idea of DP as if it were this really trendy new energy drink or video game that I would just love. Never mind the fact that I didn't play video games or that it was three in the morning. But I was game. If it meant we were still going to party, then I was up for anything.

"You guys have never done a DP? Oh, shit! You have got to try it. It's so much fun, and it feels really good! Ora, every girl who has ever done this with me loved it!" Apparently, Colby did them all the time in LA, and back home in Norway. He was smiling so much and was such a trusted friend. I just smiled back and sniffed a line, silently noting every time he mispronounced my name.

"Well. What? I mean, I don't know. How does that work? How is it possible? Won't I just break open? I don't think you both will fit." I was puzzled about how much my small frame could actually accommodate. Probably a lot, I figured, since women smaller than me have babies. The ecstasy, coke, and booze made me feel like anything was possible. This was true.

As soon as we started having this kind of sex, we just wanted to do it all the time. I ended up being pretty decent at taking two cocks at the same time. Each time it happened, the sex got rougher and dirtier. I started shoving my hand completely into my own mouth and down my throat. It had always felt good to do this when I was barfing up my food alone over the toilet, so I just incorporated the gratifying feeling of self-purging into our sex. Tyler, Colby, and the others would take turns putting their hands in, and then their cocks. We did so much coke that we would all get dry mouth. I solved the problem by reaching down my throat, producing enough saliva to rejuvenate even the most drug-parched tongue.

After I had cheated on him, I began to ask Tyler to grab me and pull my hair. I started to want some pain during our sexual encounters. He smacked me in the face while I blew him. He never hit me hard with his hand, but he would with his cock. I craved the physical infliction because I felt bad about myself for my infidelity. I wanted to show Tyler that he was important to me, so I gave this power over to him.

Once, I was face down on our bed, in our apartment, while high on ecstasy. All I wanted was for us all to be happy, having a good time. We all began fucking. Tyler was on one side of my ass, Colby on the other. I knew someone was in there, just not who. Tyler and Colby had decent sized penises, about seven inches each. Their dicks seemed identical to me, even though I constantly reassured Tyler that his was bigger and felt better. In my daze, I heard them giggling.

"What are you laughing at?" I was going to get upset. Were they making a joke out of fucking me?

"No, Ora. We have both of our dicks in your ass! It's fucking great!"

"Yeah, baby, this is amazing!" Both of them looked like pubescent boys who were seeing their first tit all over again. I smiled and giggled into my pillow.

With all of the recreational sex and experimenting going on in our lives, I guessed Tyler and I were ready and willing to do porn. We both thought, Okay, let's just try it out once and see how we feel. Tyler liked watching X-rated movies, but he didn't need to watch them when we lived together. He didn't even need to masturbate because I was there for him anytime he needed to fuck or get a blowjob.

Tyler was the first guy to successfully have anal sex with me. I had always wanted it but never could execute it correctly. I first tried when I was seventeen, inspired by my mother's copy of Henry Miller's *Quiet Days in Clichy*, which, among other things, is about Mr. Miller fucking French prostitutes in the ass. I didn't know it would be so tight, so I told the boy to shove it in. We were young and didn't know a thing about lube or spit. My asshole was dry when the cock went in. It was so painful I passed out. Until Tyler, each attempt at anal was similar to the first. When I finally found someone who made it feel good, I was in love even more.

Tyler and I had the same philosophy: a hedonistic approach to life. Just like any young girl does with her first love, I planned to be with Tyler forever. "Whatever," we said to one another. "It's just porn. So what? Let's try anything. Let's be open-minded and not limit ourselves to what might be out there. We might enjoy it." This is just a small sampling of the rationale Tyler and I rolled through in order to put our minds at ease for trying porn. We needed to give ourselves the proper ration of bullshit excuses. We weren't hurting anyone. No one had to know. It's not a crime. It's legal. We will do it together, to be safe. If we don't like it we'll leave and never come back. It was our secret. We'd look out for each other. I loved Tyler, and he loved me, so why not? It was crazy, but so were we.

CHAPTER TWO

TRENT AND ASHLEY

I drove us back to World Modeling. This time I was going through that door with Tyler, whom I loved to the point of insanity. More than anything, I wanted to be just like him. Tyler was a true romantic that did not let silly things, like, oh, consequences, stop him from living every moment to its fullest. I had no idea what the physical standards were in porn, but I had seen VHS cover art shelving tapes as a video store clerk years before. The faces and bodies on those boxes looked ugly and crazy. I didn't have a lot of confidence trying out to be a fashion model, but I knew I was definitely pretty enough for porn. Tyler was a good-looking guy. It felt like a joke between us, cakewalking into a porn casting interview.

Ty, the agency guy, had us sit down and fill out paperwork. I was feeling much more at ease. My Tyler looked around with a huge smile on his face. The giant posters of the girls and their tits were ridiculous.

Everyone else in that place took it all very seriously. Ty was not laughing with us, and neither were his coworkers, who remained busily focused on multiple telephones luring scores of faceless women on the other ends of the lines into spreading their legs on film for money. Tyler and I were a couple of Beavis and Butt-Heads, as if we were in a human development class encountering the word "vagina" for the first time. Not one sentence read or marked on those papers went without a "huhhuhhuhuh" from either one of us. My paper read: BLOW JOB_____, ANAL_____, DP_____, SWALLOW_____, GANG BANG_____, INTERRACIAL_____, and so on.

"What is this part? What do I put here next to FACIAL?" I was trying my hardest not to laugh. I knew what it meant. I just wanted someone to explain it to me out loud. It was too funny.

Ty let out a sigh and explained. "That is a list of what you're willing to do on camera. The smart thing for a new girl to do is to start out doing solo stills for print work. After you've done all the magazines we can get for you, you move up to girl/girl stills and eventually boy/girl. Much later on in your career, you could consider doing anal, if that is something you decide. Oh, and don't forget to mention if you have training in anything special, like dance or theatre. You know, I'll tell you, the reason I've been kept working steadily in this business both in front of the camera and behind the scenes so long is because...I can act."

He was definitely acting. I resented Ty and his advice. Who was he to tell me how to live my new professional sex life? Ty was a little slimy and way out of shape, nothing like my Tyler. It's so strange that such opposite people can have the same name. I could see that he may have once had a decent face, but he was at least forty pounds overweight, probably more. It worried me to think that there were guys this unattractive doing porno movies.

As for his take on what I should allow myself to be seen doing on camera, well, no thank you. He couldn't possibly think that I, Oriana Small, would be doing porn as a career. Maybe I'll do it once, but not for anything long-term, was my thinking. What the hell was he saying about career longevity? Do people actually plan out that they are going to be fucking in a video for the rest of their lives?

No way would I be doing this for very long. We hadn't even done one scene, so it was kind of impossible to think about the long-term. How would I know if I could handle it? Or, much less, like it? How much will I regret it and for how long will it follow me? What if my family found out? Or my friends? My enemies? My teachers? Kids that I've babysat? Old neighbors? People I see on the street? How will it change the way they feel about me?

All I knew at that moment was that I did not want a stretched-out pornography career any more than I wanted a stretched-out twat. I disregarded everything that Ty said I should do. I checked YES for every category. YES ANAL, YES BOY/GIRL, YES DP, YES BLOWJOB, YES SWALLOW, YES FACIAL, YES CRE-AMPIE.

That should do it, I thought. That should give me a quick and lucrative stint in the profession. What I did listen to Ty about was the amounts of money I would be paid for each sexual act. Since my supportive and loving boyfriend and I were already engaging in these acts in our spare time, I didn't bat an eye at doing them on film. If it was already bad enough if anyone found out I was doing porn period, then what difference would it make which deeds I'd be committing while doing it? Who cares? Boy/girl was $800. Anal paid $1,000. DP, $1,200. I thought, If I'm going to ruin my chances at running for political office or teaching school, I might as well make as much money as I can doing it.

I also wanted to be as hardcore as I could be for personal reasons. For one, it would please Tyler and our friends so much, and pleasing everyone was very, very important to me. I had to keep going the distance sexually for myself, too. I had to soar. I wanted to live fully, extraordinarily, not just eking by with some weekend gang bangs from time to time. I realized I had never pursued much in my life with pure gusto, courage, and passion, and often felt caged, dull, and bored. Now, considering the far reaches sex could be pushed to, I felt free.

Tyler just smiled and laughed and cheered the whole process on. When it came time to take the naked Polaroids, we went into a side room and stripped down. There was an old couch in the corner and a fat man with a camera waiting by the door. With Tyler there, I felt protected. He was the one who had to get his dick hard for the picture. All I had to do was undress, stick my butt out, smile, and say "cheese." I got down on my knees and rubbed Tyler's cock on my cheek and stuck it in my mouth. Tyler gave the camera his megawatt smile. His dick went up and stuck out proudly. Even in those green, dismal Polaroids, we both looked so fresh and innocent. It was awkward but painless.

Ori became Ashley that day, and Tyler became Trent—our new porno identities.

CHAPTER THREE

DIRTY DEBUTANTE

OUR first scene was booked within minutes after taking the Polaroids at World Modeling. Bill, the owner of the agency, made a call to Ed Powers. Ed always got the first scenes of anyone new to the business. He even paid for our HIV testing. Tyler and I would be paid fifteen hundred dollars. It was my suggestion that we should just do a DP. No one objected.

Fifteen hundred dollars! It was the most money I'd ever earned. All of my jobs until then were paid by the hour or in tips. I remember having a five-hundred dollar paycheck once, but I worked day and night at a restaurant for two weeks to get it. Money was never something I could hold on to, either. At eighteen I blew through a twenty-thousand dollar trust that was supposed to be for college. I took out a loan for the education and spent the cash on a car, clothes, and drugs. Then I dropped out of school.

The money was going to be for both of us. Tyler and I would split it, fifty-fifty. We were a team, an equal partnership, even though he was to be paid nothing for acting/fucking in the scene and the check was really only for me. The girls in porn always make more money than the guys. Approximately three times as much. New guys can barely get their foot in the porno door unless there is a new girl getting in with them. Established male producers, directors, and talent want the girls and gigs all to themselves. Everyone wants the new girl. Tyler and I vowed to stay together in scenes, so that both of us were actively participating in this new venture.

Ed normally used only himself in the scenes as the male talent. This was going to be something special. His line of movies, *Dirty Debutantes*, is an amateur video series with the hook being filming first-time-on-camera sex scenes. The video shop where I used to work in Ventura had an adult section that devoted an entire wall to Ed's *Dirty Debutantes*. They were yellow boxes with the title and some proletarian photos of girls in need of makeup. These young, corn-fed little girls were pictured having sex with Ed in smaller pictures on the back of the boxes. Though I had shelved porno at the video store, I had never once seen an entire adult film. I'd flipped through *Playboy*, but I could never look at one for too long—my eyeballs would start burning with fascination and confusing disgust mixed with envy. Envy would bubble inside me like natural carbonation.

How insane, they must have thought. Here's this new girl, and she's pretty and fresh and sweet, and her first scene is going to be a DP? I was thinking, *First scene? How about last scene? How am I going to go through with this?* I thought about when I lost my virginity at thirteen. It was my choice to have sex with a boy who was fourteen. Afterward, I was so worried that I was going to look different enough that people would treat me like a slut and a whore. I've always had a lot of guilt surrounding my open attitude toward sex. And here I was, about to do porn. It was my choice. I wanted to try it. Still, I felt so damn guilty.

We'd left World Modeling with our porno names Ashley and Trent to protect our true identities. Everyone jokes around with the idea in grade school, like how it has to be your street name and a pet name or middle name. I toyed with the technique, which would have been Rene Sorrento—pretty good, except that I have a cousin named Renee, and I just couldn't do that to her. I was Ashley Blue, for no deep reason other than that it was different from my own name. Honestly, I thought that using the alias would keep me anonymous. I truly believed that people wouldn't know it was really me if I changed my name. If anyone asked or accused me of doing a porn, I could just say, "No, look at the name. My name is Oriana Small. That video says Ashley Blue. It's not me."

Deciding to do porn was too scary to think about realistically. I knew that my family could never feel good about my chosen profession. Even if it was only going to be temporary, it would be upsetting. My extended family, everyone except for my mother and father, was made up of born again Christians. Every Sunday, they went to church and read the Bible. They would be sad and would pray when they found out I got involved with pornography. It would embarrass them.

However, as gut-wrenching as the idea of my family's reaction to pornography was, it wasn't as powerful as the allure. I have never been a good kid. I've always *liked* being bad. I practiced smoking cigarettes in the mirror when I was thirteen and was the first girl to have sex in the eighth grade. I was suspended on my first day of high school for smoking, then again for wearing too short a miniskirt. I knew of better ways to behave, but they were not what I preferred. Breaking the rules was much more exciting. Porn was attractive because I knew it was bad. I didn't know how I could ever face my aunts, uncles, cousins, and sister afterward, or if my actions would force them to stop loving me. I would be a bigger sinner to them, for sure. None of them would believe that this was the best I could do, or that it would make me happy. These relatives all helped raise me when my own parents failed. I didn't want to disappoint them. But disappointment was inevitable. It felt like I was choosing porn over family, and my old life was ending.

Getting the HIV test was scary. It brought in a true element of danger. It was Tyler's first one, and my second. The year before, I got tested after taking the morning-after pill. I was nineteen and fucking this older, good-looking Armenian lawyer. When we finished I discovered that the condom was broken and lodged somewhere deep inside of me. I was terrified of unwanted pregnancy.

I don't know anyone, even now, who gets regular PCR DNA HIV testing done except for porn actors. People who do pornography get them done every thirty days, mandatory. We would have to get used to it. Tyler had a huge fear of needles back then. I only wish he could have held on to some of that fear in the future.

After all of the heavy stuff at the Adult Industry Medical Healthcare Foundation clinic in Sherman Oaks, just around the corner from World Modeling, we had to go home and celebrate. Ernesto, our neighbor three doors away, was a cocaine dealer. He'd become our close friend and confidante. He was the first person to whom we confessed our new adventure. He didn't judge or lecture us. Ernesto's job was way more exploitive and immoral than porn, anyway. The whole thing brought us much closer.

Tyler was the one who really got me into cocaine. I'd tried it once before when I was eighteen. I was standing outside of Club Blue on Las Palmas and jumped into some stranger's limo. I didn't think it was all that great because I was already on speed when some old dude told me to close my eyes and take a sniff of blow. I'd been going through some months when I would do speed for a couple of days straight with different people. Thankfully, meth was never a long-term problem for me. Pot is something I've detested since my junior year in high school. It bores me. Stimulation, not sedation, was what I was after. I got into those liquor store diet pills called Mini Thins for a semester in junior college. Since they were basically pure ephedra, I developed an eye twitch and chronic dry mouth. Not the sexiest drug to take, but I liked to take drugs. Except heroin and painkillers. And pot.

Tyler kept reassuring me that I would like cocaine. "Just keep trying it. Sometimes it takes people like five times before they really feel it. You'll love it. Trust me." He was so right. After we did it together four or five times, I loved it. Cocaine was the best discovery since flavored lip-gloss. It revolutionized my world. It felt amazing. Better than speed, which made me feel dirty and a little isolated. Coke brought the world together. It was a happy drug. I didn't understand why there was so much propaganda against it. It didn't seem harmful at all. The coke users we met were young and beautiful, not at all like dirty-ass tweakers. Why didn't I know about this stuff in high school or elementary school?

Doing coke brought Tyler and me much closer. So did doing ecstasy. We didn't consider ourselves drunks or druggies, just partiers. We were only after a good time, not a fix. I will honestly say that we were not drug addicts then. In the beginning, it was all very innocent. We had no idea when or how the problem was going to start.

Tyler got some sleep the night before our first scene. I stayed up doing coke the entire time. Our HIV tests results came back negative, thank god. We were scheduled to be at Ed's house in Northridge in the mid-afternoon. I drove us there. I had no trouble with the idea of driving high. I had just started doing coke on a regular basis a couple months earlier. I hadn't yet become a paranoid wreck. The world was still just opening up like a bouquet for stargazers. Before we left for the big event, Ernesto extended a line of credit for a couple more grams to take with us. Ernesto was always looking out for us in this way.

Ed's house was a big, two-story building with a long, winding driveway. It looked like a nice, normal valley home. Any unsuspecting passerby wouldn't assume that this was the location for about two thousand porno scenes. Nobody knew, as we turned up the driveway that sunny March afternoon, that we were going to shoot for *More Dirty Debutantes Volume 227.*

Ed smiled warmly as he answered the door and led us into his home. He was a fifty year old bachelor pornographer. He looked just like he did on the video boxes, about five-foot-five, bald on top, long, graying stringy hair in the back. His thick eyebrows accentuated his welcoming gestures. He wore round glasses and had a mustache and goatee. He was dressed in a black tee shirt and sweats. He had a belly on him. He used expressions such as "make love" and "climax." He called himself old-fashioned. The house was large and clean. The clutter around was nothing unusual, just what you would expect from a middle-aged, childless man. Papers on the desks, dressers, and tables. Bad art and '80s furniture. There weren't any posters of tits like there were inside World Modeling.

The massive amount of coke I had been doing for the past two days made me jumpy. I was incredibly high. I'm not sure if I would have made it if I hadn't been on drugs. Coke helped me ignore the risks I was taking. I proceeded without caution. My life was in the moment. Nothing wrong with that, right? Buddhists live their lives that way, like the *om?* I told myself giant heaps of nonsense to rationalize the hazards that I put myself in daily. Ed showed me where to get ready, in his large bathroom upstairs, next to the master bedroom. Perfect, because I had to do some more coke before we started. I stayed in there with the door shut for quite a while, doing line after line and brushing my hair a lot. Tyler joined me for a couple lines and warned me not to do it all. I had a way with coke, usually finishing it all in the first thirty minutes.

My boyfriend led me to where the action was to take place. Ed snapped some photos of us standing side by side with our shirts off, and then he shot some just of me. We might as well have stepped off a Greyhound bus from Arkansas. There was a tripod with a video camera set up, pointed directly at a four-poster bed. It was all completely generic, cheap sheets on the bed. Ed was the king of this amateur formula, and he definitely nailed the décor. I can't remember what I said in response to the light interview Ed wanted for the intro to the sex. I am sure my nose was red and running the whole time. I was so fucked up and nervous. I just wanted to look good. A lot of the naked bodies on the boxes of porn movies were unflattering. With that camera pointed at me, alone, I was hot and sweaty, the bright lights frozen on my twitchy face. Now I was supposed to tell the camera—and everyone who would watch the video—what my name was, and where I was from. "Ashley, from Southern California," I said.

When the sex began, I was able to relax. Crazy sex was what I went there to do, and felt more familiar than talking to the camera. My racing mind shut off, and my body came alive. It was hardcore, since that was what Tyler and I liked. He shoved the back of my head as I deep-throated his cock, and then Ed's. Ed's cock was extremely small. He was very polite with it, too. He didn't like any rough stuff. He even wore a condom. Both sex partners stayed completely hard during it all. I was impressed because of Ed's age and the amount of cocaine Tyler had done before we started. Coke is usually kryptonite to an erection.

It was the ultimate kink experience. I didn't think I would like porno as much as when we fucked other people at home. The presence of the camera was intimidating and sexy in the same way that a person who was way out of my league was. How did I look in front of it? Was I hot enough for it? Even though I still wasn't entirely confident about myself, I wanted to be the most beautiful thing that ever fucked. It meant something greater than what we were actually doing. Yeah, the three of us were fucking, but there was going to be an audience for it. In my head, I was everywhere, the future, the present; I was getting fucked while smiling and trying to enjoy myself. This first scene was telling me that I liked doing porn.

Ed's body wasn't one I would normally fuck, with that big, white belly. My focus wasn't on him so much as it was the *idea* of him. I was high and completely into the idea of letting this older guy fuck my ass and pay me for it. It was for a movie. It wasn't real life. My relationship was with that camera, and I wanted to turn it on and shock it. I wanted to shove it in the faces of everyone who would be watching someday: I was wild, a crazy girl, and I didn't care. I was an exhibitionist.

Tyler loved to see me get fucked by other guys, so long as he was a part of it. Not only did it bring us together in a new and unusual way, there was just as much importance put on bonding with the other men. Tyler wanted to create and strengthen friendships with the other guys fucking me, in a brotherly or fraternal way. He liked to put the "team" in "tag team." The size of Ed's penis definitely gave Tyler a boost of confidence. Maybe that's why Ed's movies were so popular, I thought. Every guy watching could feel good about the size of his own cock by watching Ed's.

We did a few clumsy and easy-going positions. Our DP was just like any regular one we did at home. All of it was purely amateur. Tyler came, a creampie in my puss. Ed came in his condom and then squeezed out the contents onto my chest. I guess it's what he had to do to prove to the viewers that he still had it in him. When everyone's fluids had been properly secreted and exchanged, we were done. The tripod didn't have to budge. Everything was captured on tape. From beginning to end, Tyler and I were out of there in about four hours. We left happy and fifteen hundred dollars richer. The ass-fucking sobered me up, as it always does. We cheerfully said goodbye to nice old Ed, thanking one another for such a good experience.

Backing down the long driveway, I noticed that it was still the same lovely spring day. I wasn't nervous anymore. I was giddy and elated. I felt light and excited in my stomach and on the bottoms of my feet. There was a strong momentum going straight up and forward in my body. I could have pushed the car back to Hollywood with all the excitement that I felt.

"Tyler, do you feel bad?"

"No! No way, I feel great! That was so cool and so easy."

"Yeah, neither do I. I mean. I feel...good. I thought it would suck and be scary, but it was the opposite!"

"Can you believe we just did that?" He laughed as he steered the wheel.

"No!" I was smiling and laughing. We were so happy. It was such an authentic and unexpected feeling. I thought we would be devastated, hanging our heads, regretting it all straightaway. Phrases such as "What have we done?!" were supposed to come out of our mouths, not "cool and easy!"

"It's not like we'll do it forever, just for now," Tyler rationalized.

"Yeah, I want to keep doing it, but not long-term," I agreed.

"We'll just make a bunch of money, and we'll get out of it."

"I can save up money for school. Back to college in the fall!"

"We can do this and open up a restaurant! I'll start cooking again!" Tyler had lived in Barcelona for three years, where he studied gastronomy and culinary arts at a prestigious school before moving to Los Angeles. Originally from Houston, Texas, he spoke the most beautifully fluent Spanish I'd ever heard coming out of a white person.

It all seemed so simple and inspirational. Porno was how we would subsidize our dreams. We felt lucky. By the time our movies came out, we would be long gone from this business. I would be back in school, studying for my fine arts degree. Tyler would be opening up his own restaurant. He would call it Chez Naomi, after his grandmother. We had so much hope. Porno was the land of opportunity.

We continued to chuckle and discuss the highlights all the way home. Our friends would never believe it. I thought that I would feel more like a prostitute when it was all over. We were paid for sex, technically. But that wasn't how it felt at all. What we did was completely legal, no matter how taboo. We didn't get paid for fucking Ed. We were paid to make a movie, a product. Videotape was the focal point. It wasn't all about getting this old guy off. Our job was to make a sex tape. There is a difference.

Tyler drove and I sat in the passenger seat doing key bumps of coke out of the leftover gram. It was still our little secret, porn. Our own little moment to share. We had just put one over bigtime on everyone. We felt like we'd broken the rules, and it was magnificent. It was all just some big, unreal, and crazy joke.

CHAPTER FOUR

BREAKING ME IN

WE started to get more work, sometimes alone, usually together, and we didn't get all of our porno references from World Modeling. Coincidentally, our casual DP partner, Colby, did some music for a porn company called Anabolic. Anabolic produces "gonzo" porn—very hardcore movies that have no story, no script, and a handheld camera pointed at the girl getting fucked. There are no frills. It's all bare mattresses and butt-fucking. The attitude is Go For It, with no distraction from the penetration. Gonzo is notorious for guys getting rough with the girls. The object of an Anabolic porno is for the girl to be degraded and fucked very, very hard. Not for anyone sensitive to the word "whore."

Tyler was a big fan of the Anabolic movies. Anabolic produced films with three or more guys on one girl, with lots of anal and ass-to-mouth, or ATMs. Tyler bought a couple of Anabolic movies with a porn star named Belladonna in them so I could see what "cool porn" was. The name calling, slapping, and choking made a lasting impression on me. It did not intimidate me because it was similar to games that I already played during sex, but it made me want to take it all to a higher—a professional—level. Tyler called me slut and whore and got rough and slapped me when we fucked. I would hold my chin steady and try not to tear up. I knew he couldn't really mean it. Sex allows people to lose their rationality. Tyler got to be a tough guy when we had sex. I loved him and wanted him to enjoy that.

Colby was so excited for us. He wanted to help us out in any way he could. Having a close friend not judge us or think less of what we were doing was a huge relief. Colby was upbeat about the whole thing. He congratulated us in his thick Norwegian accent. It was as if we'd just announced our wedding engagement.

"I know you two will do really good in it! I'll introduce you to all the people I know at Anabolic. I'm friends with all those guys. I'm going to call my really good friend right now. Have you guys heard of Victor Viewer? I just saw him today. We're going to have lunch together tomorrow."

The next afternoon, a Tuesday, Tyler and I drove to Woodland Hills. Among a group of newly constructed, peach colored condos, we found Victor's. Tyler's eyes lit up when he saw Victor Viewer open the door. You'd have thought he had a gay crush, but *Wow, I want to be just like you*, was the sentiment. *The best.* Pure envy. Dozens of times, Tyler had watched this guy fuck in videos, and now we were at his house. Tyler was ecstatic to meet him. He assured Victor that we were crazy for sex and told him all about our orgies with Colby, but it all dripped off Victor without impression. With blasé resignation, he agreed to take some photos of us.

I started to feel uneasy. I was coked out of my mind, but that was normal. I instantly got the vibe that Victor was not a kind person. I didn't know my instincts well enough back then to trust or act upon them. I was so young and on drugs, I just went along. *Everyone deserves a chance, right?* I told myself. *Don't be so judgmental!* So instead of his demeanor, I just tried to focus on Victor's body, which was interesting enough to look at—a miniature body builder, big biceps and pectorals, dark silky hair.

Victor told us to take a seat on the couch. I didn't notice how short he really was until Tyler stood up to undress for the naked Polaroids. At six foot one, Tyler towered over this man, who could have only been five foot four. Victor was handsome in the face, despite his cold eyes. He talked to us condescendingly about the business. I wasn't listening to what he said. I just kept smiling and using my big, straight, white set of teeth as armor for my trepidation. I've never had braces. Somehow, I have been blessed with a terrific set of teeth. It is a rarity to find healthy, pretty, and authentic teeth in pornography. Mine were often my shield. There was just something that radiated from Victor that made me ill at ease. I can't point out one specific thing he said or did to give me the fear, just an overall eeriness, an aura of badness. Tyler and I got naked for our Polaroids, which was the ritual of every porn director thus far. For me, a frontal, back, and bent-over shot.

Tyler had to be hard for his photo. To his (and my) horror, he couldn't get it up. He jiggled, wiggled, and jacked, but his dick just hung limp, lifeless. I think Victor's bad energy got to Tyler's dick and poisoned it. We went into the bathroom for a couple of minutes. Tyler kissed me, felt up my boobs and ass, trying to make the connection. I sucked it for a minute. Nothing was bringing blood into that shaft. It might have been all the coke we did right before our arrival. I don't know. His dick just refused to work.

"Well, look, if you can't even take this picture, I can't use you in any of my scenes. Sorry, man." Victor shrugged it off, smirking at Tyler's failure. Then he added, "I need my guys to be solid. One hundred percent. No exceptions."

Victor could definitely use me in a movie though. How about Thursday? Sure, a DP, and I do interracial, right? Of course! I wanted to prove to the world that I wasn't a racist. I'd never even kissed a black guy before porno, but I loved to fuck them on film. Amorously, I have always been into tall, pale, blue-eyed artists. I was afraid I'd end up becoming a racist if I never fucked a black man. I wasn't a bigot, but I also didn't fully understand how people became bigots. Members of my own family are shameless racists, and I was willing to do anything to dissociate myself from them. I thought about doing black guys the first day I walked into World Modeling. I wanted the opportunity to deconstruct myself and society with no emotional strings attached. Porno gave me that.

When we left Victor's place, we felt awful. Tyler was humiliated, and I felt guilty for succeeding alone in what we came to do together. Tyler started yelling at me.

"Why didn't you help me out? You could have paid more attention to me! Act like you love me once in a while? I thought we were only going to work together, with each other. Why didn't you insist that I be in the scene? You didn't stick up for me at all! Don't you fucking love me? Do you?" Tyler's hands were punching the passenger seat. He lit a cigarette, blowing the smoke against the windshield as he became more and more upset. One thing that I cannot stand—that always escalated arguments behind the wheel—was smoking in the car.

"I'm sorry, Tyler! I'm so sorry! I do love you, more than anyone." I thought he wanted me to do a scene for Victor. Victor, his hero. And we had worked with other people, so far we both had. "You got that blowjob scene for Cinderella without me," I reminded him. "And I'm sorry, but I was shy in front of Victor. It's not fair that he put me on the spot like that. I just couldn't think straight. I'm still fucked up!" We flew down the 101 toward Hollywood, screaming. Then Tyler conceded.

"You're right. We have worked with other people. I'm sorry. I'll go back and prove myself to him another time. Maybe Colby can get us all to hang out together and we can show him how crazy we are off camera. I can show him how good I can fuck with you and Colby." Tyler was staring straight ahead, fantasizing about the great big orgy we would all have with Victor, how he would show this guy what a great fucker he was.

"Yeah, sure. Sounds good," I lied. No way did I want to hang out with Victor. He made both of us feel like shit. I solved the quandary by saying, "Hey, Tyler. Call Ernesto. Make sure he's on his way home."

I was supposed to be at Victor's eight o'clock Wednesday morning to do a cover shoot—or so I was told, anyway—for the video he was putting me in. Terrified that I would oversleep and make this guy angry, I stayed up all night on Tuesday. I never stopped doing coke. I arrived shaky, but not late. We weren't doing the scene until Thursday, so I felt like it was a real honor. He must think I am special, I guessed. I didn't know anything.

A very cute pregnant girl was there to do my makeup. I'd never had my makeup done professionally before. Too bad I was too coked up to enjoy the experience. Her name was Charley and she made me feel happy about being in a porno. She was sweet, bubbly, and from Simi Valley, close to where I grew up in Thousand Oaks. After she finished by putting a barrette in my hair, Charley packed up her stuff and left. What? Why did she have to leave? Now I was alone in the house with Victor. I tried to keep as calm and agreeable a façade as I could. Secretly, I panicked.

Victor led me up the stairs to a bright pastel yellow bedroom. The photos were going to be taken in there, on the bed. It was a very plain room with an open window, big enough to jump out of. Victor was cold and calm. He wasn't mean, but he ordered me to kneel on the bed. He didn't ask.

"Turn around and bend over. Push your ass out. Arch your back."

I strained a smile as he snapped off a couple of pictures. Then he left the room. I was confused. He just left me there on my knees in my white cotton panties. What am I supposed to do now? Should I stay in this position until I am told to relax? Is this how it is in porn? Does everyone assume the right to tell me what to do because I'm here, I'm the slut, and I'm asking for it? I was still trying to distinguish between the blunt feeling of a filmmaker's direction and the bluntness of feeling manipulated. When Victor walked back into the room, he had a video camera in his hands. He wasn't looking at my body directly anymore. He viewed it through the LCD screen. He came close to my face with the lens.

"Pull my cock out and suck it."

The camera was on me, and I didn't know if this was going to end up as part of the scene or what. Sex was not scheduled for this day, just the photo shoot. I did what he told me to do. The camera made it safe, I thought. I feared Victor would be mad at me if I said no. He was the director, and I was the actress who was supposed to like this—or, at least, to act like I like it. This is my job, I thought. If I say no, I shouldn't be doing porno, right?

"Suck it, all the way down," he muttered. He held my head firmly and offered up some banal groans of praise. It was a big, thick cock, and I put it all the way down my throat. I submitted completely to whatever Victor wanted. I was afraid not to. I never wanted anyone in the business to be mad at me.

Victor pulled his cock out of my mouth, and I sat on the edge of the bed, leaning back on my arms. My ass hung off the bed now, and Victor pointed the camera between my spread legs. Without saying a word, he pulled my white underwear to the side and pressed his erection against my butthole. The object itself spread my cheeks apart. I didn't move or make a sound. This was supposed to be enjoyable? How was I going to make this look enjoyable on film? Victor pushed his hard dick into my asshole. It was dry, no lube or spit. None of this felt good. It burned as my skin was torn apart. Once he got it in, he went deep and just methodically fucked me in a monotonous rhythm. I sat there, facing Victor as he held the camera and watched himself penetrate my ass through the lens. It must have felt good for him; nobody as big as Victor had ever been in there. I held onto the backs of my thighs, paralyzed by the pain, my mind racing with questions I didn't know how to answer. Should he have asked? Will Tyler be upset with me? Is he going to put this in a movie? Is Tyler going to accuse me of cheating again?

I didn't know what normal behavior was anymore. Victor hadn't shown me his current HIV test.

The doorbell rang downstairs. Victor's face changed immediately. He was emotionless, as if the last half hour had never happened. He pulled his cock out of my ass, put it back in his pants, and zipped up. He never even took his clothes off. He walked out of the pastel yellow room to go answer the door. I just sat there stunned on the bed, with my panties dangling from my right ankle.

Victor returned with a skinny guy in a floppy baseball cap carrying some more professional looking photo equipment. "This is the still photographer. He's going to get some different poses. Keep it really young-girl and innocent looking. This is for the box cover." Victor then moved about the room, looking busy. He and I didn't make eye contact at all. I still had no idea what was going on. I wish I had asked, but I didn't know I had to: What the fuck? I thought Victor was taking the picture for the box cover. Why did I have to get there two and a half hours early? So he could fuck and molest me?

I felt ashamed of being so clueless. I let Victor force his cock in and dry fuck my asshole. I didn't even know if it was okay to be upset about it. The guilt from being so high on coke and doing porno in the first place outweighed everything else. I assumed I had signed over my basic rights as a human being— respect, personal will, self-determination—as soon as I decided to be a porno girl.

The real photo shoot only took about forty-five minutes. When I got home, Tyler eagerly asked how it was. I replied, "It was fine. I think I did a good job."

"Did anything happen? Did he try anything with you?" Colby told Tyler that Victor was notorious for fucking all the new girls he shoots off-scene. Thanks for the heads-up. I'd had no knowledge of this. How could I tell him that his hero Victor was a sexual predator?

"No, nothing happened. Nothing like that at all. He was really nice. He said to tell you hello." God, I am such a horrible liar. It shows all over my face and in my body language. I have a tell: When I lie I shake my head and plead with my eyes. My upper cheeks scrunch, which creates a forced dimple, a liar's dimple.

Tyler wouldn't understand, I thought. He would never believe that I didn't like it. He thought Victor was a superstar. In Tyler's eyes influential, attractive people, especially porn stars like Victor, don't have to force someone to fuck them.

I worked for Victor a few more times. I did what I thought was the professional thing a performer should do: I didn't talk bad about him to anyone. He was more popular and powerful in the business than I was. I was afraid that I would look like someone who made trouble. Producers and directors don't like girls who cause trouble. What legitimate accusations could I make and be taken seriously? Rape? I was new to the business, fucked-up on coke, and not yet aware of the power I still had to say no. Victor took advantage of that, sexually and otherwise.

Several other girls I've come to know in the business have told me their own stories about Victor. The girls were all young, pretty, new, and on drugs, too. Like me, they were scheduled to get to the shoot hours before anyone else arrived. One girl told me she ran out of the house screaming. She had to borrow a phone to call her agent for a ride. She told everyone that Victor tried to rape her. Nobody cared or did a thing, because this girl was a beautiful, nineteen year old, crystal meth addict. There would be plenty more naïve, messed-up girls for Victor to prey upon.

CHAPTER FIVE

SPRING CHICKEN

ONE scene I did for Anabolic was for a movie called *Spring Chickens*. It was the debut title in a new series of videos. Colby called the director, Brett, on my behalf. Brett was a "good friend" of Colby's. All of the people Colby knew were either his "good friends," his "really good friends," or his "best friends." Tyler had the same rating system. I was not so quick to call anyone a good friend. Colby was Tyler's "really good friend," so we trusted his opinion.

Brett's porno name was John and he'd been doing scenes since the eighties. He was in porn's Hall of Fame and was another one of Tyler's idols. Brett/John committed suicide in 2006. Since we'd already met one of Colby's other "really good friends," Victor, I didn't expect Brett to be cool. He was pretty laid back on the phone. He wasn't rude, but quick and straight-forward. It would be a DP with him and Mr. Marcus. Brett said it would be okay if Tyler came to the shoot, too.

We arrived at a huge house on Mulholland, basically in Cala-basas. It was a new, sprawling, Spanish-style stucco monster with a long driveway that wrapped around the property. My instincts told me this wasn't Brett's place but belonged to someone a lot richer. Colby assured Brett on the phone that I was "real cute. Super cute." I had no makeup on, and there wasn't a makeup artist on set. It's what Brett wanted, a young look—too young for makeup—and I had it all right. I was as fresh as could be. My hair was shoulder-length and flipped-out at the ends, and I had such an innocent smile. Except for the little cocaine addiction, I was the Girl Next Door.

Tyler hung out and tried to keep his spirits up by watching me take the naked stills before the scene. He was bummed out again because he didn't get chosen to fuck. He longed to be in an Anabolic movie so he could wear his Anabolic hat and tee shirt with pride. Every so often I would look over at him, in between snaps of the camera, and he would be rubbing his dick on the outside of his jeans. He looked at me, my body, and would nod his head in approval. He smiled. It made me feel better.

I had a growing fear of Tyler becoming too resentful of me for getting all the attention. I didn't want it all. He could have it. But I was the girl, and Tyler was sort of pimping me out. I didn't mind how it was going so far. Everything seemed almost too easy for me, anyway. We did share all the money. It was "our" success. We were equal partners. I needed Tyler's encouragement just like he needed me to keep getting fucked by all these other guys.

Nonetheless, I began to prefer doing scenes without him. Together, it had become too dramatic. I had to cater to Tyler's feelings above anyone else's during the sex. Not an easy task when there are at least one or two other people in the scene giving orders. Male talent want to own your ass for the two hours that they fuck you, and it was getting difficult to keep Tyler's ego lubed. Tyler would get jealous if he thought I was too enthusiastic sucking some other guy's cock when we were in scenes together. I thought that's what I was expected to do, to act! All I wanted was to be agreeable and make everyone happy. Deeply, desperately, I wanted everyone to love me.

Marcus is a large, muscular, handsome black man, the second black man I would have sex with in my life. The first was

Daryl, in the scene I did for Victor. Years later, in 2004, Daryl caught HIV. Marcus was another porno star that Tyler admired, a solid guy with a shit-eating grin. Brett, on the other hand, looked like a walking mug shot from the Aryan Brotherhood. Pornography should get more credit for bringing people of such different walks of life together harmoniously. Here we all were, gathered at this empty estate on multimillion dollar property in a wreck of a house with no furniture, ready to do acts that are considered illegal in some states. Is this what happens to mansions that house porno shoots?

The scene did not take place inside the mansion. Brett led us around the driveway to a garage. The four of us climbed a narrow staircase to a little attic. The ceiling was sloped so you couldn't stand straight up at one end of the room. There was a bathroom and a stained twin mattress in the middle of the floor.

Good thing I was too embarrassed to ask things like, "Where are we going to do it and for how long?" Brett and Victor had said at separate times that one of the lamest things a girl can do is ask questions. It pissed off most directors to have a girl wanting to know when she'd be done. They called it the Hooker Mentality. Girls that just went along with everything were the cool girls. I wanted to be cool. I didn't ask about—or object to—anything. Brett took the lead. I tried to be the perfect girl. We were getting started. Brett held the camera and put it close, right to my face. Then, in a gruff voice, he asked, "What's your name? Why are you here?"

I didn't know how I was supposed to answer, so I just smiled and looked really happy. "Ashley...I'm here to get fucked." Marcus grabbed my face and pulled out his giant black cock. Both he and Brett were still in their jeans and had their cocks out through the zippers. Very roughly, they pushed my face onto each one, all the way down my throat. I sucked and gagged, spit flowing out of my mouth. It was all so fast. I didn't have any control whatsoever. They just tugged me back and forth, like a rag doll or a party favor. Although it was much more intense than I could have imagined, I liked it. I said I liked it rough, and I could take it. I knew that at any time I could have called to Tyler to come save me. But I didn't need saving. This was *my* pornographic experience.

Tyler sat in the corner of the room, near the tiny bathroom. He was watching and dying to jump in and be part of the scene. He was probably taking a few notes in his head, learning a few techniques from Brett. This guy did it all. He slapped me a little, held my head down on his cock while I deep throated it. He called me a whore and mercilessly shoved his dick into my ass. There was lube this time, but it still hurt. Brett had one of the biggest heads that a penis could have. The whole dick was big, too, eight inches and thick enough. But this huge helmet of a tip seemed like double the width of the entire thing. He just popped it in. I actually felt it go "pop" when it went in and out. I don't think the Anabolic video rulebook contains an item instructing male talent to ease large cocks into the new girls' assholes.

When I had to take a second to collect myself, trying to hold back tears from the pain, Brett rolled his eyes. He looked at Marcus as if to say, "Oh, so this girl said she can really take it, and now she wants to cry. I guess she's not so ready for this after all." It killed me to have to admit any defeat or that I was hurting. My ass was stinging and burning from Brett's enormous mushroom cap being rammed in all at once. I rubbed my butthole and wiped the forming tears from my eyes. "I'm fine. I'm okay. Can you just be a little easier on me? I'm not used to them being so big"—my way of compromising.

Marcus nodded his head and agreed to take it easier. He was stroking his cock with some lube, getting ready for his turn to go in. This big, beautiful, childish grin came over his face and convinced me that he wasn't there to hurt anyone. Brett looked pissed off and said, "You know, we're not even some of the biggest guys. You'll have to get used to it if you're going to stay in this business. Everyone is a least this big or bigger." I hated him for saying it.

I was bent over in doggy when Marcus started fucking my ass. His was much thicker but felt better because he didn't have that awful head that Brett did. Still, I could barely take Marcus all the way in. This was still one of my early scenes, and these were definitely the biggest cocks so far. I smiled through the pain and tried to enjoy it.

Then Marcus pulled his dick out of my ass and shoved it straight into my mouth. That was something I'd never done, not even at home. I was too afraid to put anything from my ass into my mouth. Didn't they teach us in school to never do that? I was afraid to stop and ask if I was going to get sick from it. Brett became so irritated the last time I had to take a break that I just kept going; even if I wanted to, I *couldn't* stop to ask, because my mouth was stuffed full of cock. Sympathy be damned.

After I did it once, the ass-to-mouth didn't stop. They fucked me until they had enough footage. It was about an hour of the hardest sex my body could take. Two positions of DP, a double blowjob, and a couple positions of anal were all I could handle. When it came to the pop shots, Brett told me, "Get down on your fucking knees, whore." I kneeled on the floor with my head back and eyes open. They both came on my face, one and then the other.

With the press of the pause button on the video camera, the whole thing was over. Brett jumped into the shower faster than anyone I'd ever seen. He mentioned before we started, during a little pre-fucking chitchat, that showering after the scene was the first line of defense against sexually transmitted diseases. Bright guy.

I got up and rinsed out my mouth with soap and water. The cum in my eyes was not my main concern. My main concern was the ass in my mouth. I gathered enough courage to ask Marcus if what we did would make me sick. "Is it okay to go in my mouth after it's been in my ass?" I felt so stupid, but who else was I going to ask? I thought a professional would have the best answer.

"Yeah, it's fine. Girls do it all the time. You'll be all right." He laughed at my innocence. But Marcus was correct. I was fine. My body was built for it, I suppose.

Tyler was beaming with pride. He was the fly on the wall and even got to hold the camera for Brett at one point during one of the DP positions. We all dressed hurriedly. I got paid twelve hundred dollars in a check. *Hopefully we'll see each other soon, bye!* I got into the passenger seat of my car and Tyler drove. He couldn't stop raving about the performance.

"You were so great, baby! That was fucking hot and you were so sexy. You looked so innocent and sweet while they DP'd you. I want to do ass-to-mouth with you, too. You have to do it with me now. Did you see me hold the camera? I should start shooting, directing. Do you think they'll use me some time? They'd be stupid not to hire you again. You have to tell them I have to be in it, too, okay?" Tyler was totally turned on by watching me get completely dominated by these two huge men. He still had a boner in his jeans that he couldn't stop rubbing as he steered us back up the winding road on our way home. Tyler didn't want me to cheat on him, but he encouraged me to slut it up for porn.

I was beat. Literally beat. My holes took a lot of pounding. It was as if the space between my twat and my ass was a thin thread holding on for dear life. I was hungry and exhausted. I didn't even want any more coke. Since it was a long drive back to Hollywood, I did a few big bumps anyway.

CHAPTER SIX

JOLLY ROGER

IT was cold and foggy like it always is in West Los Angeles in the morning. My call time was nine thirty, and I was going to be on time because Tyler wasn't coming with me. He actually wasn't allowed to come to this shoot. The director, Spike, specifically said, "No boyfriends."

Though it wasn't the first time I was to go alone to a porno shoot, Tyler threw an absolute fit. Again, it was for an Anabolic director. He so badly wanted to come and meet Spike. Maybe this director would give him a chance to be in a scene with me? Not today. Tyler wanted me to cancel. I refused. Tyler started packing up a bag to leave me after he yelled about how I didn't love him anymore. It was five in the morning, and we were still up doing coke. I cried, "Tyler, please don't go! I love you! I'm sorry," same as always, lying sobbing on the floor of our tiny apartment. Half-naked, he continued to throw some of his clothes into a backpack. His face was a blood-shot mess of tears and runny coke nose.

"No, Ori! I am leaving you! You don't fucking love me at all. Go to your scene and have a great time fucking without me!" He was so frantic as he screamed that he couldn't even tie his shoes. He wasn't upset that I was off to fuck another man on film, but only that he wasn't going to be part of it. Tyler slung the backpack over one shoulder, opened the door, and left, slamming it so hard the entire building shook. He left without any money and no car keys. When he returned, he told me he just walked to the corner of Santa Monica, and he realized how stupid this was. He probably looked like one of the many hitchhiking male prostitutes out trolling the same corner. After a few more hours of rolling around, crying on the carpet, we made up. Tyler gave me the blessing to go to work.

We fought all the time. Tyler's feelings bruised easily, especially when we'd been up all night. I hated wasting the cocaine buzz on arguing. Often, I would try to go silent and cold when he got upset. It never worked. It made Tyler even more insane. The only thing to do was scream and cry with him, often over things we would not even remember the next day. It didn't matter so much that I hadn't slept all night and was still super high on coke. The important thing was that my relationship was still intact. Tyler still loved me, so everything else would be fine. I got in the car and headed out to shoot some more porno.

Heading west on Washington Boulevard, I passed the address. It just didn't seem right. My expectations of where we would shoot the scene were not terribly high, but I didn't think I would be going to some sketchy crack den with hourly rates. I made a U-turn and pulled into the parking lot of the Jolly Roger Motel. Sitting in my car, I fumbled for my cell phone. "Um. Hi. This is Ashley. I think I'm here. Can you come find me?"

"Oh, yeah. I see you. I'm in room 213, upstairs. Meet me in the lobby, down in front."

Spike sounded a lot mellower than Brett. Hopefully he wasn't as grumpy and impatient. I grabbed my one small duffle bag containing all of my wardrobe selections. I traveled light in an effort to be as inconspicuous as possible. A lot of porno girls drag gigantic suitcases full of bikinis, heels, and other gear with them to scenes. I couldn't bring myself to do that. A lesser parcel made me feel like less of a whore. I didn't like to parade around in public. When I was among the general population, I didn't want anyone to know what I did for a living, as if my porno life was still secret.

Spike was a pleasant guy. He was probably in his late thirties, and he had the look of a heavy drinker. His skin was tanned and weathered, and his eyes were glassy blue—an ex-surfer type. He seemed sluggishly tired but prepared. He emanated such a lack of enthusiasm that I suspected the scene would be with some other guy—that Spike would just be filming it, the camera guy. When we got into the room he started checking the camera and labeling the tape. I showed him the clothes I brought, which were all cute, normal, young-looking girlish outfits. He chose a skirt and light blue crocheted top. Funny, I thought: I technically still shared that top with my cousin. Her sister gave it to us after she went to Bali. If only they knew what was about to become of it.

I excused myself to the bathroom to prepare. I had to do an enema and keep doing coke. Luckily, I had almost an entire gram with me. I needed it to stay alert and have energy for the scene. When I emerged about fifteen minutes later, it was still only Spike and me in the room. He shot a roll of photos of me alone on the bed being sexy. I'd spent more time applying coke to my face than makeup, but that was okay. I looked fresh without makeup. Young and innocent.

"Um, Spike, when is the guy supposed to get here?" I finally asked.

"It's with me. This is a POV. I have a POV series. That's okay, right?"

I was relieved. I didn't have to ask what the initials stood for. I figured out that it meant point of view. Spike would be holding the camera and fucking me at the same time. I didn't have a problem with that. I was actually quite curious how he was going to manage both tasks. This would be interesting. One of his hands would be tied. Maybe I would even have control.

Spike courteously showed me his HIV test, not making me ask for it, which was still awkward for me to do. I didn't ask any more questions. This director had my trust now, he seemed like he'd done this a hundred times. I didn't come to have orgasms. I was there to fulfill my strange desire to be videotaped having crude sex with a stranger and then go home with a thousand dollars.

"So, since this is POV, I want you to look directly into the camera. Talk to me through the lens. Be vocal and say stuff to it, like you're talking to the guys watching this at home. They should feel like they're the ones here fucking you." Spike directed me well. Basically, he was just the prop and it was my show. I could do that. He got naked and we started with the obligatory blowjob.

Getting naked was always the uneasy part of having sex with strangers when I did it outside of porn—the point when I thought the guy could be having second thoughts or might be scrutinizing my body. Regret might sink in. Porn wipes away any such fears and criticisms. It's a sure thing that we both wanted it—especially if we wanted to make money. Stripping down nude was just preliminary to the course work. The pressure was off as soon as the clothes were.

I looked up at the lens as I was down on my knees sucking Spike's cock. He said few words. It was like there wasn't a man there at all. Just a camera with a dick. It's always easier looking up at a camera than it is into someone's eyes. Spike's body was tan all over, and he had muscles underneath his slouchy posture. We were alone in a skanky motel shooting a scene for a porn movie.

It was an anal porn movie. Spike was a stranger, but I felt safe. I was turned on by the taboo of it all. It reminded me of when I would have one-night stands with strange, older men when I was a teenager. I was no stranger to sex with strangers. Maybe I would have been doing this even if there weren't a camera and a bag of coke in the room and a check waiting for me at the end.

I didn't care about the world outside of this Jolly Roger Motel room. Spike held the camera very steadily even as I got on top of him, forward and reversed, and bounced on his cock. I leaned back on top of him with his dick in my ass, and I stared into the camera. It was pointed at the penetration. Every so often, I would take a glance at the screen. I loved it. I truly got off on this experience. Not in an orgasmic way. It was more in my head than my body. I didn't know this guy at all. So much business in porn relies on trusting the word and arrangements of others. We just met, but I wasn't just fucking Spike. I was fucking Spike *and* the camera.

We fucked until Spike got about forty minutes of usable footage. His cock wasn't a monster like Marcus's or Brett's. I took it in my ass no problem. My asshole was getting used to the big dicks now. Brett was right about that, I had to adapt to the larger-sized penises. I was proud to be able to take them, with a smile. As soon as the last cum drop had drizzled into my mouth, Spike pressed the pause button on the video camera. He let out a gasp. He did a beautiful job of keeping quiet during the entire scene. Now his soul could be allowed into the room. He looked refreshed and alive. He was hardly the same person that first greeted me in the lobby.

"Wow, Ashley, you're great! That was a good scene." He was happy with me, he liked me. That meant everything. I picked up the strewn articles of clothing from around the bed. I found my panties, skirt, and I wiped my face off with that crocheted top from Bali. While Spike took a two-minute shower, I shoveled in as much coke as my nose could hold. He got out and dried off before writing my check. We set a date to shoot another scene. Now that I had passed the tryout, I could be booked for a DP.

As I drove home, down Lincoln to Venice Boulevard, I couldn't help but feel good about myself. Leaving a good sex scene with all that money gave me a feeling of accomplishment. I was young and hadn't done much in my twenty years on this planet. When porno directors praised me and paid me, it was powerful.

There was a Bank of America inside of a Von's on Lincoln. I needed to deposit my check. I didn't like to have the checks in my possession for very long. I was on drugs all the time and really bad at misplacing important papers. I always used the automatic teller machines to make the deposits. I hated seeing the bank tellers reading who the check was written from, looking at me weird with their suspicious eyes. I felt like a total whore in the bank, depositing all of my dirty money. I didn't need some snarky bank clerk being inquisitive about my big check from Spike Johnson Productions.

As I was slipping the envelope into the ATM machine, I reached up to my face to brush some hair off my forehead, when I felt something stuck there. It was some crusty stuff in a trail down my cheek, chin, and neck. It was dried cum, and it was all over my face and a little on my chest. I looked around to see if anybody was watching while I finished my transaction.

A couple of soccer moms passed by as I bolted from the store. I pressed the automatic unlock button to my car and dove in headfirst. I looked into the rearview mirror and saw where I had completely missed wiping off the load. I scraped some off with my fingernails. Then I stopped. I was laughing so hard. What kind of filthy sex-worker shit was this? Just a new occupational hazard, like bruises on the knees. The feeling of disgust only lasted a second. I was secretly proud of myself.

CHAPTER SEVEN

DOUBLE ANAL

A rare occasion: I showed up sober to my next shoot with Spike. There wasn't a huge fight with Tyler beforehand to send me off, either. I was happy to shoot with Spike again. I respected him after shooting the POV. He didn't try to come on to me outside of our professional sex scene. I thought we were on the same page when it came to making porno. It was good and "real" when the camera was rolling, but we didn't need to pretend that there was anything else going on afterward. Spike didn't need any validation besides what he got from the movie, and certainly neither did I. My plate was full of Tyler when I got done with my scenes.

The location for our next scene was in Venice, at the old Anabolic office, basically an empty warehouse with some carpeted offices upstairs. It really didn't matter what the rooms looked like. We didn't need any furniture or civilized surroundings. Bare essential Gonzo hardcore fucking and no story was definitely my specialty. Just a camera in my face and on the areas being penetrated for all of you wonderful watchers at home.

This time, Spike was only directing and holding the camera. He would not be fucking me. I was all set up to get DP'd by two other performers. Their names were Jack and Mick. Both of them were white, normal dudes. Mick was tall and had a huge, thick, nine-inch cock. Jack's was a lot smaller than what I was used to.

They were both totally pleasant to be around because of their nice blue eyes. Since I was already very comfortable around Spike, I was eager to have him tell me what to do. There was a sense of camaraderie now that we had fucked. It was like I was "in."

It seemed to me that I was now a pro at doing DPs. My asshole had been trained to take more and bigger cocks than when I had first started doing them for porn. Mick and Jack were funny and nice to me. I went back and forth from cock to cock, blowing and drooling all over them for the double blowjob. Having two dicks to suck was also very normal for me. Tyler and Colby had me well versed in double cock-sucking from our private late-night group sex sessions.

Mick and Jack took turns fucking my ass. Each of them slammed it in hard and it was far from easy. I was ready for it though, and willing. By now, I knew what to expect from porn fucking. It was going to be hard because it had to be, or else it wouldn't be worth watching. The kind of porn I wanted to be in was the kind that was rough and insane, where even a smaller dick like Jack's could do some damage. If either of these guys had started kissing me, or gently caressing my body, I would have felt weird. I didn't want to be physically comforted by these strangers. My intention was to make a porno, not to make love.

Tyler and I agreed that it didn't look good when a girl got fucked slowly. It was a bore. It looked dead. If people were going to be watching, I should be getting slammed. Give the camera and the voyeurs the maximum heat. My mascara should be running down my cheeks, my eyes watering during a blowjob, a good gagging. Always, I had to make sure and swallow, too. Or else, what's the point? Happily, I bounced along from cock to cock. My entire body was dribbled like a basketball between both guys during the DP positions. Mick and Jack were really into me, and I liked that. I was having so much fun that when we took a small break for some water, Spike pressed the pause button on the camera and asked, "So, Ashley, do you want to try double anal?"

"Sure," I answered without reservation. "I could try it. If you think we can do it, then, okay. I've never done it on camera. But I've done it at home." I shrugged and took a sip from my water bottle.

I could trust these guys. I'd only just met them, but they were decent enough. I wanted to do a memorable scene for Spike again. I wanted everyone to think I was a great performer and that I could rise to any sort of challenge. There was so much I had to prove to myself, too. If I did things like double penetration and double anal, could it mean that I belonged in porn and didn't have to feel guilty for doing it anymore?

I sat on Mick's dick while he was lying on the floor. Jack faced us both and crouched on one knee. He got between my legs, missionary style, but instead of putting it in my twat, he crammed it into my asshole. Both cocks were now side by side, rubbing and pulsing in and out of my ass and against each other. My hands were clenched into fists as I endured the pain. All the lube in the world couldn't make it easy, but it made it easier. Thank god for lube. It was a happy agony. I was yelling out "Aaahh!" as I held my legs back. That hole was so stuffed. It felt like it was going to breach like a dam on the brink. We tried another position of double anal after, my body facing the other direction. The cocks went in my butt again with me in doggy. Have you ever seen stars? I saw them, with a smile. After that, my ass was ruptured. The levee broke. I could take no more cock. It was time for the pop shots.

Spike was really excited. "All right! That was great! I'll pay you extra for this, too." He was smiling as he wiped his lens.

The scene was phenomenal. I wasn't just a trooper—that wasn't enough to describe me. I was a captain! An admiral! A decorated soldier of sex hell-bent for glory! Jolly Roger Spike paid me fifteen hundred dollars for doing double anal. I was showered with praise and compliments. Compliments were a temporary and empty sort of love I began to fiend for to keep me from feeling used. Everyone agreed that I was going to do very well in this business.

CHAPTER EIGHT

TYLER'S BLUE PILL AND
ASHLEY'S LITTLE BROWN PREDICAMENT

WORLD Modeling booked Tyler and me to shoot together for a scene in *Barely Legal*. This time we were both getting paid to fuck. Tyler was to get five hundred, and I would get a thousand, my going rate for anal. This was exciting. Not only would we get to fuck each other we were doing it for Hustler, about as close to mainstream as hardcore porn gets. Tyler already had a Hustler tee shirt. He loved to advertise that we did porn with what was written on his clothes. His wardrobe included an array of Hustler and Anabolic wear.

The producer, Cosmo, and his wife were kind to us. They made us feel like we were both very cute and special creatures. They went on about how groundbreaking the *Barely Legal* series was. Porno producers love to brag about their work. Tyler and I were to feature in number twenty-seven. At first I didn't know how to feel about being cast for all of these "young girl" roles. I couldn't understand why it was so sexy to be a "young girl"—maybe because I still was one. The term *Barely Legal* didn't seem like a compliment back then. The women I thought of as sexy were adults, not teens. I was greasy-faced and an emotional wreck as a teen. In many ways, the teen years were gross. I wanted to be a hot, grown woman. Tyler assured me it was far better to be thought of as a "young girl." When

I asked why, he replied with something about pigtails being used as handlebars for sucking dick. Tyler drove us in my car to the location. I usually insisted on driving us to the shoots. Tyler was an absentminded driver and a daydreamer. I would catch him staring at his shoe instead of watching the road. He would always be singing loudly along to the radio and miss freeway exits or forget to turn the right way. Being his passenger was an infuriating experience for the control freak and coked-out, paranoid nag in me.

The only reason he was driving on this particular morning was because I needed to do more coke in preparation for work. I couldn't drive and sniff cocaine at the same time. Tyler went slow and careful so I didn't spill all the drugs. He wanted me to save some for him. He had just taught me how to balance small amounts on the end of a credit card. I quickly moved up to getting huge piles of it up my nose that way. All of my credit cards had cocaine stuck in the numbers. The GapCard was my favorite because it was a slick, translucent white and you couldn't see how much of the stuff was crusted on it.

There was an actual crew of people hired for this movie, a feature with more production value than we were used to. There were lights set up and an all-day make up person. It seemed so legitimate. There was even food provided. Not that that mattered to me. I was so high that I couldn't appreciate it. The only makeup applied to my face was lip gloss and mascara, which is all I usually wore anyway. I couldn't use foundation on my skin because I would get sweaty from doing drugs. Sweat and foundation is the perfect storm for volcanic pimples. Thankfully, my skin had drastically improved from what it was when I was a teenager. Once I turned twenty, nature decided I'd done enough time in bad-skin hell. Now it is lovely almost all the time. I don't even need foundation.

There was no script, which was normal. Good, because Tyler and I would have made a mockery of it. Both of us could only act one way when we were together, which was goofball stupid. Plus, it felt false to have to act from a script when we knew the only thing that mattered was the fucking. There was a story, however. Fantasy is great if you get to put your own dialogue to it. We were to play a young couple named Trent and Ashley who were being shown a house by a real estate agent. When the agent leaves us in the house alone to decide if we want to make an offer, we have sex in it. Later on, I learned the real reason why some producers feel that pornos need stories to lead into the sex. It protects the movie from looking too much like prostitution or rape. People need a wholesome reason to fuck or else it seems too obscene. Even if the movie is about prostitution or rape, there still needs to be a story.

Aside from all the coke I was on, I was nervous because of Tyler. All I could think about was his cock and that it had to stay hard. If it didn't, I would be the one to blame. He would tell me that I wasn't being attentive to his needs and that I cared more about the movie than him. Every time his dick had gone limp in front of other people he would start frowning and holding his breath. He would shake his head in disapproval while he shook his wet ropy noodle of a penis. When it happened, I knew he was resenting me, that it was my fault somehow. Even if the cause was obviously drugs, Tyler expected me to remedy the problem ASAP.

Not a lot of directors like to shoot real couples having sex on film. Couples tend to bring all of their relationship problems into the sex scene and feelings always get hurt. Tyler and I were one of those couples. I preferred to wait until we got in the car to fight, but he liked to slam bathroom doors and pull me aside in front of the other porn people. We would be standing just a couple of feet away from the camera, naked with tears in our eyes, arguing about the amount of love I actually had for him. Every little thing he did at home to irritate me got dragged into the scene. If he smoked in my car or forgot to replace the roll of toilet paper, I would complain about his fingers being too rough in my ass or not let him slap my face during the blowjob.

Our sex life was great at home. We spent every second of the day together. Days and nights were just time slots to fill with different ways to have a good time. All we did was go out to restaurants, shop, go to the movies, drive around, do coke, and hang out with our friends. Porn paid a lot and left us with plenty of free time to just screw around. Sex was habitual once it became a job. We fucked every day. If I was too sore during my off days I would give Tyler blowjobs. I hated having oral performed on myself. I didn't like being bored, just waiting for my man to come back up so we could get to the penetration. I like to be in action. I was way too impatient to let Tyler go down on me for very long. I prefer to be the giver rather than the receiver.

To my relief, Tyler had a rock-hard and reliable erection throughout the whole *Barely Legal* shoot. About halfway through, we took a break. I used the opportunity to run for the bathroom and fill my nose with coke. Tyler joined me for a line before we had to get back to the sex. He was excited to show me something.

"Look," he was holding out a blue pill that was shaped like a football. "Cosmo gave me a Viagra. Should I try it? He says he gives them to new guys when he's never shot them. Just as insurance to do the scene. I'm going to take it." He grabbed my water from off the bathroom counter and gulped the pill. He was thrilled. Tyler got off on new drugs.

The last half of the scene was reserved for anal and the cum shot. Anal is the only way that sex really feels like work. It takes such preparation to do it well and keep it clean. Initially, I had no idea what an enema was. I would just starve myself for two days before a scene or when we did anal at home. I learned quickly on that day why enemas are a must-have.

Tyler bent me over on the couch and eased his straight and solid cock into my asshole. Getting fucked in the ass was nothing new, but before porn we never had to change positions or get "long strokes" in there. Doing it for the camera meant a lot more minutes. Having anal sex at home is not the same as performing it in front of other people. You want to be clinically clean when the camera is rolling. Any unsightly poo or blood is absolutely mortifying!

Tyler pulled out his cock after we'd done it long enough in doggy. There was a little piece of poop on the end of his cock. It came from my ass, and everyone saw it. The director noticed and called out in his thick, Scottish accent, "Aye. We've got a little poop." He seemed a little excited by it. I, on the other hand, was horrified! I wanted to die. I walked off set to the bathroom to wipe my ass. There was none on me. The little turd came from deep inside my intestine. The cock must have dredged it out. It had been at least two days since I had eaten a bite of food. This was impossible. My diet had been strictly cocaine and zero-calorie soda.

Nobody else seemed to be affected by any of this. For me, it was the end of the world. Tyler had never even seen me poop at home. Now, in front of ten strangers and my boyfriend, I had a piece of shit come out of my ass. I can't think of any other situation in which shitting in front of a group of people is part of the norm. Shit is an everyday occurrence in porn. But when it comes out unexpectedly during sex in front of an audience for the first time, it's the most unwanted thing, ever. It's so crushing. I think I really finally understood the true and entire meaning of the word humility. No longer did I feel like this little "sex star," but instead a lowly human being. The fantasy I had built up around what I was doing, and the fictitious person I pretended to be, came to a screeching halt when the poop appeared.

Now, I really love seeing poop. It fascinates me. When it comes out of other girls during their sex scenes, it's interesting. As long as it's just a little bit. Something about an unexpected and small amount of feces makes me feel like what I'm watching is real. You can't fake a turd like you can an orgasm.

I returned to the scene. I told them all I was too sore to do any more anal. They all saw the poop. I knew that. I also knew that they had all probably seen worse. I was being lame, acting like it never happened. *Too sore*, that was the story and I stuck to it. I apologized for it, and we went on to the pop shot.

After the scene was finished and we had hung around long enough to make new friends, we got in my car to leave. We were fifteen hundred dollars wealthier once again. As I drove the car, I thought, Screw the poo, this porno stuff is so damn easy! It felt pretty good to be doing this full-time. I wanted to get better at it. I needed to practice doing enemas and keep working on getting used to some insanely big cocks in my ass. This could be something I could do really well, I thought. Tyler sat next to me in the passenger side with his shirt off. He went shirtless a lot. He had a good body and he knew it. But he looked unusually red. His face was really flushed and his eyes were more spacey than normal. His hands were feeling around on his chest. Alarmed, I asked, "What's the matter, Tyler? What's wrong, are you still fucked up?" I wasn't anymore. I'd finished the coke by the end of the shoot.

"No, I'm not okay. I don't know. I just feel high, really high. Like I'm on some kind of super speed. My heart is beating so fast and hard. I am so fucked up. I think it was that pill."

Tyler grabbed my hand and squeezed it. I didn't know what to do. He was running so hot. I had the air conditioner on, his shirt was off, and he never wore underwear. I panicked. His pants were unbuttoned. "Look," he managed a crippled laugh and pointed to his cock. He pulled it out of his pants and it was cement hard. It was all red and looking like it was ready to lift off into outer space. He just held his cock out of his jeans all the way down the freeway. It mesmerized him. He was in awe of his penis and all its Viagra glory. His heart palpitations and other symptoms of cardiac arrest persisted but took a back-burner to the miracle between his legs.

"Isn't that stuff for older people? Like for guys in their thirties? You are only twenty-five! You don't need to take it." I had an ex-boyfriend who took Viagra, and he was in his mid-thirties. Little did I know it was actually for guys in their sixties. I didn't tell Tyler I'd seen the pill used before because it was the guy I'd cheated on him with. "What are you going to do? Why is it still hard? You came over an hour ago." He didn't answer. The look on his face told me the entire plan.

As soon as we got back to the apartment, I was on my knees blowing him. He came in my mouth. Then we fucked and I blew him again. The boner lasted all night. It withstood an entire gram of cocaine, too. Tyler was thrilled about being able to keep hard and do coke all night. It was a new discovery, yet another drug Tyler could not get enough of.

CHAPTER NINE

ECSTASY DEALERS?

TAKING ecstasy was one of our favorite ways to party. Tyler and I convinced ourselves that it was helping our relationship. We'd heard somewhere that the history of the ecstasy pill originated with couple's sex therapy. We said it made us stronger and was something we could share to become more intimate. For whatever bullshit reason, we took that drug regularly. It did make me more open to the double anal and double penetration going on at home, but that isn't exactly couple's sex therapy.

Ecstasy made us into emotional idiots. For every night of "ecstasy" there was at least a week of intense depression, but that did not dissuade us. While cocaine made me numb and powerful, ecstasy was a "feel-good" high, all about sharing and equality. I wanted everyone else to feel good on ecstasy, too.

What money we didn't spend on coke went into the pill fund. Even before the porno started, Tyler and I would foolishly buy "E" pills with what little money we had to spare. I remembered simpler days when Tyler and I were so broke that we lived off of frozen edamame and ice cream. That is when you really feel in love for the first time, when you're poor. We had nothing but each other for comfort and entertainment. It was a beautiful time.

Now we had all of this money. Overnight, we had instant success in the porno business and could buy as many drugs as we wanted. We were still young and had our looks, too. The party never had to end.

There were many different people who sold us drugs. Tyler always found someone with stuff for sale. He was like a divining rod in a crowd. His inner coke-fiend would gravitate to whoever had anything for sale. This boy had no shame, no bashfulness about asking as many people for drugs as he needed to in public, even in broad daylight. We would be at our favorite bars, like Birds or The Cat & Fiddle, and Tyler would be hitting up random people for coke. I used to be embarrassed when he would walk right up to strangers and ask, "Hey man, do you party?" Time after time, Tyler's charm prevailed. I had to hand it to him.

One of our dealers was this scrawny dude named Jay-Jay who hung out at Perversion, the Thursday gothic-industrial nights at Club World. This was the first club I ever went to when I turned eighteen. I was there almost every weekend, dancing to eighties music and looking for guys to fuck before Tyler had entered my life.

Jay-Jay never wore a shirt. He didn't need to. His chest, back and arms were completely littered with tattoos. He always had a backpack. Anyone sporting a backpack at a club sells drugs. You can spot them a mile away. Jay-Jay liked us. We bought pills from him every weekend. We had such a reliable reputation for buying that Jay-Jay would extend us a line of credit when we ran out of cash for the night.

After buying six pills off of Jay-Jay one night and taking them all, Tyler had a plan. "Hey, these pills are really good, these new ones he has now. We should buy what he has left and sell them ourselves. To our own friends." Tyler's attempt to be business savvy. We were going to invest our porno money in the ecstasy market.

"I don't know. What if we get caught?" I had issues with dealing. It crossed a line. Doing them and ruining my own life was one thing. Selling them to ruin other people's lives was immoral.

"Listen Ori, I know how to do it. I've sold drugs lots of times. I sold hash when I lived in Barcelona. When I was in high school, I sold acid to seventh graders," he proclaimed, as if that made it okay.

"What? You sold drugs to little kids?" I had to chuckle to hide my disgust. "That's awful."

"It wasn't real acid. I just took postage stamps and dipped them in Drano. These dumb kids down the street would buy them for five dollars apiece. They'd take them and always come back for more the next week saying, 'Whoa, that shit was so good. We were wasted, do you have any more?' So I'd go, 'Let me go see.' And I'd just go dip some more stamps."

I remembered buying a twenty-dollar bag of oregano when I was thirteen. "No Tyler, it would be weird to take money from our friends. I'd rather just give them away."

"Ori, it's easy. It's not brain surgery. Lots of our friends will buy them if we just take them with us and pull them out when we all want them. How many times have you heard someone say 'I wish we had some ecstasy right now?' Almost every night. We'll go to Colby's house or to a party and everyone will want one. I'll take the money from people. Come on, we'll make all of our money back and still have some for ourselves. Don't you trust me?"

I gave in. It wasn't like he was going to stop bringing it up if I said no. I decided to try it out before judging the idea too hard and putting it down completely. Ultimately, I didn't care, as long as I could do some, too.

Jay-Jay sold us fifteen pills for eleven dollars each; a perfect amount, because we already decided not to get too caught up and become drug lords. We were quiet about it. Someone might set us up. We were ecstasy dealers now.

When we got home, I went ahead and took a pill. It was my obligation as a supplier to test my own product. Tyler did two pills with me. It was customary to split each pill in half, take a half first, then, thirty minutes later, take the other half. The process solidifies the high. You want to peak as long as possible. When you start to peak, swallowing the second half will keep it going. An hour went by, and I didn't feel anything. Something was wrong with the pill. I hadn't done coke in hours, so the feeling of the ecstasy should have been stronger than usual. "I'm not feeling it at all. Let's take more." I never thought about the risks of overdosing. My mother and my father were drug addicts. Drug abuse was in my DNA. Nothing was ever going to kill me. I was built to withstand any kind of self-abuse possible. Overdosing never crossed my mind for even a second.

"Let's split one more, I still can't tell if it's working." The only change in my body was a slight stomachache from my cocaine and cigarettes diet. Two and a half hours after we first started, we were lying on the bed, feeling weird. What was in these pills? Not ecstasy. Maybe it was mescaline or speed? No. We felt wretched and tired. I wanted to go to sleep. Our pills seemed to be duds.

We got under the covers and turned out the little green lamp at the foot of the bed. It was totally dark except for a small nightlight in the bathroom. That light stayed on because I was scared of the dark. Things got even weirder on the pills in the dark. Oddly, I couldn't close my eyes. They would only blink for a split second, snapping open again. What the hell? The room wasn't still. It was quiet, but things were moving on the ceiling. I couldn't tell if what I was seeing was just the normal blobs that are present while adjusting to darkness.

"Can you sleep?" I asked Tyler.

"No, I can't. I'm wide awake now," he sighed. Then he started laughing.

"Tyler, why is the ceiling moving around? And the walls! Do you see that?" I was pointing at the fragments of foam insulation dancing above our heads, and laughing too. But it wasn't funny.

"Yeah, I see it. Oh hell," he busted up with laughter. "I think what we took had a little bit of white blotter, or something like it."

"What do you mean, like acid?" I spoke up in a loud voice that sounded like someone else's. Who said that? Fuck! I didn't want to take acid!

"The ecstasy must have been mixed with it. That's why we felt so different from the last times. It's all right. It's not too strong." Tyler had lots of experience with this drug, I presumed. He wasn't upset at all.

I was trying to be pissed about it, but I couldn't stop smiling. It was involuntary. I had no control of my facial expressions. "I don't want to be on this. I hate acid. I took it when I was fifteen and I wanted to rip my face off in the mirror. What are we supposed to do? When will it wear off?"

"Uh. That's the bad thing about acid. It lasts for at least twelve hours. Maybe more. We just have to sit it out. We'll just stay in here and trip until it wears off. But who knows when that could be. We took a lot of pills." Tyler calmly put his arm around me, and we let the acid kick in.

Hours and hours went by in our little studio apartment. Galaxies of particles danced around in midair. If I looked at Tyler for too long he would become something hilarious, then quickly something frightening. The sun came up and shone through the window. It was too bright for our dilated pupils. LSD makes the eyes super sensitive to sunlight. I tore apart the cabinets, looking for sunglasses. The only shades I could find were two ridiculously huge ravers. One had purple lenses, the other had blue. I used to actually wear them during a phase I went through. Two summers before, I bought a Paul Oakenfold album and wore these stupid glasses. I thought electronica was awesome for about a minute.

Nothing could stop the acid trip. Objects in the room were dancing. The walls would shrink and then get further apart, like they were breathing, like lungs filling up and then letting out. We couldn't leave the bed. The carpet was a dark sea of the unknown, crawling with small organisms. I couldn't make any shapes out from all of the living things that had now coated our apartment like the inside of a petri dish. Every time I looked at Tyler, I would lose control, laughing so hard. My hands kept going down to my underwear to check if I had peed my pants. It felt like there was pee all over me, but I remained dry. We had sex repeatedly. It felt good, but again, there was this hallucination of piss all over me and the bed the entire time. Tyler even came. After the first two times, I let him come inside my vagina. I was on the pill back then. Typically, on a non-acid day, Tyler would just come in my mouth. Acid gave Tyler a massive boner for some reason, and we fucked close to ten times. Maybe it was because LSD makes you literally insane.

All we did was fuck and talk. Tyler spilled his guts to me. Stories from his childhood he'd never told me before. He had me laughing so much I forgot how to breathe. When he was seven years old, he decided to walk down his street naked. He said it was because he felt sexy! None of his neighbors saw him, as far as he knows. When he got halfway down the street, he said he realized what he was actually doing, and he ran back into his house. He does live in a dreamlike state as an adult. I guess it started at a very young age.

In the second grade, Tyler used to bring baggies full of white flour to school. The purpose was to roll up pieces of notebook paper and sniff it up with other kids in his class. He said he saw his mom and stepdad doing it, so he wanted to do it too. He and the other children he hung out with in elementary school would cut huge lines and act crazy, saying that they were wasted. Tyler also smoked weed when he was in second grade. He gathered the seeds and stems his mom and stepdad left in the ashtrays. Soon he had a large baggie of what he called pot. After school one day, a fellow seven year old friend came over to Tyler's house. Without any adults home to watch them, the kids rolled the marijuana stems and seeds into joints using big sheets of notebook paper. Tyler's little friend ate a seed and freaked out. He went home to his mother and said that he'd eaten drugs. The police came to Tyler's house later to speak with his mother. Tyler's mom talked her way out of it somehow, and no charges were pressed. She and her husband were both dealing pot out of that house. They had several pounds of it in the basement.

Eighteen hours went by before we thought that maybe the acid was easing up. We had stopped feeling high and began feeling shitty. The world was an ugly, scary place now. Instead of comet trails, we saw ghastly shadows creeping into our periphery. Though we weren't hungry, we decided to drive to a Jack in the Box. Fast food is supposed to sober you up. It worked with every other form of intoxication. We layered our clothing with shirts and sweaters and jackets. It wasn't cold, but it was dark outside. Who knows what could be out there? The layers made us feel safer. The closest Jack in the Box was on Sunset at Cahuenga. It took a lot of courage for us to get out of the car and go inside to order. Our minds were unable to handle any challenges that a drive-thru could possibly bring. We got the food, sat down at one of the little tables. My eyes were sprung but really dry. We needed to drink water, not the giant Dr. Peppers that we'd just ordered.

Tyler squeezed out some ketchup and I lost it. "No! These fries are too curly! This place is fucked up! Let's go! This place is scaring me! I can't be in here right now! Take me home, or somewhere. Anywhere but this place!" I didn't want anyone to hear me. Everyone seemed to be watching us. The clerks and the customers were all freaks, secret monsters, and they were closing in on us.

Tyler just nodded his head and agreed. Fuck this place. He tossed down his fry before it got to his mouth. He put his arm around my shoulders and we walked out. "You can have the thirty dollars of fast food back!" We had to go home and get back under the covers. Fucking was the only relief. We fucked for another day and a half until it was finally over.

CHAPTER TEN

I got another scene request from a director at Anabolic. It was for someone named Pro Trusion. This was not his real name, of course. The video line he directed was called *Oral Consumption*. I was hired for a blowjob scene that included some male ass-licking and man-toe sucking. Fine with me. I hadn't licked any man-ass before, but I was always up for trying new things. I didn't care what I put in my mouth. I was literally a sucker for a new sexual experience.

Tyler wanted to come with me. He still wanted to be in with the guys at Anabolic, and I was glad he was coming with me to this shoot. It was at night, and I had to drive all the way out to some remote part of Chatsworth. I didn't know that Chatsworth even existed until I did porn. Apparently, the district of Chatsworth, deep in the San Fernando Valley in the city of Los Angeles, has a higher concentration of porno companies doing business than any other place in the world. Every major street is decorated with adult industry offices. Anabolic was on Nordhoff Street, at the corner of Owensmouth. The building was ominous, a grey cement two-story warehouse that said ANA-BOLIC and DIABOLIC in large letters on the front.

Tyler's eyes were shining like it was Christmas. He was told that any chick who went to the Anabolic warehouse and blew someone could have free shirts and hats. Tyler really wanted

some free Anabolic gear. I told him that I would not blow a guy
for clothes. That was where I drew the line. What would be next?
Fucking for food? Tyler remained hopeful though. He knew he
could persuade me to do anything if he threw a fit or made a big
enough commotion about it. I was easily convinced. All he had
to say was, "Ori, do you love me? Well, then...?" How could I
argue? Of course I loved him.

We met a friendly Asian-American guy in the parking lot.
His name was Voltron. And Wanker. We could address him by
either name. He had a big beer gut and brown skin. He was probably in his late twenties, but I couldn't be sure. I always thought
Asian people had great skin. My mom is half Chinese and
has almost no wrinkles. I immediately liked this guy, Voltron
or Wanker. He giggled constantly. His face had an infectious
humorous expression that seemed to suggest everything around
him was a permanent joke. I liked that he didn't take this porno
shit so seriously. I felt the same way, that all of this was still a big
laughing matter. The sex I was having and the money people
paid me felt kind of silly. This was supposed to be a brief detour
I would one day look back on and laugh at.

Voltron seemed completely harmless. He didn't even seem
like he had a dick. He was entirely void of sexuality. He had a
mean sense of humor, but so did I.

He was, as it turned out, a very sick person, though. He had
previously done time for pistol-whipping an ex-girlfriend, and was
a serious drug addict. He is still suspected of murdering his girlfriend, a porno girl named Haley. We will never truly know because
Voltron, aka Wanker, killed himself shortly after her death.

We walked with Voltron through the empty office building
to the back, near the warehouse. It was past seven at night, and
all the employees had long since gone home. There were several

lights, called Kino Flos, set up near a couch. Kino Flos are packages of fluorescent lights, the most common lighting equipment in porn. A few dudes were there getting things ready for the shoot. I can't remember who they were because they were shy. And I was still embarrassed to be there. I wasn't able to proudly say, as I can now, "I'm Ashley Blue, and I'm here for the blowjob scene and ass-licking."

Pro Trusion introduced himself. "Hello, pleased to meet you, I'm Pro. Ashley Blue? And, is this your boyfriend?" He was sneering too much to be sincere. He was downright sarcastic. But he was funny. He meant to be entertaining. It was clear that he liked attention. Pro Trusion had a speech impediment and sounded like an exaggerated character from *The Simpsons*, sniveling, as if his dentist was perpetually drilling him without using the saliva ejector tool. Maybe he had to develop the comedic personality because of his lifelong problem. Spit, white spittle, was flying as he talked.

Bitterness also exuded from this man. He was around fifty years old and was bald and a tad overweight. He told us right away what he wanted us to know about him, his own story, his mythology. At the time, Tyler and I believed everything people told us about themselves. I didn't think anyone had a reason to lie in porno. I thought everyone was already a degenerate, so there was no reason to lie and make yourself sound better, because everyone already thought of you as a lowlife. I was wrong about that. Pro explained that he was a rich real estate developer and just directed porno for fun. What he really got off on was rough sex. His *Rough Sex* series of videos were so abusive that he had to discontinue them. Stores banned his work for the sheer violence toward women. This made him prouder than anything else he'd accomplished in life, he said.

Pro was an incessant talker. When he spoke, he looked straight into our eyes for reactions. He wanted us to be scared and shocked. He seemed desperately excited to put fear into me. It was confusing, because he also made us laugh with his clever humor. He was obviously a smart guy. But at the same time we were made uncomfortable by his vulgarity. He smoked a putrid smelling cigar and bared his yellow-brown teeth around its soggy butt as he talked. He used intellectual words. He was testing my comprehension, trying to see how intelligent I was. He even remarked a couple of condescending times that I was "pretty smart for an ass-licking, little anal whore."

I just let Pro Trusion talk to me any way he wanted, which was down and rude. Yet another thing to get used to in this porno business, I thought. I shouldn't expect any better treatment from these pornographers, really. Why seek his respect? In a few minutes he's going to see me with my tongue in some guy's asshole.

Respectfulness had a vague meaning to me. It didn't really bother me to be disrespected on a porn level. Pro wasn't going to be my friend. I was young and seeking his approval as a porn director, not his respect as a human being. Some sick and sad people are incapable of paying even the most common of dignities. I wanted this cretin, Pro Trusion, to be singing my professional praises by the end of this blowjob scene. No matter how he treated me as a person, through sexual performance, I was going to gain—I was going to earn—some recognition.

I sat on the couch with a light pointed at my face. The dude I was about to blow, Bent Brent, was sitting nearby on a chair. He was rubbing his cock through his pants. So was Tyler. Voltron worked the video camera, and Pro Trusion started with his questions. One of his specialties was to ask a girl just the right questions to make her cry on film. His interviews always came first, before the sex. He asked me about my parents—did they know? No, they didn't, and I didn't care if they did. He inquired about my aspirations before I decided to suck cock for a living. His goal was to make me feel like a piece of shit. He said, "...because that's what you are, aren't you, a piece of shit?" I told him I wanted to be an artist. I was unshaken by his insults. He couldn't make me feel bad about myself, no matter how much of a jerk he tried to be. How could this guy think he had any grounds to judge me? To Pro's disappointment, I didn't cry. He said he wanted to continue the interview some other time, for another scene. Good. Another gig meant more money.

We had to start the blowjob. Bent Brent had a long, uncircumcised penis. It was about ten inches, with a curve in the middle. It was like an elephant's trunk, but I managed to get the entire thing down my throat. It was better to deep throat than to suck because of the foreskin. The smell underneath foreskin grosses me out. It's sour and resembles the stench of what's between sweaty toes. Brent's had a lot of white, cheesy stuff under it too. Every time he stroked his cock, more would appear. It was like a butter churn.

During the blowjob and ass-eating, Pro berated me. I just licked away at the butthole. It was freshly swabbed with a baby wipe. The ass was much less offensive than the cock cheese. Brent had pretty clean toes, too. There wasn't any visible fungus, like so many other porno guys had. His feet were dry and rough with calluses. I sucked each toe individually, then stuck the whole foot into my mouth, as far down as I could. Then I choked myself, taking the extra step. I wanted to show everyone how into this I was. I didn't want anyone to pity me or think I was doing it just for the money. I don't—I didn't—think I was doing it just for the money.

Pro saw me choking myself with Brent's cock and foot. "Do you like to get choked?" he asked after Bent Brent had dumped his load all over my face. Tyler had gotten turned on during the scene and decided to pop on me as well. Now I was wiping both of their cum off of me. Without much thought, I replied with a yes. I remarked how much I liked it when Mark Davis had done it to me, that I loved it. Mark Davis was the sexiest porno guy ever. He was English and handsome. It didn't even matter that he was uncircumcised. He could make it work—he could make you feel happy about foreskin. I swooned when I worked with him. He was charming and sexy, just like my own boyfriend, only a little more. Doing scenes with Mark Davis was like acting out a romance novel.

"Can I choke you?" Pro asked with a dark gleam in his eyes. My compliments about Mark Davis struck a nerve. Pro Trusion didn't like it when girls talked about Mark Davis choking them. According to Pro, Mark couldn't do it the right way. "I am the only one who does it right. Let me choke you." I said it would have to wait until the next shoot. Fair enough.

"Do you like to get pissed on?" Pro asked. He was relentless.

I thought about it, then laughed, looking at Tyler. "No, no one's ever done that to me."

Pro gasped, "What? You're kidding me! You have to try it. You'll love it! I swear on my children! All girls love piss. Every girl I've ever pissed on absolutely loved it! We can do it right now. Can I piss on you?" His yellow-brown teeth were gnashing together with delight. This was a real treat.

I stared at Tyler, sort of in disbelief. I never thought anyone would be asking if they could piss on me. Especially someone I barely knew. I didn't have a ready answer. So, I responded, "No, you can't piss on me. If I were ever going to do that, it would

only be with my boyfriend. He's the only one who ever could."
Assuming Tyler was on the same page, I thought I had gracefully
dodged the situation. I didn't want to get pissed on for the first
time in front of people. I liked to do everything at home first.
Instead of remaining on the same level, Tyler lit up with excitement. "Okay, let's do it! I'll piss on you!" This was his chance to
finally be in on the action. He'd been sitting on the sidelines for
so many shoots and wasn't satisfied with just being an extra pop
shot. He jumped at the chance to piss in my mouth. I don't know
why I thought he wouldn't.

"No, Tyler, you can't just piss on me right now. Your pee is
too yellow. It's gross." I was looking for any reason at all to stop
what was already sadly in motion.

"My pee is always clear. Can I piss on you?" Pro wouldn't give
up trying to gain first pissing rights to my mouth.

"No! I'll drink water. Look, I'm drinking right now." Tyler
chugged down the bottle in his hand, and Voltron handed
him another.

"All right, fine." I gave up and laughed at myself. Not ten
minutes earlier had I wiped the cum of two guys out of my eyes.
Soon, I would be wiping out piss. Who knows, I thought, maybe
I really will love it. I did love it in the ass. Part of me looked
forward to any possibility of enjoyment. It would definitely be
the most hardcore thing I'd ever done. Anal sex and piss. There
was a ring to it.

Tyler filled up his bladder as much as he could. Voltron and
Pro went into one of Anabolic's employee bathrooms with Tyler
and me. The door was wide open for all of the others to watch.
I got down on my knees and made sure my face was positioned
over the toilet bowl. *Ha, now I'm the toilet bowl,* I thought. I
looked up at Tyler as he unzipped and pulled out his soft dick. I

asked him to hold my hand. He did. I watched the peehole until the pee stream appeared. Then it was steadily flowing into my mouth. It was warm and gross, salty and stinky, all vinegar and sour herbs. There wasn't a lot of yellow to it, but it was still sour. All the water he drank didn't make it exactly clean.

The piss filled up my mouth a couple of times, there was so much of it. I just spit it into the bowl. No way was I going to swallow it. After about thirty seconds, Tyler stopped pissing. He couldn't pee anymore. He was completely hard. Pissing in my mouth gave him a huge boner. I looked at him and said, "Are you serious?" His erection was very serious. It turned him on big time that I was kneeling over a toilet getting pissed on. I even put my hair into pigtails for him, at his request.

I took the piss into my open mouth with a smile. It was totally ridiculous. I was thinking, *Okay, done.* Now I've tried piss and I can say so with truth and conviction whenever someone asks me about it: It's not that big of a deal. I didn't love it, and I didn't totally despise it. I guess it was more for the guy to get off on. Voltron captured it all on video. I consented to have it be taped, and Pro paid me an extra two hundred dollars in cash. He said it would never be seen by anyone else but him, that he had a whole collection of private videos that he kept at home to jerk off to. Stupid me, I believed him.

A few months later, the piss scene in the bathroom ended up on one of Pro's websites called *PissMops.com*. I felt like an idiot for trusting this guy. It was out of my control. Once you sign that model release, it's over. As the performer, I surrendered absolute consent after I was paid for the footage. To tell the truth, I like that people can watch me getting pissed on my first time. I like piss now. By the time *Piss Mops #2* was put onto DVD, I was ready for it. Pro Trusion even put me on the front cover.

CHAPTER ELEVEN

GONORRHEA

IT happened only two months after we started doing porn. While HIV tests once a month were mandatory, back in 2002, the syphilis, chlamydia, and gonorrhea testing was free but optional. Tyler and I decided to get tested for all four diseases. Give us the works, the full panel! We felt proud to be doing at least one healthy thing for our bodies. "It's the right thing to do," we said. "We have to take care of ourselves now that we are in porn."

The results came back a week later. HIV: negative. Syphilis: negative. Gonorrhea and chlamydia both came back positive. We got a courtesy telephone call from the Adult Industry Medical clinic. They needed us to come in and get medicated. They also needed us to give to them a list of the people we'd had sex with in the last month. I wanted to die. I felt so filthy, from the inside out. Welcome to porn.

I must have wailed "Oh my god, Tyler," over and over, for hours. We sat on the floor of our apartment feeling stunned and sorry for ourselves. "Why did we have to get this? Why?"

"Well, we fucked a lot of people," Tyler said. "It's normal, I guess. I mean, to get this stuff in porn. I mean, we were going to get it sooner or later. Everybody does."

It is not normal to fuck more than ten or twenty different people in a month. You catch stuff called gonorrhea. What was it? Was it diarrhea in your pussy? It was awful to dissect all the ways I felt I had become so sickening. I wanted to hide from the daylight people. People who got up before noon and went to work, people whose job liabilities did not include the risk of gonorrhea. *We are no longer allowed in society*, I thought to myself, *we're being punished*. This was karma for staying up all night every night doing cocaine and having threesomes. Waking up at 3:00 p.m. and doing porn has consequences. They are called gonorrhea and chlamydia.

"Look, Ori. Calm down. It's going to be all right. We just have to go in and get some medication. At least this is curable. We don't have AIDS. We're lucky."

"Lucky? I don't feel lucky! And I don't want to talk about or think about the possibility of us catching AIDS. That's awful, Tyler! Don't say that! I can't fucking handle the thought of that." I was throwing a complete fit. I rolled around on the floor on my back, crying and kicking my feet. All my life, I've gotten the most out of good tantrums. As a kid, they felt so viscerally good. Now when they happen, they're cathartic.

Tyler got up off the floor and walked into the bathroom to pee. I remained on the carpet, being morbid and negative. When he stepped out of the bathroom, he had a frown on his face.

"Um, I think I feel it. My dick doesn't feel right. It's hurting to take a piss right now. I think we should hurry up and get that medicine. Get up!" Now he was worried. So much for being the calm one. "Ori! Come on! I'm fucking serious! My dick hurts. We need to get there by five, hurry up!"

I was contemplating the devastating scenario of Tyler and me catching AIDS. We'd be shunned from everyone in porn. Our faces would be all over the news. We would have to live in an assisted living establishment because no one would want to help take care of us. Suicide would be the only solution.

"Ori, my dick feels really weird! Look at it!" he shouted, not in anger, but with fear. He'd shuffled out of the bathroom with his pants around his ankles. The cock looked tiny and frail. The white briefs he was wearing had yellowish green stains on the crotch.

"Ew, Tyler. What's that? Is that why they call it the drip?" I was probably the one who gave it to him, and he was feeling all the symptoms. I didn't have any. Who knows how long I had been infected. It didn't even burn when I peed. There were no yellow or green stains on my panties.

We decided our gonorrhea and chlamydia were good excuses to leave town. That night, after getting the medication from Sherman Oaks, we drove to Houston. I have always had warm feelings about Texans. My dad's family all live in Texas, but I don't speak to them. Maybe it's more like they don't speak to me. I haven't seen my father since he disappeared when I was fourteen. But I lived with him in Texas, briefly. It was in a town called Pflugerville, just outside of Austin.

Tyler and I made it to Houston the next morning. We drove all night, through the darkest parts of New Mexico and West Texas. We did cocaine the entire drive, so we were paranoid about every single light we saw in the middle of the desert. There were dozens of tiny red flashing ones. We were convinced we were being tracked by UFOs.

Tyler's grandparents let us stay with them. They had a neat 1970s house that reminded me of *The Brady Bunch*. Tyler's grandmother made us Frito pie. We stayed in Tyler's old room, which was right next to his great-grandmother's room. Tyler had been raised by his grandparents, Emmett and Naomi. They called him Scooter. I thought it was darling. He had such a loving family. The only thing wrong with them that I could see was that they were solid George Bush and George W. Bush fans.

We stayed at Tyler's grandparents' house for five days. That was how long our gonorrhea and chlamydia lasted. It was a pleasant way to live through the duration of our STDs, except for the constant lies we told to all of Tyler's family. Why did we have so much money? How did our jobs allow us to take off for five days on such short notice? What exactly did each of us do? I couldn't take being around Tyler's family for very long because it felt too awful to lie. And it was too hard to keep track. Was I a secretary, a personal assistant, or a production assistant? Did Tyler sell cars or was he in sales? Did I get a big tax refund, or did I have a trust fund? We kept on having to go into detail with the lies, which accidentally got changed from person to person sometimes. We lied to everyone but Tyler's younger sister, Desiree. She'd already witnessed firsthand what we did.

Desiree had come to visit us for the annual Coachella Valley Music and Arts Festival, a giant gathering in the desert outside of Los Angeles. Coachella was a major reason Tyler and I continued to do porn. Tickets for the thing were rather pricey, and we were so hungry to attend that we used it to justify selling our bodies. The event takes place every year in April. We began doing porn in March. Porno funded our party pilgrimage. We could buy as much coke and ecstasy as we needed, which was a couple thousand dollars' worth. I remember saying how exciting it was to see all of these infamous bands. Now, I can't even remember who played.

We flew Desiree out from Houston. She and Tyler had the same mother, but different fathers. Half-siblings, like me and my sisters. Tyler's mom was married more times than my mother, but they are both named Cheryl. Desiree looked like her mother in the face. She was pale and very pretty. Her eyebrows were severely plucked, but she had big, blue eyes and a perfectly straight nose. Her whole family treated her like she was much older than seventeen. She quit going to high school but claimed she was on "independent study." I knew what that meant. It's a legal version of her mother letting her drop out of school. My mom did the same thing and put me in the "independent study" program when I was the same age. It's for mothers who just give up making their kids go to school when parenting becomes too tough for them.

Before I met Desiree, I imagined her to be this hard-ass and worldly woman. She had a job as a hostess at some fancy restaurant in Houston—something I could never handle. I did the same type of job and got fired for sleeping at the front desk, just prior to entering porn. Desiree was also a full-time drug dealer. She used and sold crystal methamphetamine. Tyler was proud of her for her street smarts and for making so much money at such a young age. Desiree was proud of her business, too. She and Tyler spoke often on the phone. They were close. I'm sure she knew that he sold hash in Barcelona while he was going to culinary school, but I'm not sure if she knew about the Drāno acid he'd sold to the neighborhood schoolchildren. She looked up to him and found nothing wrong with making extra cash just like her big brother. She even sent us some product in the mail. As a surprise, Desiree would call the night before to tell us a present was coming. The next day, a FedEx envelope would arrive at our doorstep. I'd even signed for it. Delivered to our door with love, a bag of crystal meth and a couple bars of Xanax!

Bringing Desiree to LA was our way of saying thanks for all the packages of drugs she sent us out of the kindness of her little Texan heart. We never gave her any money for the meth she sent because we hardly had enough to pay our bills at the time. That was all over now—being broke was a thing of the past. Porno economy. There would be no limits to spending on all the fun we could have.

Desiree was a sweet little girl. I was taken aback by how young she really was. Her baby face was seventeen, no matter how much crystal she was doing. She tried to like me, but I could tell she didn't trust me. Tyler told her I was a cheater, and that spoiled any chances of our being friends. It must have been so strange for her while Tyler tried to explain and substantiate the fact we did porn. She didn't want to hear it, but she nodded and smiled, accepting it. I was so wrapped up in my own battles with morality that I didn't really think about her well-being too much. The fact that she was seventeen and visiting us to hang out and do drugs should have been a bigger issue than my doing porn. Desiree said she could handle herself and had her life under control. Only three years older than her, I was the furthest thing from a good example. I tried to respect her decisions. She wanted to quit school and sell drugs.

Within the first hour of hanging out in our apartment, Desiree and Tyler taught me how to smoke crystal meth. Desiree fashioned a foil pipe into something that looked like an aluminum volcano. Tyler hollowed out a cheap ballpoint pen that served as a straw. Using the straw, we three chased the dragon together. After one of us lit the meth, melting it, we would take turns sucking up the smoke. The effects of smoking it, as opposed to sniffing lines, were much stronger. It smelled like a smokestack from a plastic factory. The smoke was a light grey and I could definitely taste every single chemical when it filled up my mouth. I tried to hold it in as long as I could, because that supposedly got you higher. Smoking meth made my whole body numb and light, without the burn that comes from sniffing it. It turned my brain into a ball of helium and lifted my body off the floor.

For days, the three of us smoked crystal, did coke, ate ecstasy, and drank booze. We made it out to the concert, four hours away near Palm Springs. I really can't remember much, but I do have some snapshots from the trip. We look fucked up and very happy. Desiree, Tyler, and I are so skinny holding on to each other in the photos. A group of degenerates. Tyler's eyes are half open and rolling back into his skull. We all have maniacal smiles on our mouths. It was supposed to be a good time. We had all the drugs we could possibly want.

On the third day of her visit, I had a shoot in Woodland Hills. It was for a movie called *Grrl Power*. My call time wasn't until the afternoon. It didn't really matter, because I was planning on being late. I was a few hours late, in fact. Tyler and Desiree dropped me off at the location. We were all super high on ecstasy, too out of it to leave Desiree at home alone. I didn't feel good. But the director and production manager told me I was fine, so Tyler and Desiree left. It was probably for the best. Having an underage girl at a porn shoot could get everyone arrested. I stayed there to do my scene, but I was rolling so hard I could barely open my eyes during the stills. I'd already gotten the cold shoulder from the makeup artist.

Two different men on set lectured me about taking drugs before scenes and how it looked bad. They asked me what I was on and I told them, "Mmmm, ecstasy..." But I had no idea who they were or why anyone cared. This was porno, right? I was on the road to ruin, not success! Not one part of me felt guilty or sorry for doing drugs. I was a total mess, but they shot me anyway. I did a great scene, despite the bad looks and worse vibes

I got from the entire crew. They were happy when I left. Tyler picked me up a few hours later, without Desiree. The director wrote out my check and told Tyler not to let me take as many pills next time.

When our infections cleared up, I was ready to leave Texas. We could retest and go back to work seven days after starting the antibiotics. We needed to get back to LA All of our shoots were rescheduled because of the STDs. No one in porno really cared that we got sick. Everyone was very sympathetic and understanding. We were not ostracized or treated poorly because of it. I was looking forward to going back. Porno had become the world in which we thrived.

After not being able to talk about porn and our involvement in it for so many days, I began to miss it dearly. I wanted nothing more than to speak freely about it and not have to hide from it. Even if I wasn't proud of it or bragging about it, I wanted to be able to mention it if I wished. Tyler and I needed to get back where things were happening. LA was where people would be open-minded again. Where the Republicans were outnumbered and the weather was nice. Home to cocaine and pornography. Home to Trent and Ashley. Home, where we fit in. Hollywood. Home.

CHAPTER TWELVE

HEART ATTACK

BECAUSE Tyler and I were doing coke every day and every night, and booze was just as excessive as the cocaine—we drank it all, beer, Scotch, vodka, whiskey, tequila, wine coolers, red wine, Goldschläger, gin and tonic, etc.—all of our porno money was spent as soon as we fucked for it. It was a blast to live in such a grand city and have the time and means to enjoy everything Dionysian within it. Los Angeles is the best place to live, period. Tyler and I frequented The Cat & Fiddle, Barfly, The Abbey, Improv, The Viper Room, Saddle Ranch, La Poubelle, and Birds. We went out dancing at Joya, 7969 Santa Monica, Hollywood Athletic Club, Three Clubs, and Fubar. We ate at Matsuhisa, Water Grill, The Pig, Cobras and Matadors, and French Market Place. We went anywhere we damn well pleased. Carousing was all that mattered, our skewed version of everyday, normal life. Our lives revolved around the next outing, the next party.

We remained living in the same cheap studio apartment. Even though we were making a few thousand per week in porn, we still only paid $575 a month for rent. Our neighborhood was full of transsexual prostitutes and drug dealers, so it was cool. Much better than the closed-minded and uninspiring suburb of Thousand Oaks. The filthy and unsafe elements suited us. It got unbearably hot in the summer without air conditioning. But we could be as loud as we wanted since it was so loud on the streets at night. There were fights, car crashes, police helicopters, and drunks. It was scary and fun at the same time.

Our place was cute. We painted the walls light blue with lavender borders. The bathroom was bright purple with a day-glow shower curtain. I painted little red roses in various spots on each wall. On the dark green fridge, I painted "I like food, food tastes good!" in honor of one of my favorite bands, the Descendents.

My little Sony boom box provided music when we smoked and drank all night. There was also a television and a PlayStation. Sometimes Tyler would challenge one of our friends to a coked-out marathon of Tony Hawk. I asked him to buy a DVD player after shooting a POV scene with some creepy producer. Tyler bought the video game player instead. I hate video games. There was a time when I got hooked on Nintendo, but I was seven years old. Now, it's just Nofriendo.

We kept our cheap apartment relatively clean. You could catch me vacuuming at three in the morning. I refused to have a garbage bin in the place for fear of tempting the cockroaches that are just about everywhere in Los Angeles. Maybe it's because the weather is so nice. Even on the cleanest streets in Beverly Hills, there are cockroaches. Roaches on our street were dark, fearless, mysterious. Diseased. I often had nightmares about them, and still do.

The best thing about the apartment was the twenty-four hour unlimited access to as much cocaine as we needed, thanks to Ernesto. Tyler and I were Ernesto's best clients. We spent a thousand dollars a week on cocaine. He would even allow us to go in and get it when he wasn't home. Tyler had a special method of breaking the screen off Ernesto's kitchen window. All he had to do was slide it to the right and it would open just enough to crawl through. Tyler and I were such trusted friends that we knew where Ernesto hid the stash. It was always in a coffee mug right above the pantry. We would break off however much we needed and weigh it on the tiny drug scale. Usually a couple grams. The money was left on the counter. It was a beautiful system.

I never realized at the time how much of an addict I was. I had only tried coke a couple of times before Tyler found such a steady source in Ernesto. We would hang out in his apartment and before we were in porn he would give the coke to us for free. Soon it went from a weekend thing to a nightly activity. The word "addict" never applied to me though, or so I thought. I didn't even consider myself a cigarette addict. I'd been smoking since I was fourteen, but I just thought it was because I liked it, not that I needed it. Tyler and I weren't addicts, we said. We just liked to party. Drugs feed your mind such bullshit. It's amazing.

Ever since Tyler had that first Viagra he became obsessed with the little blue pills. He insisted on getting his own prescription. He got it from a drug-dealer doctor that ran an urgent care clinic in Canoga Park. All the porno people went to him for pills. Without checking any vitals or stats, Dr. Dope prescribed my twenty-five year old cokehead boyfriend Viagra. We didn't know very much about the drug, except that it was for old men. That, and if you mixed it with any nitrates you could die. Tyler wasn't worried about harming himself since it was a porn director that gave him one in the first place. It had to be safe, right? As long as he didn't do any poppers or sniff any VCR head cleaner, he'd be fine.

One night, Tyler and I were hanging out at home doing coke instead of eating dinner, the usual. Coke was our dinner. It was laundry night, so we got an extra gram to stay focused. We thought having after-coke coke was the same as having coffee after a meal, only stronger. Ernesto had drinks and did lines with us while we washed our clothes. By 2:30 in the morning, it was just Tyler and I with a huge pile of clean, unfolded clothes in the middle of the floor. We never folded. There weren't enough drugs in the world to get us to fold. Out of nowhere, Tyler started pacing the apartment. He was totally jacked up and wanted to smoke inside. I wouldn't let him. He grabbed his chest, took a deep breath and held it for a second. When he let it out loudly, he put his fingers around his left wrist to check his pulse. His eyes darted all around the apartment. His mind was racing and he didn't hold long enough to properly count the beats. He didn't need to. It was too fast to count.

"Tyler, what are you doing?" I asked, very sweetly. I was concerned, but I didn't want to sound alarmed. He was freaking me out.

"My heart's just banging. I think there's something wrong." He barely made eye contact with me as he walked to the porch to have a cigarette.

"Maybe you shouldn't smoke right now. Cigarettes are a stimulant. Have some water or go get in the shower. A cold shower will snap you out of this," I optimistically suggested.

Tyler just took another loud, deep breath and felt his bare chest again. He had this look in his eyes that happens only when he's done way too much coke. It's a crazy, paranoid expression that shuts him off from anyone else. He goes into his own fucked-up world and acts like a complete asshole in the real one. Every time Tyler had gone psycho on me with jealousy and yelled at me, accusing me of being "against him," he had this exact look about him. Telescopic fish-eyes.

"Are you okay? Is there something I can do for you?" I was scared now.

He looked at me with fear and hate. Like I was a bitch for asking him if he was okay. "No. Ori. I'm not 'okay.' Do I look 'okay' to you? My heart is going way too fast. I have chest pains. I took a Viagra a little while ago, and I feel bad, really bad."

"What did you take a Viagra for? It's so late." I couldn't hide how stupid I thought it was.

Tyler yelled at me, "Because I wanted to be crazy, Ori! I don't know, maybe I wanted to fuck! Or do you only want to fuck on camera, for money? Is that it?"

"What? No, Tyler. That's not true," I said in a small voice. It always hurt my feelings when he said things like this. I wasn't really sure what I liked more, sex at home or sex in the movies. Tyler always knew where to hit me when I was feeling vulnerable. Only hookers like it more in the pornos, I thought. If I like getting paid for sex more, it means I am just a prostitute. Being called a hooker is way worse than being a porn star.

"Ori. I feel really, really bad. Call 911!"

"No. I can't. You're all right. You're just freaking out."

"ORI! Call fucking 911! I'm having a fucking heart attack!" He screamed at me, his eyes bulging out in terror.

"No! You're fine, Tyler. You're just too hot. Look, I'll get a cold washcloth to put on your neck. Just take some deep breaths and calm down!"

"Fuck it! I'll call myself if you won't do it. This is serious! I'm having a fucking heart attack and you don't even fucking care!" He flopped down on the bed and picked up the phone with the free hand not clutching his chest. "I can't believe you're making me call my own ambulance, Ori. You won't even do this for me. You don't love me at all! I could die, Ori! You don't fucking love me, do you?"

I loved him more than I loved anyone else in the world. I was fucked up, too, and scared that he was going to get us in deep trouble. You never call the police when you're on drugs. They will arrest you. Didn't he know that? Was his heart attack as real as our paranoia? "Tyler, please don't call! Please! We'll get in trouble. We are so fucked up!" I begged him not to call.

He dialed 911.

I ran downstairs and pounded on Ernesto's door. The only person I had to help me was the dealer. He grabbed Tyler by the arm, "Look, man, you gotta listen to me. Don't smoke right now. Don't drink any alcohol. You need some water. I've seen this happen a lot of times. You're not having a heart attack. You gotta chill out, man. You don't need an ambulance, man. Relax." Ernesto was a lot better at this than I was. He wasn't screaming at Tyler or sobbing, calling him "baby." But all of Ernesto's pragmatic drug wisdom bounced off of Tyler's fixed gaze. It was no use. His mind was set on heart attack.

The sirens came blaring down the street and an ambulance and fire engine stopped outside of the gate. Red and white lights flashed in the night sky. I held on to Tyler's arm as we walked down the steps and out the gate, as if we were leaving one altar for another, ill-omened one. He was my man. I had to stand by him, no matter how stupid he was being.

"Who called?" The fireman boomed in a loud, clear voice. He was the first sober person we'd seen in ten hours.

"I did. It was me. But it was a mistake," Tyler backed down. He did look a lot better. His crazy-eye disappeared. He was now standing in front of the emergency medical technicians, very humbled.

"You called about a heart attack?" the fireman asked. He knew the story. Young, fit men don't have heart attacks unless it's because of drugs.

"Yeah, I was feeling chest pain, but it's starting to feel better. I think I'm okay now." Tyler was calming, crashing, doing his best to look innocent.

"Have you been taking any drugs tonight?" fireman number two asked.

"We took some ecstasy that someone gave us at a party. I don't know what was in them. We never do this. We thought we'd try it just once. It was stupid. We're more mature than that. They're wearing off now. I'm okay."

Tyler seemed quite fine all of the sudden and talked us out of having to get in the ambulance. It was as if Ferris Bueller were the star of an ABC Afterschool Special. He pulled it off, but it had a sobering effect on both of us. Back in our apartment, we were again alone. All was calm, and we were safe. I began picking through the clothes pile, looking for some pajamas.

"Where's the coke? What did you do with the rest that was on this plate?" Tyler asked.

I was shocked that he wanted to do more after everything that'd happened. "I'm sorry, Tyler, I got scared and flushed it in the toilet when you called 911. I didn't know what to do. I thought we would get in trouble. I'm sorry," I cried.

"You did what? You flushed it? How could you do that? Oh fuck, Ori! That was so much, and you just flushed it! I really could use some right now. I just need a few lines to go to sleep and unwind. You flushed it!" He just needed a few lines to go to sleep.

"I'm sorry Tyler," I sobbed. I was exhausted. I couldn't argue anymore.

"Will you go down and get some more from Ernesto? Please?" He was serious.

"No! It's too late. You don't need anymore! Let's just get it tomorrow," I pleaded.

"You're the one who threw it all in the toilet without asking me! You should go get more. Don't you love me?"

Of course I loved him. So, down, down, down to Ernesto's I went.

CHAPTER THIRTEEN

CHOKED OUT

T**ECHNICALLY**, I did ask for it. When Pro Trusion had asked me if he could choke me, I told him he could. I liked it when Tyler and Mark Davis had done it to me during sex. It was erotic. My experience with it had been good, so far. I was very trusting to let men do what they thought was best. I never wanted to say no. I thought that saying no meant that I was holding myself back from something new. Experience was very important to me. I got off, emotionally, on being persuaded. "No" was not a very strong word in my vocabulary.

Tyler and I were asked to do another shoot for Pro Trusion. It was to be a very rough blowjob scene with some slapping. Both Tyler and Trusion would be choking and slapping me. This information was provided up front. I thought I knew what I was committing myself to. I thought it was safe because Tyler would be there with me.

It was a gorgeous day. Tyler and I casually strolled up to the door of the condo. The building was nice and new, on a peaceful street in Tarzana. We'd been there before, when Tyler was hired to get a blowjob from some girl named Gemstone. I tagged along to watch his performance. He throat fucked this chick and she threw up In-N-Out burger all over his dick. It was disgusting. I could smell it. She refused to clean it up, so I stepped in. I wiped the grey, lumpy mess off of Tyler's cock and lap. Then I got him hard, sucking his vomit-coated penis until he was solid enough to stick it in Gemstone again.

Voltron met us at the door. He led us upstairs to the master bedroom. The entire condo was almost empty. It looked like nobody had ever even lived in it. A couch, desk, and a lamp were the only items of furniture. The place was large, three stories and three bedrooms. Pro Trusion bragged about how he owned it and had built the entire complex. We just shrugged and told him that it was great. It was not a great place, but it was spacious. We climbed the steps to the top floor and entered the room where the scene was going to be shot. There were some lights set up, and a bed. Pro Trusion sat in a chair. He was cheerful. He talked nonstop as soon as we entered the room. He went on and on about how excited he was to choke me. I was finally going to know how it's really done, the right way. I just smiled and went along. Whatever they wanted to do, I was game.

The camera was rolling and Pro began with his preliminary questions. He was so vile. Looking at him made me shudder. His teeth were brown, his breath like rancid garbage. He was smart enough to intimidate me, but I didn't think he was better than me. I didn't look up to him or admire him the way I did Tyler or Mark Davis. Pro Trusion was just an old, gross pervert. Any submissiveness I felt was merely a game. I really didn't think I had any reason to fear Pro.

He leaned in close to my face and looked into my eyes. It was like he was trying to use his eyes to stomp all over mine. Then he pinched my nose and held my mouth shut, suffocating me. He twisted my nose, hard, and I started to cry. He released me.

"It's just the nose that made you cry, right?" he said, and he put his hands around my throat. His mouth was watering. "So if

I go like this, this isn't going to make you cry, is it? This is scary, isn't it? Is it scary?"

"Yes..."

Not another ounce of air went into my lungs before Pro Trusion clenched my throat. He squeezed with both of his big hands, tightly. One hand was in front and one behind, cutting air off completely. He stood up as he choked me. Pro stared into my gaze. It was obvious that I wasn't expecting this, and I was terrified. It's what he wanted. His grip was so hard that his teeth were clenching. When his mouth parted, a smile formed. He was sneering at me. Darkness and murder filled his eyes. He was strong, and he had me. I couldn't protest. I didn't know what to do. I wasn't ready. Pro was hurting me. I was naked and this man was strangling me.

"We're proud of you, okay? Alright, you're a good girl. So now your nose is not being hurt, so you're not going to cry, are you? Huh? Don't move your hands! Put your hands behind your back!" His grip went even tighter.

Tyler just watched. Voltron filmed. I thought I was just going to give Tyler and Pro blowjobs. It was too late to stop it. I couldn't do anything while Pro's hands wrung my neck. My legs went numb. The rest of my body felt a wave of warmth, but it was not a good warmth. I had no oxygen and was beyond dizzy. Big white and black spots appeared. I could no longer see, yet my eyes were still open. I was fighting to keep my eyes open—for fear that they would not reopen. I lost control of my muscles. My tongue started flopping in and out of my mouth.

I need help, I thought. I couldn't speak. I couldn't form the words to call for Tyler, who still sat and watched me. Everything went limp. My arms dropped from where they were trying to pry Pro's hands away. My eyes fluttered in one final attempt to live. My face went crimson and I passed out, gurgling. Then, I died.

I saw it. I saw that tunnel with the light at the end. There is definitive credence to the lore. I was alone in a dark place, but it was peaceful. When I looked into the light, I not only saw my entire life, but I felt it, too, passing through me like a specter. No specifics, but each primary emotion I had ever lived through I felt all at once in that light. All I can remember explicitly are visions from childhood. Then, I died a horrible death. At the end of it, I felt safety in the tunnel. It was real.

As suddenly as it all went black, I found myself back in the room, on the bed. My eyes opened. *This isn't Heaven.* I was looking at the white ceiling. I was lying on my back, on the bed in Tarzana. Tyler was there, staring at me, and a camera was rolling. I sucked in some air and let out a sob. Deep sobs kept coming from the bottom of my lungs, hyperventilation. How long had I been passed out? I was disoriented, scared and crying. Pro Trusion looked at me with self-satisfaction. I had broken down, finally, in front of this man. All he wanted was to see me cower in fear of him.

"That's what you get for not going on a date with me."

Nobody acted like it was a big deal. Pro Trusion was smiling. Tyler was eager to finish the blowjob scene. I was hysterical. Voltron kept at the camera.

Pro said, "Well, when I was younger I used to ask girls like you out on dates all the time and they would say 'no,' so now I'm forced to do this. You understand what I'm saying? You sure? *I'm dead serious.* You're very lucky I'm not in the scene. We could do that for three hours."

Tyler put his hands around my throat, saying, "I know you can do this. I promise I won't choke you out like he did. I've seen you do this before without crying."

After Tyler's failed attempt to slap me around and shove his cock in my throat, Pro cancelled the scene. I couldn't stop crying, so we had to stop. I felt like I was the problem. It was embarrassing. I was the only one who was upset. Was I crazy or fucked up? I was so confused after letting a man I trusted professionally try to choke me to death. Why couldn't I stop crying while they all acted like the day was perfectly fine?

To make himself into the big hero for the day, Pro Trusion paid Tyler and me a couple hundred dollars for a "kill fee." It was almost a real kill fee. Pro almost killed me. And I let him. So did Tyler. We took the money, gladly, and went to sushi with this man afterward. I was a shell of a person the whole rest of that day, cracking skin of the locust. I was still in shock, traumatized.

I tried to forget any of it had happened. I didn't want to let it stop me from doing porno scenes. I still wanted to be in porn, so I kept partying and performing in all the movies I could. I even did more scenes for Pro Trusion with Tyler. I acted like the choking didn't bother me because I didn't want to show any of them how much this horrible man had scared me. I would just roll my eyes and laugh about it.

The footage of me getting choked ended up on Pro's website. His knuckles are red around my neck. Many people saw it. It was so brutal that I got phone calls from producers that I didn't even know asking if I was okay. When I saw the video, it upset me all over again. It was an embarrassing first impression to present to people that didn't know me. I was still relatively new to the business and already crying and getting choked on the internet. It was so disturbing that Pro himself even took it off the site soon after it was made public. Nothing about it was sexual except that I was naked. It just looked like I was being attacked. The sole purpose of Pro's actions was to hurt and scare me. It's what he always and ultimately had in store for any porno girl that he hired for a scene. Pro Trusion is a sick person—I wouldn't even call him a sadist because that would sexualize him too much. I was green and vulnerable enough to allow myself into the situation. Though scared and shocked, I did not get fully angry about it until a year and a half later. Tyler and I even rented the very same condo in which I was choked to death. We lived there for a year and slept in the bedroom where it happened.

I stay away from creeps now. It took me a few years to finally shake Pro Trusion. I thought it would prove how much I'd grown as a person if I could be friendly with this man. I even asked him to be my date to an awards show. It didn't prove a thing. Only that I am capable of being wrong and naïve and savagely hopeful over and over. Instead of making me the bigger person, befriending Pro afterward only served to legitimize and glorify his actions.

I thought that I needed to "get over it." So I did. Like a lot of traumatic events that happen in life, it just had to be put aside. People close to me, like Tyler, continued to act like it wasn't a big deal. I was fine, and that's all that mattered. It was even funny to some people, because it didn't happen to them. It happened to me. I was choked to death. Then I woke up.

CHAPTER FOURTEEN

ANAL FISTING

IT was a little before eight in the morning. Tyler and I left Hollywood for Tujunga. We were working for a new director. He was hiring us together as a couple. The director's name was Roach. It was stressed by Roach not to be late. Maybe he had heard about our legendary tardiness. We always showed up to porno shoots at least a half hour late. Sometimes Tyler and I were hours late. Other times, we didn't show up at all. Love and cocaine were the biggest things in our lives. Porno came third and suffered because of the first two.

Luckily, Tyler and I were getting along great that morning. We were excited to meet this guy, Roach. He sought us out and spoke to both of us on the phone for hours. He told us all about the porn business and how he made a success out of his wife, Guinevere. They were millionaires from doing porn. Guinevere was the anal queen and he taught her everything she knew about anal sex.

Tyler was eager to work for this man because Roach was the first person who was happy that I had a boyfriend. Everyone up until then had been very rude to Tyler. He tried to prove we were a cool couple and that he loved the fact that I fucked other guys. Tyler was actually the opposite of all of the other porno boyfriends we'd met, guys who stared at the ground and seethed with anger while their girlfriends got fucked. Some just chain-smoked cheap cigarettes and fidgeted, waiting for the girlfriend's paycheck. The boyfriends tried to act tough, talking about how they're used to beating asses. There were a lot of what we called suitcase pimps, boyfriends that carried their girlfriends' porno clothes and shoes and drove them to set. Pussy guys that don't like to work. They spend their days controlling the money of the porno girlfriend. The suitcase pimp is a staple in the porn industry. It's a full-time job created by these special circumstances. For instance, when a girl is too drugged-out or belligerent to make it to a shoot, her suitcase pimp will drive her to work and wait for her to finish getting fucked. Many suitcase pimps sit around and smoke pot and drink soda on a given day of production.

Different directors and other male talent made it a point to try to make Tyler feel insecure. Victor disrespected Tyler and said plainly that we would probably be broken up by the business. So did some other male porno stars. They were all jealous of us, we thought. Nothing was ever going to break us up. Porn was just porn, not our entire lives. We were in love. They just didn't understand. My boyfriend was special. He encouraged me during my scenes. He wanted to see me get double penetrated and get covered in cum. Without Tyler behind me all the way, I wouldn't have been pushing the limits of my sexuality. I had his full support.

Roach told Tyler to hold on to me, that I would be a star and that we could be a very successful couple just like him and Guinevere. Instead of predicting the time it would take for us to break up, Roach gave Tyler and I hoards of advice. Save the money. Do every scene we can. Work for everyone. Don't have an agent. Don't be late. Work together as much as possible. Don't let me get a star attitude or put on airs once I'm famous. Always call him if we needed to talk about someone or something going wrong. We could count on Roach. He was on our side.

We made it to Tujunga at exactly eight o'clock. It was the first time Tyler and I had ever been on time going to a shoot together. We made sure not to oversleep. I took the extra precaution by staying up all night, sniffing coke, the ritual. I was high, as usual, and ready to shoot my porno scene. I could get away with it, somehow. I guess it's because I was only twenty. Despite the runny nose, I still looked sweet and innocent. I was happy. I knew that all the attention would be focused on me when I shot a scene.

Roach looked nothing like I'd imagined. Hearing his voice on the phone, I could only think of a friendly, nurturing, and only sort-of insane nice man. *Totally harmless*, I thought when we spoke. But Roach *looked* like a person who would harm you. He had tattoos covering every inch of his body, except his face. His neck, arms, chest, back, and fingers were inked. All of them crappy jail tattoos. One of them on his chest read "WHITE TRASH." He was bald, but covered it up with a black bandana tied around his head. I wasn't sure if he was sensitive about his hairline or if it was a skinhead thing. All of his clothes were black, including his boots. He smoked Winstons and wore silver jewelry.

"Ashley Blue! And Trent! It's great to meet you. We are going to have a killer and knockout scene today, right? I hear that your scenes are the best around right now. It's going to be all hardcore and anal. We've got to have high energy and hard fucking today! Let's get you ready, and then we'll go upstairs to start the scene. Before we begin, let's fill out the paperwork, then talk about what we are going to do. We've got to go for the extreme. Ashley, are you going to show me how you can push yourself to the outermost limits? Are you going to give me the hardest-core scene of your entire career?" Hardcore anal were the movies Roach was all about, what mattered most in life.

Of course I would do my hardest scene. Roach's enthusiasm made me feel loved. Tyler and I felt appreciated. I got ready as best as I could. There was no makeup artist to turn me into a whore. I had to do it myself. I didn't really know how. Roach wanted big hair and dark eye makeup. How do I look like that? I didn't even own dark makeup. My look was a fresh, young girl, not a cheap, overly-done stripper. As for the hair, it's still a mystery how some porno stars can even get it that big. When I had done all I could with a can of aerosol hairspray and some sticky Mac lip gloss, I emerged from the bathroom. I was plenty high. I brought extra coke with me to get me through the day. I always brought more with me when I was doing heavy anal scenes. It was a way for me to get energy without having to eat. Eating before and during an anal scene is taboo. Your bowels have to be completely empty when big porno cocks are pounding and gaping the asshole. If you eat, there will be shit. It's like Newton's Law or something.

Two massive Kino Flos were lying on the brown carpet in the bedroom upstairs. The room was plain as usual. Only a bed and a dresser for furniture. There was plenty of room for a guy named Quasar to move around. He was the cameraman. Roach came in to direct us all into what he called one of his masterpieces. He was absolutely radiant. I had never seen a man so enthusiastic and crazy about shooting pornography before. Roach called it "decadent anal love."

"Ashley Blue, would you follow me, please," Roach ordered, not asked. He had the best intentions though, I was sure. "You come, too, Trent. I want to show you both something." He guided us over to a laptop. The images on the screen were ones Roach had taken for Guinevere's website. "This is Guinevere's site," he said with pride. "It makes thousands of dollars a month. Do you know why?

I'll tell you. Because it has the most extreme and hardcore content. That is what sets her above the rest of the girls in porn. Guinevere has broken world records with what has gone into her ass. She holds the world record for putting the most chopsticks into her ass—one hundred chopsticks. Look at this."

Roach clicked on a photo gallery and a startling image appeared. Guinevere was lying on her side and looking back over her right shoulder, smiling. Her tiny arm reached back behind her, reaching her ass. The hand was not in the picture. Or was it? It was. Only, the hand wasn't visible because it was completely encased inside of her butthole. She was fisting her ass. It looked incredible!

"Is she fisting it?" I gasped.

"Yes. She's fisting her own ass. Isn't it amazing? I taught her how to do that. Today, I'm going to teach you, Ashley Blue." Roach grinned and put his hand on my shoulder. His blue eyes were sparkling.

"What? I don't know. How is it going to get in there? It's too big!" I looked at my own hand. Involuntarily, it had already gone into a fist as soon as I thought about the possibility.

Roach grabbed my fist. He wrapped his own fingers around my knuckles. Then he pulled his hand away, sizing my hand. "See that," he pointed to the measurement of my fist in the open "O" of his hand. "That's Mark Davis, right there. His dick's no smaller than your fist. You can do this, easy. You've taken Marcus in the ass. He's way bigger than your hand. Don't worry, I'll show you."

I lied down on the bed. With the camera rolling, we began the intro to the scene. Roach needed some build-up to the fisting and the sex. He handed Tyler some things to stick in my ass. A beer bottle and a candle, which they lit. It was just for show. I wasn't going to get fucked with those. Then Tyler's fingers went in. They were big and rough. I hate scratchy man fingers going into my ass. They are never manicured and often have gnarly hangnails or jagged edges. His callused digits continued to dry-fuck my hole, in an effort to stretch it. It only made me tighten up from being so uncomfortable.

I was relieved when it was my turn to put fingers in. Thank god it was my own hand that was going to do the fisting. My hands are lovely, I must say. I am vain about my hands. Roach poured an oil-based lubricant all over the hand that was going inside. I was on my side lying down. My arm came around my side; I put my hand in between the ass cheeks. I found the butt-hole. Slowly, I pushed all four fingers in. The thumb went next. All of the fingers were in and I kept on easing the rest into the anal cavity. It was a shock how easily my knuckles slid in there. I was relaxed and eager to accomplish putting the whole fist in.

Once my hand got past the knuckles, Roach gave me the final cue. "Okay, Ashley Blue, close your hand," he said.

I folded all four of my fingers and one thumb into a fist, while they were still in my ass. As soon as I did this, my hand went in a little further, too. Closing the fist made room for the entire hand. I did it! I could fist my own ass. I could trust my own hand. I could control it and it couldn't hurt me unless I commanded it to. It was a different kind of power than being at the mercy of taking a big cock controlled by another person. The feeling in my hand was different than I expected; in a warm, wonderful little pocket, it seemed like the walls of my pussy were muscular and firm in comparison. No wonder guys love fucking girls in the ass. I was so excited and proud of myself. Everyone else was proud, too. From that point on, Tyler and I had the utmost respect and faith in this new friend of ours, Roach.

The fact that I was now an anal-fisting porno girl changed my status as a performer. I was as hardcore as it gets. To me, it meant confidence. I could take on anything now, and it would be no problem. Directors saw me as unbreakable. I wouldn't go so far as to say that it made me a star. It did give me a false sense of durability, though, that nothing could ever hurt me. I thought, Hey, if I can fist my own ass, then I am the toughest girl on the planet. I came to find out later, the hard way, that I was wrong.

CHAPTER FIFTEEN

ASS HERPES

TYLER and I had to start grooming like professionals. Every couple of days, we would take turns shaving each other's ass. He would take a shower and soap up between his legs and butt cheeks and bend over. I would help him spread it open and glide a razor up and down the area. Everybody in porno shaved their pubic and butt hair and we wanted to fit in. Everyone said it was much cleaner to be hairless. It must have been helpful to some degree because we'd never heard of anyone having a case of crabs on set.

I shaved my vagina a little at first, but not much. The stubble on my twat was much more disgusting than any amount of hair could be. So, I let mine stay, but I trimmed it with a pair of eyebrow scissors to keep it nice and short. Guys I fucked told me I had nice hair. Their opinions meant everything to me. My self worth has always depended on what men have or have *not* said to me—determining how attractive I feel.

Tyler became really self-conscious about his body hair as soon as he'd done a few scenes. Some girl called him Sasquatch during one shoot. He bought an electric trimmer for his legs because he thought it was too effeminate for him to completely shave those. Many men in porno had shaved arms and legs. It scared Tyler to trust me with the razor. I am a little rough with sharp objects, such as knives and scissors. My moves are more

117

abrupt than delicate or careful. Twice, when Tyler was bent over
with cheeks spread, I accidentally nicked his hole. He screamed
and snapped straight upright, swinging the shower curtain in
my face.

"Aaaaaaaaaagggghhhhhhh!! You cut me! I can't believe you
cut me! Get away from me."

I would laugh at him. Not for the fact he was bleeding from
his butthole, but because he was scared of me. "Ooops! I'm so
sorry. I didn't mean to do that, I swear!" I'd cover my face with
my hand so he wouldn't see my amusement.

"You think this is funny? You're sick!" he would shriek at me
from within the pink-tiled shower. I peeked inside and laughed
even more at the sight of him huddling in fear under the stream
of hot water.

I cut his balls, too. On a different occasion. He wanted to
try my way of grooming. Instead of shaving his ball sack, Tyler
wanted to just snip the longer hairs, so it would be more natural
looking. I was flattered because he wanted his pubes to mirror
my style, and also because he was going to trust me with a sharp
utensil again. I'd ruined my shot with the razor on his ass for the
last time when I went over a little red bump and skinned it off.
There was blood.

In our purple and pink bathroom, Tyler stood naked with
his legs apart and his fingers lifting his balls. This would be no
problem. "I do it all the time to myself, it's easy," I reassured him.
The eyebrow trimmers were in my firm grip and I began to snip
the blonde pubic hair. He let out whimpers of cowardice every
time I got too close to the skin. I scoffed at him. He had to put
one of his legs up on the toilet for me to get in between his ass
and sack. In porn, this position is called standing doggy. This
was the trickiest part of all, the taint. It was dark under there

and I couldn't really see. I didn't think it was all that important, so I just cut without looking. I did it all the time to myself, and I was fine.

"Ooooooowwwwww, not again! Psycho! Get the hell away from me with those!" Tyler jumped away. I'd been kneeling on the floor to get a good angle. One of his hands gripped what was left of his genitalia, the other swatted at me.

I looked at what I'd done. The skin on his ball sack had a half-inch long cut on the left side. It was near the bottom and dripping blood. My eyebrow scissors had blood on them. From then on, Tyler shaved his own ass and balls, without my help whatsoever. It's actually quite easy to do yourself. I managed to shave my butt solo just fine by feeling for the stubble and going slow. I imagine that's what every person (who has ever shaved their own butt crack) already knows.

One afternoon, Tyler called me into the bathroom. Maybe he had forgiven me for my clumsiness and was going to give me another try with the blades. Something about grooming him got me off. I liked it, similar to how monkeys care for each other. The intimacy was primal.

"Ori, what's this?" He bent over and spread his butt cheeks wide with both hands. "It hurts. I don't know, I think it just started. What does it look like?"

I lowered my face down, really close to his asshole. Nothing struck me as being odd. "I don't know, Tyler. What do you mean?"

"I'm not sure. I just want to know what it looks like right there. Is there something? Like a rash or something? Do you think we caught something again? Is it herpes?"

"No, I don't think so. I don't see any bumps, but it is kind of red." I was concerned, but not in a fret like him. His butt just looked like he'd wiped it too hard too much. "Don't worry. If you have something, then I probably have it, too. It's okay." A rare moment of equanimity on my part.

"I hope not! Do you feel anything? It probably came from you, because you've done more scenes than me! You've been with way more guys than I have girls."

So much for composure. I started crying. Now I was the one who brought herpes into our lives. First it was gonorrhea and chlamydia, and now herpes. Tyler was convinced of it, and the guilt felt heavy enough to bury me underground. Then Tyler leaned down to where I knelt on the bathroom floor. It was a tiny space, but he squeezed his tall body around me and put his arms around my sobbing shoulders.

"Hey, I'm sorry. I didn't mean that. It's not all your fault. I could have gotten it from one of those nasty chicks I've fucked. Don't cry. It doesn't matter who gave it to whom. Please, baby, don't be sad."

I stripped down and he checked my ass for anything unusual. There was some redness around my butthole. That was normal though. My asshole got pounded a few times a week by large cocks. It was bound to have a fair amount of tenderness. There wasn't enough irritation to tell what was going on in my butt. We did do cocaine every night, so the bathroom was frequently used, too.

Tyler would not be pacified by just having me look at his problem. We did the right thing and went back to the Adult Industry Medical Healthcare Foundation clinic. For a medical facility, it was filthy. The floor was always dirty and sometimes there were junkies there getting clean needles. It smelled sour. Other medical offices smelled like pressed linen and the air had a cold crispness, like the carnation cooler in a florist's shop. Our adult clinic was dusty and warm. A giant birdcage with a green macaw was a fixture in the waiting room. The workers were visibly flustered and held back nothing when it came to expressing how tired they were or how annoyed they felt. As untidy as the place was, we were all very lucky to have it. The people who ran it did so because they cared. If it weren't for AIM, who knows how many more cases of HIV would have infected the adult community? They even helped drug addicts with rehabilitation resources, in addition to giving out clean rigs. You can go in crying, bleeding, yelling, high, dripping in green stuff, and they will help you. No matter how ornery they can sometimes be, the people at AIM truly care about the talent and all of their fucked-up drama. The poor staff is flawed and criticized, abused and taken for granted every day. They are not superheroes, just superb human beings when all is said and done. They were heroes to us. They do a job that I never fucking want to do. Listening to so many problems and flaky people, trying to heal them and send them back to the industry, prepped to get their next infection. It's a thankless toil. Damn it, we needed AIM.

The alternatives to risky porno sex are not promising. The Los Angeles county bureaucracy wants to enforce safer sex, but people won't want to watch it, download it, or buy it. Condom requirements? I don't think anyone will shoot in Los Angeles anymore if condoms become mandatory. No swallowing? The SoCal adult film industry would collapse. The dream will be over. The Truffula Trees will all be gone, and the Lorax will disappear, too. Fly off one day by the seat of his pants.

Aside from the previous STDs, we regularly tested for HIV and hepatitis. Last time we'd gone to get tested for HIV, we were hassled by a wife of the late, legendary porn star John Holmes, who died of AIDS in the eighties. She worked drawing blood at

AIM. A good handful of aging, retired porn stars worked at the clinic. She could see that Tyler and I were high on coke when we came in. We also would take turns doing bumps of it in the bathroom when we had to piss in a cup.

This woman did not like addicts coming in high to AIM. "YOU KNOW, COCAINE IS A TERRIBLE, TERRIBLE DRUG." She squeezed my arm hard, tied it off with a strip of rubber, and slammed the needle into my vein. The blood filled up the plastic vial. The woman snatched a nearby cotton ball from a jar. Her skinny fingers grabbed me around the elbow, and she pressed the cotton ball firmly over the blood spot from the needle. She sharply threw the needle into the biohazard trashcan. I got up as fast as I could from the seat. Tyler looked at me with a nervous smile. He had a way of puffing his lips out bigger than normal when he got uneasy. He flopped down in the plastic chair, like a big kid would.

"COCAINE IS HIGHLY ADDICTIVE. IT RUINS PEOPLE'S LIVES. IT'S DANGEROUS. YOU CAN CATCH DISEASES AND SPREAD THEM IN THE INDUSTRY AND TO PARTNERS OUTSIDE OF THE BUSINESS. I HAVE KNOWN SOME HORRIBLE COCAINE ADDICTS IN ALL MY YEARS IN THE BUSINESS." The woman's bedside manner only grew worse. She pinched Tyler with those bony fingers, using both hands to squeeze his arm. She found a vein without a problem. That should have made her relax. At least we weren't shooting anything up. She had seen it all with drug addicts, albums of bad memories. Her own dead husband had prostituted himself for drugs and had contracted HIV. Before he died, John Holmes knowingly had sex with other porno performers and could have spread it to many scene partners.

The woman got this faraway look in her eyes and stabbed Tyler with the needle. I saw it jam in, poking the skin hard. Tyler looked at me and took a deep breath. He was still skittish about needles at the time. This was his worst nightmare. When the blood container had filled up, she yanked the needle out. A cotton ball and a large piece of masking tape were wrapped around the blood spot. Tyler jumped up and stormed out the door. He needed a cigarette.

When we returned to AIM to get Tyler's ass rash checked, we saw the main lady, a very wonderful woman named Sharon who was an ex-porn star turned doctor and who devoted her medical career to keeping the porno industry workers free of AIDS.

Sharon showed Tyler and me to the examination room. It was an eight-by-six-foot space with a gynecological table covered in butcher paper. There were posters on the wall of syphilis and genital warts. Tyler pulled his pants off and climbed up on the table. He got on all fours in a receiving doggy position and looked down at his hands.

"Do I have herpes?" he gulped.

Sharon pulled a light over to his rear and looked closely at the affected area. She had a flashlight, too, to be thorough. "Well, I don't see anything that looks like herpes. You just have some sort of a rash. It is red and irritated. But I don't think it's a breakout." She snapped off the light and put her flashlight down. She was so calm, a breath of fresh air.

Tyler stood up. "You don't think it's herpes? Then what could it be? Why is my ass sore?"

We both looked at her as if she were a great oracle about to speak. Like she was a Greek goddess. Goddess Sharon: patron protector of our private parts. "It could be a few things. Have you changed your soap or laundry detergent in the last few days? Or it could be an allergy to a fabric—how about new clothes?

What about food? Maybe you ate something you had a reaction to." She was so nonchalant; it was exactly what we needed, her soothing tones to rid us of the hypochondria.

I piped up, "What about toilet paper? Could it be from that?" I had just remembered that Tyler had recently insisted we buy the environmental "green" toilet paper from Whole Foods. We'd had it for about a week. It was rough and coarse, unlike the usual pink and fragranced kind we bought. I hated it. The stuff rubbed my ass raw after anal shoots.

"Definitely. We'll test you both for herpes today anyway. But I don't think that's what's on your butt. I'm pretty sure of it. Okay?" She left us in the room to soak it all in. What was on his ass wasn't a case of herpes, but a wiping rash from recycled toilet paper. If we weren't such cokeheads we probably wouldn't have gotten a rash. Less coke equals less shitting equals less wiping. Tyler pulled up his pants and let out a sigh of relief.

Our tests came back a few days later. The rash was indeed due to the toilet paper, but we weren't spared. We both were negative for herpes simplex two; both of us were positive for herpes simplex one. By the book, it meant we had the kind spread by mouth, not by genitals. None of that simplex stuff means anything in real life. We had the virus and that was that. Just because it originated in the mouth on someone doesn't mean it can't be spread elsewhere. A person can have simplex one in the genitals and the mouth. It just depends on where you breakout. Herpes is everywhere.

CHAPTER SIXTEEN

A NIGHT WITH MAX HARDCORE

MAX Hardcore movies were the first porno that Tyler and I ever watched together. The night after we first walked out of World Modeling as Trent and Ashley, Tyler gave me a crash course in his favorite porn stars. He found Max Hardcore's website and bought a three-day membership for $7.95. An investment for our future. I had to learn how to do porn the right way, like the girls in Max Hardcore's movies.

For three days, I sat on Tyler's lap at our computer and we watched the girls on the site get ass-fucked and ass-fisted. Their heads were upside down, they were throat-fucked until they vomited. Max Hardcore girls wore little schoolgirls' outfits with hooker heels. They wore their hair in pigtails and baby barrettes. Max pounded each one in the ass, hard, and made the holes gape when he pulled his dick out. Max pissed on their faces and into their mouths. Each girl gulped down his pee. These "little girls," these women, all had exaggerated amounts of makeup and lipstick on. They looked like clowns.

Tyler said, "Look, these girls are hot! You've got to be nasty. It's fucking sexy."

Tyler was totally turned on by the extremity of the sex. He also showed me movies starring Belladonna and Gauge, his top two favorite porn stars. Gauge *was* a little girl, quite petite (under five feet tall), with big, innocent blue eyes. Tyler showed me a tape of her sucking a big cock and gagging on it. She threw up during the blow job, then kept going, right back to sucking it. Belladonna took on four guys in her movie. She smiled as she got her ass fucked and eagerly went after each cock. The guys were mean and rough with her, but she seemed to love it. Both girls were quite pretty.

With Tyler's guidance, my pornographic style would be influenced by the grand masters: Belladonna, Gauge, and Max Hardcore. Each performer stood out not only because of the sex, but because they all looked good. They weren't fake. The girls didn't have Tijuana boob jobs. Belladonna, Gauge, and Max Hardcore were actually attractive *and* doing really dirty things. When I saw them, I thought, *If I could look half as hot as these chicks fucking, that would be great!* Max was a blue-eyed and blonde-haired cowboy with an even tan. He was a little older, but he had a strong body and an incredibly animated persona. He smiled at the girls as they were being defiled. He praised them for being whores that liked to throw up. Max was the most memorable man to watch in a porno.

Max had an office right next door to World Modeling. He wasn't in it when Tyler and I signed up to do porn. Otherwise, I think I would have been booked to do a scene with him on my first day. Tyler really wanted me to work with Max. I did scenes for a lot of different people. Several of them told me not to work with Max.

"Don't do a scene for him. He's dangerous."

"He once had a girl come to his house to do a 'test shoot.' Do you know what he did? He fucked her in the ass for three hours and then said it wasn't part of the scene. And he didn't pay her!"

"Stay away from that guy Max Hardcore. It's bad for your career. Once you're a 'Max girl,' people just won't hire you as much."

"You'll never be in a Vivid movie once you've worked for Max."
Tyler and I were impressionable, so we heeded the advice. I
didn't pursue doing a scene for Max Hardcore. Max remained
one of Tyler's idols, and we both continued to admire his scenes,
but I was afraid to work with him after hearing so much about
what a horrible person he was.

All of what we had heard about Max Hardcore could not be
further from the truth. Tyler and I ended up meeting Max at
his house. He was letting some other director shoot some scenes
there, and Tyler and I happened to be the talent. Max was hos-
pitable. He smiled and invited us into his office to watch some
movies of him pissing all over some European girls. We really
hit it off. Max became our friend that day. I still wasn't going to
shoot for him, but we wanted to hang out socially. The fact that
I didn't want to be in one of his videos never got in the way of
our friendship.

It's an experience unlike any other to go out with Max Hardcore. First of all, Max Hardcore doesn't break character when
he's not in his movies, like the rest of us porn stars do. Though
it's not his real name, he lives his life as Max. He wears a big yellow cowboy hat at all times. His jacket is a big denim and leather
bomber that says *"TEAM MAX"* on the back in huge letters. Tyler
and I accompanied him to Universal City Walk, Sky Bar, and
the Hollywood Hustler store. Max brought a few skanky whores
with him at all times, his "Max Girls." He toted them around
in public, and they also were in character. They were skeleton
skinny and wore tiny schoolgirl outfits, ankle socks with ruffles,
and platform hooker heels. It was a spectacle each time we went
out with him. Men scrambled to get Max's autograph and to
worship him. Little children would just stare at the whores and
wonder who Max was. He looked like a superhero.

Tyler of course loved it and wanted me to dress like a school-girl prostitute when we went out. It didn't look as charming on me as the Max Girls. Max Girls were all size 00. I couldn't get down to below a three, even on the heaviest amounts of cocaine and bulimia. Max Girls smoked crystal meth and threw up their food all the time. When it comes to bingeing and purging, I'm only a part-timer. I could never be as skinny as the Max girls. It would kill me.

Max invited us to spend a night at his love shack. We were all going to continue partying after leaving the Sky Bar one night. I just wanted to go home. Tyler wanted to go back to Max's place so we could have a threesome with him. It was a dream of Tyler's to fuck me with Max Hardcore. He couldn't believe I was being so selfish by refusing. I got my way, despite Tyler's pouting. I was sick of being so porno and hanging around with Max's whores. It can be a tiresome act. I don't like to be in character, so to speak, twenty-four hours a day. I didn't want my entire social life to revolve around sex. Tyler thought differently.

Thinking we were going to settle in for the night, I turned our little CD player on at a low volume. I put on Radiohead's *The Bends* and tended to a huge mess of clothes on the floor. Tyler went on the computer in the kitchen and shut the door. I thought maybe he was doing his dick exercises. He had joined one of those websites for penis enlargement, and would shut himself in the kitchen from time to time. He forbade me to watch. The exercises involved many humiliating movements. Pelvic thrusting and fondling, mostly. I had no idea that Tyler had gone off to the kitchen because he was still mad at me for not wanting to go to Max's. When he opened the door again, I could see that he was pissed.

"Why can't we just go over to Max's? I just want to go party with him and get a little crazy. Why don't you want to? Do you only like to do it for the money now?" That old line. The color of his eyes had darkened, and I prepared myself for more mean things to come.

We had an entire eight ball of coke and half of it was dumped out on a dinner plate. This is how we always did coke at home. We never ate our dinner on plates. Dinner served in our home was typically in white powder form. Using a credit card, Tyler cut small, thin lines and sniffed them up with a cut-up drinking straw from Jack in the Box. You could always tell whose lines they were by the size. Mine were always thick and long.

Tyler knew he could get to me. He knew I was confused about what I was doing with my body. I was at odds with myself over the sex for money. Was it wrong? Was it more wrong than other things we do for money? Was I a whore? Was I no good? I asked him all these things daily, and I asked them of myself as well. The answers remained elusive. I wanted to be a good person, inside. I wasn't sure if I could be a good person anymore because of the porn and drugs that consumed my life, even though I enjoyed them.

"You never want to do anything crazy anymore with anyone else, Ori! The only time you like it is when you're getting paid. Admit it! You've got the whole hooker mentality, don't you?"

"No I don't! I do get crazy! I do like sex and not just when someone's paying me!" We were going into another full-fledged argument about whether or not I still liked off-camera sex with other people, and I wanted to outsmart Tyler. If I lost the argument, I would have to give in to what he wanted: I would have to have sex with whomever Tyler wanted me to. It was all a game. This was the reality of my relationship, and Tyler always won.

"Well, then how come you never want to do anything anymore? We hardly ever go over to Colby's house to have fun, now that we're in porn. All you do is scenes! You don't have as much anal at home. You just do it when you get paid. Porn is changing you, Ori! You're not the same person as when we started." He shook his head at me, like it was hard to look at who I'd become.

"We do still party! I thought you wanted me to make money for us, right? Don't call me a hooker! I'm not! I still want to do crazy things, and I do want to do anal at home! I just get worn out and I'm tired after the scenes. What am I supposed to do? Just want to fuck all the time?" It was all so frustrating because the only explanation I had for why we didn't fuck our friends as much had to do with the fact that porn was hard work. Tyler used my "excuse" to call me a hooker. Only hookers thought of sex as work. I must be one.

"See! You just think of sex as a job now! You should still want to come home and fuck after work. It shouldn't matter! Now I know you're only doing this for the money. You're not really into sex, are you? I can't believe you're so fake, Ori! We shouldn't be in this business if you're in it for all the wrong reasons." Tyler cut out a few more lines, threatening to quit porn because I was turning into a prostitute.

I was too coked out and confused to argue anymore. I couldn't figure out my feelings, and the drugs made me unable to articulate what I wanted to say.

"Okay, Ori, if you're not a hooker and you still like fucking for fun, then *prove* it to me." Checkmate. "Let's go to Max's. Tonight. I'll call him right now and we'll drive over and party with him."

We forgot all about the risk of getting DUIs and headed to Alta Dena. All of the fighting and the drugs made us like caged rats. Tyler wanted to take a drink in the car. I freaked out and made him put all the booze in the trunk. Tyler did bump after bump of cocaine in the passenger seat as I drove us to Max's house, and, to rub it all in, he even smoked inside the car. It was near 3:00 a.m., and we had a thirty-minute drive ahead of us. I could no longer drive on coke the way I used to. My pupils were huge. Every streetlight and road reflector was a bright white blur. There was no way my eyes could focus correctly. There were trails of white light everywhere slicing the darkness. Then, it was pitch black out on the 210 east except for the headlights on my little Toyota Corolla and the cherry on Tyler's burning cigarette hitting the asphalt. We were the only ones on the big, desolate freeway. The rest of the eight ball lay tucked safely inside of Tyler's pocket. The partially consumed bottle of Absolut rolled around in the trunk.

Max Hardcore lives at the top of Alta Dena, a charming and picturesque neighborhood in scenic Pasadena—one of the top ten cities to raise your children in. Close enough to metropolitan Los Angeles to take advantage of city life without any of the grime, Alta Dena is nice and safe. The most extreme pornography I have ever watched is filmed in this lovely little town. Max's house stands out like a magnificent fluorescent piss stain, a multi-million dollar, bright yellow three-story home with Miami-inspired architecture among streets full of mock Tudor-style mansions.

The streets in Max's neighborhood are terribly winding and woodsy. I could hardly maneuver the car around each dark corner. Tyler kept calling Max, over and over. No one answered. It was past three o'clock. Was everyone in bed? We finally found the monster of a house and parked on the street in front of it. We sat in the car feeling like fools. Tears of "I didn't want to come in the first place" started welling up in my eyes, but I didn't dare speak. Marching up the steps of the quarter-mile-long drive-way, we both continued to call Max's phone numbers.

"Let's just ring the doorbell until he answers," Tyler demanded, refusing to give up on his dream. "We are not turning around and going home."

We got up to the door and ferociously rang the bell. We switched places for ten minutes straight, just poking the button over and over. I knocked and pounded on the front door, and Tyler yelled, "Max! Max! Let us in! You told us to come over! Max! Max! Hello!"

Then, it opened. Max appeared, just like that. There was a sudden burst of light and energy when we saw him. He was standing in front of us, smiling and happy. "Come on in, guys! You finally made it," he boomed. Max wasn't a big fellow, but his personality was huge. He's actually a little bit shorter than Tyler and has a normal-sized cock. I guess it just goes to show that a huge cock isn't necessary to do quite a bit of damage. Normal is all you need.

The party was always happening at Max's house. He was up drinking, and all the lights were on. Since the place was so big, it's hard to really say if anyone else was there. There could have been a family of four living on one of the several stories. Tyler and I were led to the bar on the patio. Max whipped out his guitar and began strumming along to the music blasting on the stereo. Tyler mixed a couple of strong cocktails with the vodka we brought. Max pulled out a bottle of champagne. He kept a special fridge stocked full of champagne for the whores. I sipped on my glass before Tyler handed me the bag of coke. I was dying for some. I needed to relax and do some lines. I had to get much, much higher in order to prepare myself for the night to come. Almost a whole gram dumped out of the bag and onto the counter. Fuck it. I sucked it all up, from a pile. Why even bother cutting lines anymore? It was all going to the same place.

I did an enema, too. I had packed a small enema bottle in my purse. This is what we came for. Tyler wanted us to party with Max. So did I. I had to get crazy and prove to my boyfriend that the porn scenes didn't come before our real sex lives. I still wanted to fuck for free and take it in the ass for fun.

Tyler knocked on the door and I let him into the bathroom. He saw that I had done the entire amount of coke that he'd just given me. I thought he would scold me for hogging it, but he smiled at me instead. "I knew you would do it all. So I split it up, see?" He showed me two other baggies in his pocket. He shook his head in a silly way. Nothing could tick him off now that we were about to make one of his fantasies come true.

I was led by the hand down the hall to Max's master bathroom. The bathtub was filling up with hot water and bubbles. There were candles lit, and more champagne. Tyler took off my clothes and I stepped into the tub. Max and Tyler got naked and climbed in with me. The three of us drank champagne and laughed. It was all very romantic. Tyler started kissing me. His hands came out of the hot water and up to my face. He dunked my head under gently so I could suck his cock. The Jacuzzi was on in the giant tub, and it was loud. I couldn't hear anything, so I just sucked. Tyler pulled my head up by the pigtails. Max stood up and started pissing on my face. He was smiling. Tyler was grinning, too—in complete adoration of Max. Tyler shoved my head onto Max's cock and I sucked it down to the balls. Max throat-fucked me hard. That squeaking noise, from where the back of the esophagus is being crushed, resonated throughout the bathroom. Tyler stood up and started to piss on me. Both of them pissed at the same time. Max handed me my champagne glass so I could take a drink. Covered in their piss, I finished the bottle.

They helped me out of the bath and put a towel around me. The three of us climbed up onto Max's large bed. Tyler and Max took turns face-fucking me, and then they fucked my ass. I was bent over with my face down on the sheet. Tyler and Max spread my asshole apart and pounded me. Then Tyler lied down on his back and I climbed on, putting his cock into my vagina. Max came behind me and stuck his cock into my asshole. They were double-penetrating me for as long as we could hold it. Doing a DP in your private life isn't much different than on film. There is no focus on tenderness. The only difference is that the guys don't have to open up for a camera to see what's going on. At home, the limbs and bodies can collapse on each other and enclose the action. It's more like a dog pile than a position when doing a DP in real life.

Tyler slapped my face while I was getting fucked in the ass and sucking both cocks. Surprisingly, Max was the more gentlemanly one during the sex, more than my own boyfriend. After we fucked, Tyler and Max came in my ass. Max came first. I collapsed afterward, from exhaustion. All of us fell straight to sleep soon after. I rolled up next to Tyler and cuddled him close. I had all of the drugs fucked right out of my body. There was cum leaking out of my asshole.

We all emerged from Max's room at about ten the next morning. Nobody acted weird. It was just another night of partying as far as we all were concerned. As soon as I woke up and put on my swimsuit, I took a baggie of coke with me to the bathroom. Max told us to stay and hang out by the pool for the day. Why not? It was a hot summer day, and we had no other plans.

A guy introduced himself to Tyler and me in the kitchen. He

was a houseguest of Max's and was staying in one of the many rooms we didn't know about. His name was Jonah, and he said he wanted to shoot me. "I shoot solo, girl-on-girl, and blowjobs. It's internet stuff, but I pay in cash. Do you want to shoot today? A BJ? I'll pay you two-hundred-fifty in cash, today," Jonah said.

I gave Tyler a look of uncertainty. Who was this jerk putting me on the spot first thing in the morning? "I don't know. I'm not really ready to shoot today. I don't want to do it now. I just woke up and I don't even have any of my stuff. What about my makeup and hair?" Shooting a blowjob scene was the last thing I wanted to do. I was tired and needed to do more coke.

Jonah pricked up. "I shoot really fast! It will be like twenty minutes, tops. You don't need to do anything to your hair. Just wear your swimsuit. You look great. If you need makeup, then Max has some for you."

Was he fucking kidding? Max's makeup was for his Max girls, it was all bright and tacky, the secret ingredient to making his girls look like circus freaks. Tyler took a second to ponder the possibilities that he could use the cash for. "Ori, it's cash. That's a good deal. I mean, twenty minutes? We could use the cash to pay Ernesto. Come on, Ori. Just do it. It'll be a turn-on. I want you to do a blowjob scene at Max's house. Come on! Do it. For me?" Like usual, Tyler turned Jonah's proposition into something "romantic" for us to share.

"Fine. I'll do it. I'll get ready," I smiled. Tyler leaned down and kissed me for it.

"Okay. Great. Oh, and it's a POV blowjob scene. It's going to be with me, is that all right?" Jonah added that part last, purposely. I'd already said I would do it. I didn't ask who it was going to be with because I presumed it would be Max or Tyler. Not Jonah. He was disgusting. The man's stomach was the size of a beanbag chair. There's no way he could even see his toes, let alone his dick. No offense, but in this fable, Jonah *was* the whale—over three hundred pounds. But he was serious. My shocked expression didn't stop Jonah from handing me his fresh HIV test.

I'm not a mean person. So, I just acted like it was cool. I said, "Yeah, it's fine." Tyler reminded me that it would only be twenty minutes, at the most. I got ready in misery. Tyler tried to stifle laughter. "Shut-up! It's not funny, Tyler! I can't believe I'm going to blow some fat guy right now. He's so gross." I laughed, too, and shook my head. The things I do for money!

Jonah came into the bathroom when I was ready. I'd already been asked twice through the door if I needed any more time to prepare. Yes, I needed time. I didn't know how much time it would take to make me ready to suck Jonah's dick. A bell didn't go off in my head indicating that it was suddenly a good idea, something to look forward to. I gulped in the last bit of air in the bathroom that held only my smell. Soon it would mingle with the smell of some dude's butt, gut, and balls.

Tyler was outside by the pool sipping on a refreshing cocktail while I was inside working hard for our cocaine money. Jonah held the camera and filmed me in the bathtub. I got out and dropped to my knees in front of him. I'd become a master at the art of POV. I looked into the lens and talked dirty to him. I stuck my fists into my mouth and got my hands really wet. Then I felt my body all over, before going after his cock. Jonah was wearing a white tee shirt and pants. He had an odor about him, like it'd been a while since his last shower. I hadn't seen Jonah smoke, drink, or do drugs, but he smelled foul, from a poor diet, I guessed. I could feel and smell his breath all over me. I unbuckled Jonah's belt and undid his pants. I unzipped him and reached in for his wiener. It wasn't rock-hard ready, like a porno dick. I had to stroke it to get the blood going. His dick was on the small/normal size, and it was crooked. It really stunk down there. I was getting nauseous. Jonah's dick smelled like feet. I gagged myself with my hands in my mouth, my throat. I wanted to keep my hands wet so I could just jack him off mostly. I did not want to suck Jonah's cock.

However, I did shove his cock into my mouth enough to technically call it a blowjob scene. I choked on it, and I spit on it. I couldn't tell if Jonah was pleased with the performance. He stayed quiet behind the camera. If he had wanted me to suck his balls, I would have quit the scene. The smell underneath his gut was too gnarly—the sourness of old dead skin. Jonah lost his boner a couple of times, making the scene longer than twenty minutes. I didn't say anything. The best thing to do when a dick goes limp is to nurture the person it is attached to. I just smiled and stroked it so it would come back to life and put me out of my misery. We got through it, finally. Jonah ended by jerking off on my face and mouth. His cum was white and thick, like curdled milk being squirted out of a warmed triangle of cheese.

Tyler collected the money for us. Jonah thanked me for the blowjob. I didn't want to stay and hang around Max's house much after that. I needed to go home and take a Silkwood shower. We had the cash, Tyler reminded me. It worked out in the end. We stopped and got another eight ball on the way home.

CHAPTER SEVENTEEN

SWINGERS

NELSON and Hannah were a porno couple who planned on getting married one day. They were from England but had been living together in the States for over a year. I met Nelson on the set of *Guttermouths*, a video in which the girl getting fucked has a foul, trash-talking mouth. I am a natural at using crude language. I have my mom to thank for that.

Nelson was impressed by my performance, both verbally and anally. Nelson had a huge nine-inch cock. It looked even bigger on him because he was short. He stood only about five foot five, but he was intimidating. He had a frosty personality. He was muscular and tan, and obviously way into his good looks. He was a little on the fake side, though. Nelson's nose had been surgically altered to a straight line, and his front teeth were the work of some 1990s cosmetic dentistry.

After he fucked my ass and came on my face for the scene, Nelson introduced me to his girlfriend. Hannah was a tall, blonde, demure knock-out. They were a solid and striking couple. Phone numbers were exchanged, and plans were made to hang out. Later on the phone, Tyler and Nelson talked about the fact that we were all swingers and that we should go out to a swinger party together. Tyler considered us to be a swinger couple because we did porno and had threesomes on the side. We were not swingers. We were in porn and did get crazy with our friends on occasion, but that didn't qualify us to be part of "the lifestyle," as it's often called. Swingers were mostly nasty old people that sat on sex swings and "made love." The swinger "lifestyle" was portrayed on shows like *Real Sex*. Swingers were always at some log cabin retreat. The men had more stretch marks than the women. Swingers were always eating each other out in a group on the floor. Swingers made me want to suck my vagina into my stomach. I thought Tyler and I saw eye to eye on the subject of swinging—that we were not into it. To me, this party we would be attending with Nelson and Hannah was nothing more than a party. We were not going to swing.

Tyler hadn't yet met Hannah. When we arrived at their apartment, her beauty took his breath away. She was six feet tall in heels, towering over Nelson. She was Nelson's gorgeous trophy with platinum blonde hair and a top-of-the-line Beverly Hills boob job. Hannah was nineteen and already a star by porno standards. The girl with the biggest picture on the box and magazine covers. If it weren't for her incredibly alluring, sweet personality, it would have been difficult to stand next to her. I thought she was something out of this world. The girl was just a heavenly creature.

This swinger party was executed with the same measures that an upscale rave would have. You had to call and make an appointment to meet up with and buy tickets from the promoter. On the night of the party, we followed directions from a map that came with the tickets. It only gave the address of another meeting spot, not where the actual party was. We left Nelson and Hannah's apartment off Vineland and drove to a parking structure in Universal City. There, a shuttle van escorted us and the other guests to an undisclosed location in the Hills.

Tyler and I had been doing coke steadily since we woke up that morning. I was high and nervous when we got to the party, but I marched in with confidence because we were with Hannah. Everyone noticed her. I felt inadequate beside her, but I could still feed off of her radiance. She wasn't the kind of girl that invokes jealousy. She was shy and humble.

I took a turn in the bathroom with our coke. The house was grand and modern. Nelson loved the décor. Everything was polished and new but bland as could be. The carpets and walls were white. It was several stories tall and had massively high ceilings. All of the art just blended into the background. There were clear glass sculptures of human figures. Nothing so far alluded to the fact that it was a sex party. The patrons were well dressed and tame. They were young professionals, attractive, groomed, and in their twenties and thirties.

Nelson and Tyler strutted Hannah and I in and out of all the different rooms on the first floor. We got some vodka cocktails to wash down the ecstasy. Apparently everyone at this party was taking ecstasy, but you couldn't tell just by looking around. No one was acting wasted or silly. It was the best behaved drug-crowd I'd ever seen. I didn't get it. Why all the mystery and fuss for this bunch of dull, normal folk? I was still wondering if something was supposed to happen at this shindig. I was starting to get bored and uncomfortable. Mingling with the other guests didn't come so easy, not with this crowd. Tyler and I assimilated with wild partygoers. Where were all of the stupid druggies? I wanted to cut loose and whoop it up. Where was the real party?

Hannah and I grabbed onto one another once the pills kicked in. Both of us started smiling and laughing very hard at nothing. Nelson and Tyler were busy scoping people out. I pushed my way through the crowd to the bar several times. I am fairly pushy by nature. I don't hesitate shoulder-shoving or elbowing a pathway to get what I want. Hannah and I bonded as attracting opposites. She was the polite and well-mannered half of our team. I covered the loud and demanding end.

About an hour after we entered the place, Nelson, Tyler, Hannah, and I went upstairs. There were three other floors to discover. I was feeling good from the pills, drinks, and my wonderful new friendship with Hannah. The white carpeted spiral stairs led us up to another set of rooms. First, we walked into a lounge area. It looked onto the foyer and living room downstairs. It was no different than the rest we'd seen. A mini bar was set up for self-serve drinks. Groups of four and five stood around and socialized. This floor didn't have what we were looking for, whatever that was.

Floor number three was just a loft. Pillows and cushions were laid all over the space. I was beginning to have a hard time walking and seeing straight from all of the pills. We sat down on some cozy pillows. Others sat near us. Mellow electro-lounge music filled the space. Tyler turned and started talking to a girl with bouncy, buoyant tits next to us. The ecstasy was really strong. Each of us had one and a half each. Hannah sat back with me and we let our eyes roll back into our heads. Jaws clenched and unable to swallow, we let the drugs take us completely.

"This is Cait, Ori. She wants to meet you. I told her what we do, and she thinks it's great. How we're a couple and we love each other and we can still do what we do for a living," Tyler said, squeezing my hand. He and the girl with the bubbly tits, named Cait, were really chatting it up. I was too high to get mad at him for telling a stranger about our professional sex lives. Cait took my hand. Then Tyler kissed her on the lips, with lots of tongue. Cait reached for my leg as she made out with my boyfriend.

Nelson was right next to us, observing. He brought down Hannah's top, exposing her perfectly constructed breasts. Tyler followed Nelson's lead. My little boobs came out and so did Cait's buoys. She had a boyfriend with her, who came behind her and started feeling her ass. Tyler pushed my head to Cait's, wanting me to make out with her. My mouth was dry and tasted horrible from all of the shit I was on. I couldn't do it. I was too shy. I had not expected any of this.

Nelson's huge dick came out and he stuck it in Hannah's mouth. Then in Cait's mouth. Tyler nudged my head to his lap, encouraging me to get going on his. I just smiled. At least our friends were here, and the person I loved. *Is this what I have to do in order to keep proving I am a sexual being?* I thought. I didn't want to be lame. Everyone wanted to have a good time, and this was part of the fun. I didn't want to back out of it and spoil it for Tyler and Nelson, so I went along.

Cait sat on her boyfriend's dick and some more people entered the room. Others saw what was going on with our group and started forming small groups themselves. Bodies were exposed, and mouths began going back and forth. I could only catch glimpses because I was already engaged in my own small orgy. I didn't want to get fucked, though. It was looking like I was going to have to, so I got up and wandered down the hall. Tyler got up to see what I was after. Maybe he hoped I was going to go reel in another stranger.

In a daze, I drifted up another set of white carpeted stairs. Tyler caught up with me and helped me up the steps. We found ourselves amidst a group of nearly twenty people having sex. It was the top floor of the house, just one small open room. Slightly bigger than a crawl space or attic, it was the most crowded area of the party. Tyler and I were fully dressed and stepped over the naked bodies. No one noticed us coming in and trying to pass. I was still really high and just wanted to party like a normal person does on ecstasy and coke. All of the random bodies having sex got to me. While both Tyler and I liked the attention from new partners while we were working—it was easier to pretend I was someone else while on the job—I didn't look for sex with strangers in my private life. Friends from time to time were one thing, but unfamiliar people made me uncomfortable.

For the first time, I saw that Tyler could agree. He looked at the mess of sucking and grinding limbs as if it had all finally gone too far. Whatever he thought we were ready to handle as a couple didn't add up to this. He took me by the hand and we exited the top layer of the house. I still had a cocktail glass in my hand, but it had nothing left in it. I had spilled my vodka cranberry all the way up the white carpeted stairs.

We rejoined Nelson and Hannah and Cait and her boyfriend where we'd left them. They were lounging on the big, fluffy pillows on the floor, spent I supposed. I didn't want to sit down again. They all got up and we migrated downstairs to a living room full of dull people. To Hannah's and my horror, Nelson and Tyler started talking to an attractive woman and told her all four of us did porn. We didn't know any of these people, and I was always afraid of being judged, even by strangers. What we did for a living was our business. Before the solicitation of the woman went any further, I tugged at Tyler.

"I want to go now. I'm not feeling good. I think I might be sick. Let's leave, please?" I tried to look as sincere and pathetic as possible. "Hannah doesn't feel good either."

"Well, here," Tyler handed me a bag of coke. "Go to the bathroom and do some of this. Take her with you. It always makes you feel better."

It wasn't the answer I was looking for, but technically Tyler was right. Coke always made me feel better. When ecstasy got too strong, I could always right myself by doing lots of coke or speed to cancel out anything else and make me feel grounded. By the time I straightened out with the coke, we'd all had enough of the swinger party. It was time to leave. We caught a white shuttle van back to the parking garage and piled into Nelson's Jeep. He drove us back to his and Hannah's place.

"Do you have anything to drink besides energy drinks?" Tyler asked as he took a peek into the fridge. Nelson and Hannah's kitchen was full of protein powders and bottles of water. No real food and certainly no booze. They'd invited us up for a nightcap and we assumed that meant alcohol.

Nelson briskly made his way over to take a look. He had such a shrewd way about him. If he smiled or laughed, Tyler and I felt like we had accomplished something others rarely could. Nelson was naturally joyless and stiff. We didn't give up on him.

"Ah, here we are. This is something. I've had it for a long time. Somebody gave it to me as a gift. Yes. I think this will work out all right," Nelson said in his British and self-satisfied voice. It was a bottle of Cristal. Tyler and I were impressed.

Nothing about the party was discussed. We drank the Cristal and joked around as the night waned. It was late, and Tyler and I did some lines of coke on the coffee table. Hannah didn't say much. She was out of it. Nelson went into the bedroom for a minute or two. When he came out, he was naked and his big dick was fully hard. He walked right over to Hannah and pushed it into her mouth. Tyler looked at me with a distressed face. He didn't know we were all going to fuck. There was no way he'd be able to get it up after so many drugs.

Ecstasy has a nice way of telling a man's body that he's doing something very unhealthy. Cocaine has an equally humbling effect. Tyler, like millions of other men who've done both of these drugs simultaneously, had an unresponsive cock. I sucked it and he jerked it, but nothing would happen. I think it was shrinking from all of the pressure we put on it. Nelson fucked away at Hannah, who was like me and went along with anything her boyfriend wanted. Like a robot, she obeyed.

Tyler gave up after a while. No sex for him. He felt so inferior next to Nelson. It didn't seem fair. After an hour, Nelson put on some sweatpants, and Hannah a robe. Tyler was sulking, and we wanted to leave. We all said our warm goodbyes and parted ways. We made plans to get together the next weekend, just for dinner, no party.

In the car, Tyler was bummed. He wanted to fuck Hannah, and it's all he could think about. The whole next day he beat himself up for not being able to get an erection. None of this mattered to me. I was glad he couldn't fuck. I didn't want to have sex with our new friends, not this time. Hannah was nice. Couldn't I have at least one non-sexual relationship among our friends? After all, we weren't swingers.

CHAPTER EIGHTEEN

A WEEKEND IN VEGAS

"**LET'S** get out of town for the weekend. How about Vegas? We deserve it! Just a couple of nights. Do you want to?" Tyler asked while we were driving around Hollywood one afternoon. We were feeling inspired because we had actually gotten up and out of our apartment before noon. It was one of those electric summer days; anything was possible, potential could be felt with every movement.

I didn't need much persuasion. Sure, we did deserve a trip to Las Vegas! Feeling *porno riche* came with its own special sense of entitlement. I was doing scenes several times a week. We definitely had the money. We partied at home and out on the town almost every night. It was time for us to relax and take an overdue vacation in the most debauched city on the planet.

Tyler's convertible Mustang had been stolen a couple weeks before our road trip. He was feeling sad about the loss, so we rented another one to drive to Vegas, wild cherry-red with a tan leather top. It was already a hundred degrees when we started east on the 10 Freeway. I had on a pink bikini and Tyler was shirtless, the top down to get some sun. Ken and Barbie's estranged porno cousins had a weekend to kill.

Tyler and I bought an eight ball and ten extra ecstasy pills for relaxation. I booked a room at the Luxor. We called up our friends to tell them about our last-minute getaway. It was going to be a great party! Our dear pals Nelson and Hannah could meet us there. They would also bring a new girl named Carmelita, a bronze beauty from Brazil. Another couple, Cait and Jeff—the duo from the swinger party, who'd entered our circle of friends—would end up coming, too. My sexy boyfriend and I were the coolest people alive. At a second's notice, we were going to Vegas for the weekend to party with a group of attractive friends, and my shallow heart was complete.

Tyler had a crush on Nelson and Hannah. He was completely smitten with Hannah's vast beauty, and he looked up to Nelson for his keen business sense. Nelson and Hannah had just started an adult talent agency. They asked me if I would like to be one of the first girls to join. Nelson had been steadily hooking me up with porno work since we first met. I already felt like he was acting as my agent, and we'd all become close. I trusted him completely. We'd been going to parties and dinner with Nelson and Hannah for months. We had a sexual encounter at their apartment. The men initiated all of it, of course. Hannah and I remained mutually indifferent to the sex between the four of us—it was unnecessary.

Everyone else was staying at Mandalay Bay. Nelson wanted to have dinner at some Brazilian churrascaria at the MGM Grand. Nobody wanted to argue with him, because Nelson always won. Nelson had rented a big black Mercedes. He had an affinity for fine things like jewelry and foreign cars. He was a total snob with a taste for expensive clothes and cheap women. Nothing made him happier than being surrounded by fake tits and bleached blonde hair. It didn't matter to Tyler and me where we ate. I never planned on eating a thing in Vegas. Coke, pills, and booze were the only nourishment we needed. Carmelita didn't like coke, but she always adored taking ecstasy. Tyler kept hounding her to try cocaine with him, but she refused. He always wanted people to give coke a chance. He couldn't fathom the thought of a human being that was unable to benefit from all the drug had to offer. I think Carmelita wanted to, if only for Tyler. He shamelessly flirted with her, touched her, and told her how sexy she was. Tyler was going to initiate sex with her, inevitably, and he would probably want me to be part of it. It was just a matter of time.

Leaving our plates of uneaten food at the restaurant, Tyler and I wandered to a vodka bar in the MGM casino. Carmelita and Hannah came with me to the bathroom to swallow their ecstasy tabs. The pills were small, red, and had little clovers stamped on the backs. I tried to shove mine in the back of my throat before swallowing. They tasted of chemical vomit. Carmelita and Hannah made sick faces as they got theirs down. Our entire party had migrated into the bar and we joined them for drinks. Nelson and Tyler took some pills at the bar. Mine was already kicking in. I looked at Hannah and Carmelita, and could see they were feeling it too. I could barely stand up. I leaned against the wall and Tyler pulled me back up. He wasn't worried, because I was smiling. It made him feel good to know just how potent his pill was going to be.

Hannah, Carmelita, and I meandered back into the bathroom. This time our steps were loose and all over the place. We slid our hands over the walls to guide us to the sinks in the restroom, smiles branded on each of our lips. The trademark melty look was beginning to form in our eyes. Carmelita turned toward the trash can and said, "Oh god!" She opened her mouth and vomit shot out. All of the Brazilian meat was poured into the waste bin. My jaw tightened. She looked up at us and let go of the trashcan. "I'm fine, babes. I feel nice!" Carmelita had a seductive Portuguese accent with a British inflection.

Cait and Jeff knew about a club we could go to. It was off the strip, a place called Whispers. We could have gone anywhere and partied in style and comfort, but Cait and Jeff were hardcore swingers. Apparently, before they left for the trip, they scoured their online swinger message boards for a place to visit in Vegas.

Because swinger clubs are like raves, in that they move locations every night, finding Whispers was going to be a scavenger hunt. Seven people wouldn't fit in one cab, so Cait went with Tyler and me. Carmelita, Hannah, Jeff, and Nelson followed in another cab.

"It's called Whispa's. It's not on Las Vegas Boulevard," Cait told the driver. "It's off the strip." She was from Down Under and had a sexy accent, too. All four girls in our group were totally different and exotic in our own ways. My ecstasy was in full effect and I was thinking only of positive things because of it.

Whispa's was definitely off the strip. The cabs pulled into a dark, empty lot in some industrial area. The building on the lot had a portable classroom look. There was no foundation. It was an oversized trailer. We might as well have been in San Bernardino. We got out and made our way up the handicapped ramp that led to the door. I took one last look at the cabs, hoping they wouldn't stray too far.

I was still in denial that Tyler and I were swingers. A bulk of what we'd been doing at the time was hanging out with swingers and going to swinger clubs. Sometimes, we had sex with swingers. That didn't make me one, I told myself, because it didn't happen too frequently. I played the part when I needed to, but I still would have preferred to go to a normal, non-sex club. Tyler was the one who wanted sex from everyone. Not me. I got my fill of getting fucked by multiple men on film, and I enjoyed it. The porn fulfilled my every need to be sexually depraved. But Tyler couldn't get enough from porno. He always wanted more.

We were all dressed up for the night. Cait wore a catholic schoolgirl outfit, with fishnets and hooker heels. The rest of us girls looked sexy, but we were not in costume. Being the only non-porno girl in our group, Cait wanted to look like a porn star for the evening. In real life, she worked for the New Zealand Board of Tourism. She was a government official!

There was a dance floor with a stripper pole in the middle. Carmelita made a beeline for the pole. Couches lined the walls. Tyler and I found some barstools to lean on while Hannah, Nelson, Cait, and Jeff walked through a beaded doorway. There was a back room. The place was completely dark, except for black lights lining the bar area and dance floor. A disco ball acted as the Polaris.

My pupils had enlarged to the size of silver dollars. I took another pill with Tyler at the bar. Whispers could only be tolerated with the help of more drugs. I didn't want to dance, so I led Tyler through the beaded doorway and into the back room. It was covered with wall-to-wall mirrors. This room was even darker than the main area and had a black bed-like platform to lie down on. Nelson had his clothes on and was fucking Hannah doggy style. Cait was topless and sucking Jeff's cock. Tyler looked at them and then at me. He had a bloodthirsty smile on his mouth. I got a nudge in my shoulder, telling me to have a seat on the rubber mattress. I sat on the edge, stiffly. Tyler reached to feel Hannah's boobs and smiled. He looked like some college kid from a beer commercial who was having a dream sequence.

I didn't like ruining whatever fantasy he was about to live out, but I had to ditch him there. I pretended not to hear when he called to me as I left the back room. He could go ahead without me. I'd fucked on enough dirty mattresses in my porn scenes. I didn't need to come all the way to Vegas to do it for fun.

Carmelita swayed to horrible hip-hop songs while holding onto the stripper pole. There weren't many other options but to join her. I didn't notice how much the room had filled up in the hour or so that we'd been there. Couples were pacing around everywhere. They held drinks and eyeballed us. Pairs of men and women huddled in corners and at tables, looking around and sizing up the scene. These people had come to hook up and swap partners for sex. Just being here meant you were fair game.

Others made their way into the back room. It got to be a little too weird for Tyler and the rest. Most of the crowd that had taken over Whispers was not so attractive. It was an older bunch. They were all middle-aged and tacky. These were the real swingers, like I had seen on *Real Sex*, not at all like the ones from the Hollywood Hills parties. Tyler grabbed me and put his arms around me. He looked around at the creepers that had just rolled in, feeling their eyes burning into the back of his skull. We were like feeder mice being dropped into an aquarium full of snakes. Someone tapped Tyler's shoulder.

"Hi, I'm Craig and this is my wife." A man with a silvering mustache was standing there with a wrinkly-faced woman. They just smiled and held their drinks. He didn't say anything else to follow the introduction. We were supposed to know what he meant by it.

"Uh..." Tyler spoke for us. "Sorry, man. We're not swingers."

The guy and his wife looked confused and walked away. I threw my arms around Tyler and kissed him. I loved him more than ever in that moment. Finally, we weren't swingers, and I considered it official.

We got into cabs, back to Mandalay Bay. Cait and Jeff were tired and wanted to sleep. Nelson retired to his room without saying goodnight. For the rest of us, the night was half empty. We had to fill it up with more partying. Hannah, Carmelita, Tyler, and I took some more pills and got into another cab.

"Take us to a party! Or to a club! Somewhere people are partying!" I yelled at the driver.

"And dancing!" Carmelita added.

"You don't know where you want to go?" said the driver. He looked at us like we were idiots.

"Just go somewhere fun. We want to go to a party. I don't care," I told him. My friends and I cuddled in the backseat of the cab. They hugged me in approval.

"Uh, okay. There's this place I dropped some people off a minute ago. That's where they all like to go after hours. What are you guys on, anyway?" The cabbie scrutinized us in his rearview mirror.

"Ecstasy," Tyler batted his eyelashes and replied in a low purr.

"Coke and ecstasy," I corrected him. I was so sassy. We all looked at one another and laughed. "Why are you asking us that? Just take us to a party!" I was out of my mind. The cab was warm and we were warmer, a mini-spaceship flying through the desert night sky. My friends and I had left the planet Earth. Our destiny was unknown.

"Whatever. I only wanted to know because you all seem really high. I don't touch any of that coke. It's too expensive. Speed is where it's at. You get a lot more for your money's worth. It lasts longer. Coke is a waste of money, that's all," the cab driver shrugged.

I was too messed up to think about it too much. I didn't have to defend a car full of drugged-out porno actors.

The place he dropped us at was absolutely disgusting—a tweaker den. We hassled through a crowd of scummy locals to get to the doorman. Hannah was not twenty-one. I'd turned twenty-one earlier that summer. Carmelita took care of Hannah's problem by putting her arms around the bouncer's waist and saying, "Please babe?" She hypnotized the guy. He led us through the crowd and put us in the elevator. Tyler handed him forty bucks for a tip.

The club was down in the basement of the Barbary Coast Hotel and Casino. It was one of the sleaziest places I'd ever been. We breathed in concentrated sweat and smoke. It was a hundred degrees of body odor and humidity. Drenched bodies moved to the loud noise of drum and bass. We could hardly get through the densely packed room. Everybody there was on speed. Tyler found us a place to sit at some guy's table. The man had on sunglasses. His face was dripping, obviously from crystal meth. I watched his body jerk around, watched him chew on his own face.

I was starting to feel sick, with the heat and stuffiness of the club. But I couldn't be miserable. My ecstasy pills would not allow me to feel anything but excitement. Taking her hand, I led Carmelita through the crowd to the restroom. As soon as there was a clearing, Carmelita opened her mouth and shot vomit all over the wall. I faced the other wall and blasted it with my own puke.

The bouncer quickly came over and grabbed each one of us by the shoulder. "All right. You're out!" He led us toward the exit.

"No! Please! We're fine! Please, let us stay!" I cried. It was so important for us to stay. I would rather have died than gotten kicked out of that awful shithole of a club.

Carmelita placed both hands on the bouncer's hand. He was a big, pudgy guy with a soft face. Her nails lightly grazed the back of his hand as she looked up at him and pleaded, "Please, babe? Let us stay? Please?"

Who could say no to her pretty blue eyes and sad little brown face? Her voice was specially designed to speak to large men. The bouncer was merely another victim of her feminine powers. He took one look at her pleading smile and let go of us. "Okay, but keep it in your stomachs," he warned.

Back at the table, Tyler was sniffing some of our coke. The tweaker in the sunglasses passed a bullet container to Tyler. He sniffed something out of it. I stuck to our stuff. Carmelita and I puked under the table a couple more times and laughed hysterically. Hannah looked on, moving to the blaring beats and inescapable sounds of electronica. Her eyes were half closed, either from the ecstasy or her hypoglycemia, or both. We couldn't take it much longer. This place was shedding years off our lives. The smoky atmosphere clung to our biological tissues, a chemical sauna. It was time to climb out of the gas chamber.

It was difficult to drag Tyler away from the free dope and new acquaintances. Nothing gave him a better time, other than sex of course. He had a second wind, but the three of us girls were tired and wrecked. It was past four in the morning. Hannah and Carmelita got into a cab for Mandalay Bay. Another cab took Tyler and me to the Luxor. We smelled like tar. Our breath was bad. Our skin was sticky. Tyler wanted a drink, so we got a little table at one of the casino bars. I sat and waited while he went and got our vodka tonics. The ecstasy was wearing off, but I'd done some coke in the cab. My mind was straightening out.

Tyler came back with our cocktails and sat down in front of me. "Ori, you know what I've never done, and always wanted to do?" He looked into my eyes, trying to be as charming as ever. It wasn't effective. Normally, Tyler could make me melt with just a glance of his big, brown eyes and their long, curled-up lashes. Now, his eyes were red, half-open, and had dark grey circles underneath. He looked like hell. There were red spots on his skin, and his big, pouty lips were dry, cracked, and peeling.

"What, Tyler? What have you never done?" I entertained him.

"I just talked to this girl at the bar, and she's an escort. I want to get her to come up to our room for an hour."

"An escort? Like a hooker? No, Tyler! Why do you want to do that?" I was appalled.

"To fuck her! Both of us with her. Come on," his face smiling still. He was not reading me.

"No, Tyler. I wouldn't touch her. She could have fucked a hundred other people tonight. She could have AIDS, and we wouldn't even know. This isn't porn."

Tyler got serious. He tried to convince me another way. "Ori, this is something that I've always wanted to do—ever since I was a kid—and have never done. I want to try it at least once, and I want us to do it together. You should be glad that I want to share everything with you. Most guys just go out and do this shit without telling anyone."

My face twisted up in rage. What the fuck was wrong with him? Why did he need a hooker? Wasn't I enough? We did porn and had sex with friends all the time, and now even with strangers at parties sometimes. This was too much. Was he crazy—or was I? I was too wasted to trust even my own reasoning. What if Tyler was making sense? Maybe there was something wrong with me for being so judgmental about a hooker.

"Listen, Ori. Just this one time I want to know how it feels to get a prostitute in Vegas. Please do this with me. Please tell me you love me and you want me to be happy." He now had his hands on mine and spoke with intense concentration.

"Fine. I don't want to hold you back from this important experience. You should do it, then. Go get her. I don't care. Don't expect me to touch her, though. That's all for you." My consent.

"All right! I knew you'd be into it! I love you, baby, thank you!" Tyler raced off to the bar to negotiate. I sat at the little table next to the slot machines and rolled my eyes. He came back a couple minutes later, alone. For a moment, I gratefully thought it wasn't going to happen.

"Where is she?" I asked.

"Oh, she's going to come up to our room. I gave her the number. She'll be there on the hour," he replied. Tyler stood there for a second before he clasped his hands together and pleaded, "Baby, could you loan me the money, please?"

"What?" I spat out my drink onto the table.

"Baby, I'm sorry. Will you please pull out three hundred dollars from the ATM so I can pay her? She only takes cash, of course. And I've already gone over my limit of what I can take out in a day. Please? I will pay you back as soon as possible."

"Tyler," I sighed, "if you can't afford a prostitute, then you shouldn't get one. Did you ever think of that?" I was calmer than expected after having my boyfriend ask me to pull out cash for a whore.

"Look, I thought we shared money. I would pay for it, but I've taken out too much tonight." His tone took on a new nastiness. "Besides, I would give you money for anything you wanted, no matter what it was. Because I love you. Now, are you going to do the same for me? Do you love me?"

Not this again. The love card—his ace. "Yes, okay. Yes. I love you. I'll take out the money for you."

We walked by an ATM on the way to the elevators. I took out three hundred and twenty. Tyler wanted to give the prostitute a tip.

We waited in our room for her to show up. Tyler took his clothes off and started the shower.

"You're going to take a shower for her?"

"Yeah. I want to be clean. I feel disgusting after being out all night."

"It doesn't matter what you smell like to her. She's probably nasty. She has to fuck you anyway."

"Ori! Why are you being so mean? She's not nasty. I just want to take a shower. Don't make a big deal out of it." Tyler shut the bathroom door.

It was five in the morning and the sun was faintly coming in under the curtains. I chain-smoked and pulled out the contents of the mini bar. I lined up the little bottles of Absolut, Jack Daniel's, Captain Morgan, Beefeater, and Chivas. I would need them all for what I was about to endure. Of course I was going to make a big deal out of him getting ready for this hooker. Tyler never showered before going to bed with me.

Knock knock. Tyler opened the door to our hotel room. A blonde walked in. She was about five foot four with heels on. Her hair was bleached and long, but her black roots were long too. She wasn't a ball of personality. She was thick in the thighs but had fit calves and ankles. She was built like a waitress. Her boobs were big and sagging a little. These tits definitely nursed something in the recent past. Her tummy had stretch marks from pregnancy, but mostly her skin was tight, pale and milky. Nothing was wrong with her face. I searched for a missing tooth or a lazy eye, something, somewhere, but I had to admit she was attractive.

The woman was dead inside, strictly business. Tyler gave her the three hundred and offered her some of my cocaine and alcohol, but she declined. She was on duty. This was not a fantasy for her, just a job. The graveyard shift. I didn't catch her name because there wasn't a formal introduction. Her clothes had come off within the first two minutes. Tyler laid on his back and she took off her skirt and top to reveal her white flesh and black lingerie. A bra and panties from Victoria's Secret.

The hooker didn't suck Tyler's dick. He asked her to, and she replied that she didn't do that. I looked at Tyler and repeated her.

"She doesn't do that. She won't even suck your dick. Nice three hundred dollars, Tyler." I was pounding the bottles of booze and smoking cigarette upon cigarette. I sat cross-legged at a table across the room from the bed. I was still dressed in my nightclub wear. My makeup was still on, and I felt like I looked way hotter than the hooker. I cackled at them and heckled. Tyler and his whore, a one hour comedy special!

The prostitute didn't give a shit about me or what I said. Her mind was somewhere else. Her panties came off and Tyler felt her legs up and down. Her legs were bruised. She rolled a condom onto Tyler's cock. His cock was hard. He was actually turned on by this.

"She isn't even looking at you. She's looking at the wall. Wow. You must be pretty excited," I called out. I took a long drag of my cigarette. I blew it straight in their direction, with force. The sun was now up over the desert floor and shining brightly outside. I could see how thick with smoke the air inside the room was. It was foul.

The prostitute barely moved and was silent. She just rocked her hips halfheartedly with his cock stuck inside. No moans, no flailing arms, no gripping fingers. He wasn't allowed to choke her or spit on her. "Is this the experience you've always wanted, Tyler?" I taunted.

Tyler ignored me. He had to focus or he would lose his hard-on and not be able to finish. He had to get his money's—my money's—worth. He nudged her off of him and put her in doggy position. His hands grabbed her ass and he slapped it.

She let out a sound for that. It wasn't encouragement. She looked over her shoulder and said, "Do not do that again."

Tyler started pounding the woman and making noises like he was really into it. I knew he was full of shit. "You're faking it. Aren't you? That can't be any good. This is so fucking stupid! And a waste of money, isn't it?"

I was getting to him now. Tyler couldn't block out my voice anymore. He looked at me with frustration as he tried his best. Tyler pulled his latex penis out of the hooker's vagina. He got her on her back again and went in missionary. "Come here," he said.

"Are you talking to me? I told you I wouldn't touch her. No, you can do it all on your own." I was drunk and defiant.

"Ori, come here!" He needed me to help him stay turned on. The hooker was a bust. She just lay there, dead. I would have to bail him out of this lame idea, same as I paid for it. Without a remark, I went over to the bed. I took off my top and started kissing him as he fucked her. My hands were all over him in a drunken fervor, like he was the antidote to my poisoning. Tyler came to life and nailed the lazy bitch hard and fast. He was going fast enough to come. I knew his body like it was my own. When I sensed his climax, I dropped my face down to where her twat was. I didn't touch her. I could see her head was turned toward the window, gazing emptily out toward nothing.

Tyler laid a couple more strokes into the warm corpse and pulled out.

"Aaahh, aaahh! Yeeeaaahhhhsssss! Yeeeeessssss!" he shouted. He snapped off the condom and sprayed cum all over my face and into my waiting, open mouth. It was a hard orgasm because of all the drugs he'd ingested over the course of the night.

The prostitute rolled over and sat on the edge of the bed. She picked up her panties and shirt. The bra never even came all the way off. "Well, thank you guys. I hope you have a good stay. If you need me again, I'll be at the bar tomorrow night. Take care." It was the most she'd said.

Tyler gave her the extra twenty dollars. There was nothing left for us to do or say. That was it.

From 7:00 a.m. to 1:00 p.m., Tyler and I slept. Our bodies needed to recover from all of the abuse. We checked out late from the Luxor and drove the rented Mustang convertible over to Mandalay Bay. All of our friends were lounging by the pool, sipping cocktails. It was a late summer afternoon in Las Vegas. Tanned and sexed-out men and women swaggered everywhere. A busy weekend for partying.

Nelson wanted to drive home to LA It was impossible for him to think of anything but the porno business and making money. He had a new agency to get off the ground and it consumed him. Hannah's fun and contentment was a happy accident when it came to Nelson and his pursuit of making money. They did what he said, and she always went along. She didn't argue with her boyfriend like I did with mine. I thought they were some kind of perfect couple. I didn't wish to be in their shoes, but they did seem to have a system that worked. He cared for her in his own way, I guess, and she loved him. That met the limits of my comprehension of complex relationships during the time I was with Tyler. At the time, I thought that all relationships consisted of obsession. Like mine.

Cait and Jeff left with Nelson and Hannah. Carmelita rode home with us. We invited her to come over to our apartment and go out later that night back in LA. Though she was from Brazil, she lived in London. From what she told us about her childhood, the poor girl had it rough. She was an orphan raised by a cruel aunt who beat her. At sixteen, after a bad motorcycle accident, she forged immigration documents and made her way to the United Kingdom. She got a job at a McDonald's cleaning floors. When she learned English, she was promoted to assistant manager. Then she started stripping, got fired from McDonald's, and began to seek out porn.

She hired Nelson to be her agent and she stayed with him and Hannah while doing porn scenes in LA Tyler and I listened to Carmelita tell her life story as we inched along the road. The traffic was beyond terrible.

I sat behind the wheel and cursed. "I can't believe how bad this is. It's Monday night. The highway should be empty!"

Carmelita had been in the passenger seat, but as the traffic got worse she moved to the backseat with Tyler. They got quiet. Then I heard kissing sounds and a female moan. I looked in the rearview mirror. They were making out. Tyler's hands were on her tits. I heard a belt being unbuckled.

I didn't know what to do. I'd had it. They kept going at it, and I just gripped the wheel. The car was going nowhere. My boyfriend fucked this new friend of ours. We were hundreds of miles from home. Tears rolled down my cheeks, but I said nothing. What could I say at that point? It was absurd.

It took us over seven hours to drive from Las Vegas to Hollywood. There was so much traffic because it was Labor Day

Weekend. I had no idea. Nationally observed holidays had come to mean nothing to me. I rarely checked the mailbox. I hardly ever got up before three in the afternoon—and after this misadventure, I wasn't sure I ever wanted to get up again.

Tyler and Carmelita fucked and she sucked his dick for four of those seven hours. They cuddled in the interims when his cock needed a rest. But she kept her hand on it, stroking it the entire time. Halfway home, I began to hate her. At first I was only mad at Tyler, but couldn't remain so for long. He was my boyfriend. So I shifted my rage to her. She took advantage of a tempestuous relationship under odd circumstances. I dried my tears and toughed it out, letting her get fucked by the man I loved and lived with.

At last, we arrived at Nelson's place. I popped the trunk and gave Carmelita a firm hug. Tyler kissed her goodnight, deeply with tongue, and we left her outside on the curb.

CHAPTER NINETEEN

LIABILITIES

DESIREE came to LA for another visit. She needed to get away from home and be cheerful. Her life had become very sad in Houston. She was still seventeen and not going to high school. Her crystal meth use had finally gotten out of control. Little Desiree had become the hardened veteran neighborhood meth dealer, selling to friends and strangers all over her suburban Texas town. Her mother kept wondering why the heavy-duty rolls of tin foil would disappear out of her pantry.

Though still seventeen, Desiree had aged since the last time we saw her. Maybe it only seemed so because she'd kicked meth. She put on about fifteen pounds. She looked good. Seventeen years old, and sexy. The extra pounds filled her chest and hips out, and her skin was amazing. There wasn't a trace of the old cracked-out Desiree. We took her home to our apartment and began drinking and doing lines of coke with her. Coke was okay to do with her. It was crystal meth she had a problem with.

Since our place was so small and we did not have a couch, Desiree slept in our bed with us. It wasn't awkward. Sharing the bathroom was much worse.

One night, Tyler introduced Desiree to our neighbor, Oliver. He lived on the other side of our bathroom wall. Being our neighbor required a lot of tolerance. We stayed up all night and stomped in and out of the front door at odd hours. Both

of us threw things at the walls and on the floor during arguments. Tyler borrowed Oliver's dishes because we'd given up on
cleaning ours. I don't think we ever returned them on our own
accord. We had loud friends who'd come over to do drugs and
have sex with me. We indiscreetly/openly talked about porno.
But Oliver liked it. He was charmed by us. Who wouldn't have
found us interesting? When Oliver first moved into our building, Tyler made introductions on his own reconnaissance. I
never could tell if Tyler was just planning a threesome or a
regular friendship.

I didn't get excited over new relationships like Tyler did. My
life was already full of people and things I could hardly handle.
We had lots of friends and all of them were crazy. Oliver was a
quiet sort of wall-flowery type. Nothing about him was strikingly
attractive, and still nothing stood out as particularly ugly. There
are a million men like Oliver in Los Angeles trying to do the
same thing—direct movies.

Tyler and Oliver got to be pretty good friends. I barely noticed
him most of the time. He began to do coke with us, and with
Ernesto from downstairs. Our apartment building became quite
the place to party. Oliver met Desiree during one such party.
When it came time to crash, Desiree didn't want to sleep with
Tyler and me again. We hadn't done any ecstasy, so we weren't
feeling the need for the innocent, and, of course, non-sexual,
fuzzy, family-time cuddling that it often fueled. I tried to accommodate her by letting her know that Tyler and I would sleep on
the floor. She was our guest. I wanted her to be comfortable in
our home. But she didn't want to sleep in our bed alone, either.
She wanted to sleep on Oliver's couch, in his living room.

Tyler didn't think it was weird at all for Desiree to stay with
the much older Oliver. "It's fine. Oliver's all right. He's our

friend, and his place is bigger. He offered, and she wants to. She can make up her own mind."

Tyler knows best, I thought. He's the big brother, not me. It gave us a chance to do more lines without her and have sex that night.

The next morning, we woke up early to Desiree coming in through the front door. She didn't say much. She just grabbed a couple of things out of her bags and went in the bathroom to shower. I pulled on a pair of purple sweatpants and did some lines to wake up. I didn't have to convince Tyler to get out of bed because his nicotine addiction did that for him. Just like I had to have my morning lines of cocaine, Tyler needed a cigarette as soon as he opened his eyes. He was so hooked on tobacco that it would wake him up at five or six in the morning, even if we'd just gone to bed at three or four. I smoked, too, but he did it too much.

That night, we took Desiree to a Halloween costume party at Bent Brent's house, whose ass and feet I licked for one of Pro Trusion's scenes. I'd done many more scenes with him since. Desiree wanted to dress up in one of my stripper outfits. I wasn't sure about it, but Tyler said it was okay.

All of the other guests at the party were from porn. Mostly performers. Lots of guys were ogling Desiree. It's hard to blame them. She was dressed like a prostitute, and in my clothes. She was wearing a tiny plaid skirt with a black bra and white cropped top. Only a pair of G-string panties covered her ass and snatch. Fishnet thigh-high stockings went with a pair of clear heels to complete the look. I didn't want her to feel out of place, so I wore an equally slutty outfit to match.

Desiree wasn't ready to wear those clothes. I never should have let her. She was so uncomfortable when we arrived at the party. At our apartment getting ready it was all fun and games. Playing dress-up, imagining getting lots of attention. But when it was real and the guys were staring, she didn't like it. She was still a little girl. Everywhere she turned, there were real strippers and prostitutes partying for keeps. Groups of guys talked about how hard they fucked these chicks and about wood problems. Tyler and I let them know Desiree was only seventeen. All of the porno guys flirted with her, asking her when she'd turn eighteen.

Everyone thought Tyler and I brought his little sister in order to turn her out. You know, get her started early in the business. To them, she was better than barely legal. She wasn't legal at all.

Some of the partiers were having sex in the bathroom and taping it. Two girls were grinding on each other in the living room. They began making out while sitting on some guy's lap. A crowd formed around them. Desiree started freaking out. She didn't want any of these strangers to think she was like the rest of the girls at the party.

"She was the one who dressed me like this!" Desiree declared to a room full of people, finger pointing at me, then demanded to go home and put on some clothes. I let her blame me for the way she was dressed. It didn't matter to me what these other people thought.

I didn't know how to be a big sister to Desiree. In my family, I was the little sister. Tyler allowed her freedom, with little protection. He let her cut loose, but didn't seem to want to safeguard her or feel the need to beat her boyfriend's ass when she was knocked up earlier that year, things like that. I don't know exactly what it was, but they had an odd relationship. Tyler once told me that an older girl had sex with him in a shower when he was ten. He didn't consider it molestation because he enjoyed it. Knowing that made me love him more—in some ways, I'd always searched for a lost soul who would need me to resurrect him from a complicated history. Desiree had some of that in her, too. They had the sweet-natured but reckless characteristics of damaged children who had grown up a little too fast and never enough.

Tyler surprised me by buying us tickets for a trip to Europe, just the two of us. Never in my most farfetched dreams did I think I would be able to go to Europe on my own! At twenty-one years old, I'd pay for the entire trip except for airfare. Tyler purchased the tickets on a whim at a travel agency in West Hollywood. This one extravagant and impulsive buy would be one of the greatest gifts I've ever received. Tyler's irresponsibility worked in his favor half of the time.

In some ways, it's hard for me to initiate risky decisions. With Tyler, I was the one who played it safe. I got upset if a bill was mailed in late. Tyler would tell me it didn't matter. I hated eating fattening food. Tyler told me to enjoy the taste, rather than worry about the calories. I shopped at Macy's and Tyler preferred more expensive boutiques on Melrose. His grandmother always told him he had "champagne taste on a beer budget."

I grew up poor. My parents never had any money, and they were irresponsible with what little they had. It was a revelation not to have to worry about how much something cost. I had the money to buy whatever I wanted. If I wanted a thousand dollar watch, I could buy it. But I didn't. What money we didn't spend on going out and buying coke (granted, a lot), I saved. I had saved almost ten thousand dollars in just a few months. It was too easy. We didn't have to spare ourselves any luxury and could still have money in the bank.

It was unreal how quickly my scenes added up. Every porno movie I appeared in paid me over a thousand dollars.

When we left for Europe in November, only three-quarters of a year into the business, I'd already done so many scenes that I'd lost count.

I was ecstatic about the prospects of a European trip. My life's sort of in the toilet, I thought, and Europe is going to cure it. I was in love and that was the only thing I was consistently proud of at that time, no matter how tumultuous the relationship was. Waves of guilt would unexpectedly crash and gnaw down on my soul, refusing to let me feel good about myself; often, porno felt like a moral death sentence. I was always lying about it. There were too many days when I felt like I was wasting my life because I was caught up in a world of sex, drugs, love, and experience for experience's sake. I was killing my brain and abusing my body. Going to Europe would educate me, and, I hoped, inspire me to do something different with my life in the future. All roads do not lead to porn. The trip would be an accomplishment that I would be entirely proud of without mixed feelings.

The night before our trip, I was thinking of ways to get back at my mother—whom I prefer to call Cheryl—for being vile. She'd called me a few days before we were to leave, while Desiree was still in town. Cheryl knew about our planned Euro trip, but she probably didn't remember. Her brain is seriously deteriorated from doing drugs her entire life. She phoned while I was in line at In-N-Out Burger. Desiree had started her period in my car. She had bled right through her sweatpants, so she waited in the car with Tyler. I was trying to order all of our cheeseburgers correctly. Tyler wanted "no tomato, yes grilled onions, no special sauce, just ketchup only." He would throw a fit if it wasn't just so. Desiree's was simple: no onions.

I answered my cell phone and held it with my shoulder as I fished around in my purse for cash.

"So, do you have anything to tell me?" Cheryl's voice was angry. I could tell by her rhetorical tone that she knew the answer to her own question.

"What? What are you talking about?" I was handing the money over to the cashier and felt rude. I was rolling my eyes. I was annoyed at the bitchiness in my mother's voice.

"Well, do you have anything to say for yourself, young lady?" The voice got angrier. My mother hadn't been mad at me since I was in high school. There wasn't any reason for her to be. I'd been on my own since I turned eighteen. Nothing I did was any of her business. How dare she utter a demeaning phrase like "young lady?"

"Excuse me? What are you getting at? What's your problem?" I had no respect for her. I responded with the same volume of nastiness. Cheryl had put me through misery all of my life. It angered and saddened me when she tried to play "mother" with me now. She hadn't earned it.

"Well, I just saw my daughter on the internet...with a mouth full of cock!" She said it with such mean, matter-of-fact evenness.

I was disgusted and embarrassed. I could tell that her sole intention was to hurt, humiliate, and expose me. I was ashamed of her. Somehow, to hear her speak "a mouth full of cock" was cruder than me even having one. A mother isn't supposed to say things like that. I wanted to vomit into the phone. Instead of fuck you, I venomously said, "So!"

"I think you better start explaining!" She was feeling powerful, and that wounded me deeply. She was trying to corner me.

"So what, do you hate me now?" I asked her. I knew she didn't, but I had to ask.

"No," she responded flatly.

"Okay," I said back, in the same voice as hers. We sound very much alike.

"No. Not okay. I'm so mad at you! You're all over the internet. You fucking little whore. Your mouth's full of cock. I'm ashamed of you, to be your mother! You fucking little bitch!" Then she hung up on me. I didn't get a chance to rightfully respond.

When someone finally handed me the bag of fast food, I was weak in the legs, in shock. I shoved the phone back into my purse and walked out of In-N-Out. My hands were shaking. We'd only done one line apiece that morning, just to wake up. The tears came a few minutes later. I always knew that at some point I would have to talk about *it* with my family. Cheryl just had no right to be so vicious about it—she was probably with her grotesque boyfriend looking at porn when she'd found out.

I've never been scared of letting my mom down. Whether or not she's proud of me makes no difference. Cheryl is a drug addict and a manipulator. It's impossible to trust her. Just when it seems as though she cares, she's got some ulterior motive to benefit herself. I've often promised myself that I would not talk to her anymore. Cheryl would have to wait.

On Desiree's last night in LA, Tyler and I planned to take her out to dinner at Water Grill, one of the best restaurants in the entire city. Tyler made a special point to dine at all of the finest places. His culinary education in Barcelona made him an expert of exquisite cuisine. He taught me about food and opened my palate to a world of niceties I never knew existed. Being a bulimic since a young age, I'd thought of food as my enemy. I have Tyler to thank for changing that, even though I still have a serious eating disorder. I remember the first time I ever stuck my hand into my mouth and reached down my throat and puked up food on purpose. It was Thanksgiving Day, 1994. It stands out to me as much as the first time I had sex (May 27th, 1995). I was thirteen years old. Bulimia and sex started at roughly the same age. I threw up every meal, every day. It gave me pleasure, actually, even though I know it's not healthy behavior. I loved it—it was exhilarating, I could feel a rush in my entire body, a rush of fluids out of the stomach, mouth, eyes, and nose all at once. I found it more orgasmic than sex, until I finally had orgasms at age nineteen.

In 8th grade I went to camp for a week. My mom went into my room while I was gone, to investigate a foul odor coming from my closet. She opened the rickety sliding door and found six or seven tightly tied Von's grocery bags, all full of puke. I'd been hiding the purging after my mom caught on to the bathroom. My newest scheme was turning up my stereo with my bedroom door shut and vomiting in homemade barf bags from the grocery store. Food in. Food out. Back in those days, I had no pager or cell phone. So my mom sat on this horrible discovery for the entire week I was gone. She told all of her friends, my aunts, uncles, cousins; everyone I knew. She was worried, but mostly she was pissed off and disgusted. I have always had a high threshold for the gross, the vulgar, the sickening. For me, it is a source of happiness and excitement.

In junior high, I discovered that almost each one of my pretty girlfriends were also throwing up. We just flocked together, the beautiful and the vomiting. A clique, taking turns at the toilet, in my best buddy's backyard (her dog ate it), in bushes behind the school. In my bedroom closet, in a plastic bag. We were always thinking of new places to do it, and finding new girls to share it with. Sounds like a fetish now, but we were too young and lame to know what a fetish was, or to understand the damage we were doing.

Only in porn would a person's wretched habit of shoving her hand all the way down her throat be considered a talent. I was praised and encouraged to puke and fist my mouth. It was perfect. I loved myself and my eating disorder. Every time I sucked a cock, the hand had to go in first, laying bare the darkest part of my soul. And I was encouraged to take it there. This was and remains a disease that plagues my mind so heavily, and it was sexualized. And it seemed like the right thing to do.

I cannot have any kind of sex to this day until my hand goes in my throat. Pull out some of my soul's thirteen year old innocence and curiosity. That's what I'm reaching for. I can erase everything I know with that hand down my throat. Fresh tears, cleansing the mouth with watery saliva, recreating innocence—returning to an innocent state. I think it does work. I still go there.

But I can't throw up anymore. I've graduated to natural laxatives and enema bags. Not as conventionally sexy as vomit, they have their perks. I get to keep my tooth enamel. My intestines are clean enough to make blood sausage with. Now that I'm older and wiser, I have more free time and less ability to bounce back from convulsions. So I focus on the asshole now. It can take a lot of beatings and blasting. Thanks to porn, I know about this mysteriously resilient piece of the Digestive Lexicon. I'm fascinated by feces, anyway. I love to look at shit and fantasize about how it came to be. It's so disgusting. I do love that feeling of strong repulsion.

For Tyler, cooking food was an art form, to be indulged in but not to be abused afterward. Good chefs were fine artists. When Tyler cooked, it was magnificent. It filled me with hope for a better world. But cocaine is an appetite—and therefore a cooking—suppressant. Though it rarely happened—or because it rarely happened—watching Tyler cook was better than watching him fuck. You could see the creativity blazing in his head. When he first moved to LA, he had jobs in the kitchens of Patina and Asia de Cuba. Even with his degree and training in Europe, he couldn't make enough money to survive in the city on kitchen wages, not for the kind of fun that Los Angeles has to offer. Porno didn't inspire Tyler to cook. We made plenty of money for him to go back to cooking, but he lost the drive to be a determined artist. He said it was too hard to see me doing something easy like porno while he went and cooked in a competitive and fast-paced kitchen for twelve hours a day. We compensated for some of his lost chef dreams by becoming patrons of four-star restaurants.

Desiree and I got ready together. She wore an elegant strapless black dress. Her skin and tits looked great in it. I've always been a fan of small chests. My dress was black, too. It was too sexy for the place we were going. The middle was cut out of the side and it had one strap. It was a stripper dress. I made it work with a long, thin coat. Tyler wanted me to wear the dress. He picked it out because it was hot. I often turned to him for style tips because I could never go sexy enough. Clothes I chose were too plain, not fitting for a girl in porn.

Tyler went next door to Oliver's apartment to wait for us to get dressed. He probably wanted to do a couple lines and see what Oliver had to drink. Desiree shut the door behind Tyler as he left. She locked it and looked at me. Desiree confided to me that she and Oliver had fucked the night she stayed over at his apartment and that she didn't want to hang out with him on her last night here. I told her we would do whatever she wanted and that I was sorry for what had happened. All of a sudden, and way too late, I felt protective of this girl. *She's only seventeen!* I fumed.

What a creep! I felt naïve for being so blind. Oliver seemed so harmless. I never thought anything would happen between them. Oliver was supposed to be engaged to a girl back in Boston. He acted too uptight to fuck an underage girl. Tyler couldn't know. I wasn't going to tell him while Desiree was still staying with us. If she wanted to, then that was her business. Desiree was his responsibility more than mine, but I played my part. We fed her drugs and booze. Then she got fucked by the twenty-seven year old neighbor. What else could Tyler and I possibly do to help corrupt this girl?

Our reservations were at eight, but we arrived late. Just like with porno jobs, Tyler would continually make us late for dinner. We ordered caviar and wine to pair with the tasting menu. The sommelier came to our table. He was absolutely gorgeous. Desiree and I gawked. It was so hard to take our eyes off him. The man was tall, black-haired, blue-eyed, and impeccably dressed. He also knew everything about wine. Tyler made fun of us for being so adolescent. He didn't get jealous. It was too great of a night for him to act like an asshole. He didn't get wasted or embarrass us. It was lovely.

The sommelier asked Desiree her name and sat down with us for a glass of wine, on him. The four of us chitchatted, and for once not about pornography. Desiree told him she was twenty-four and in town for one last night before she would be going home to Houston to finish college. It was a pretty good story, and he bought it. Meth teaches people to tell a decent lie, the addict's survival instinct. Our party migrated to The Standard downtown for some drinks. Tyler and I thought nothing of the flirtation going on between Desiree and the sommelier. I didn't think it would go any further than a make-out session at the bar. Part of me was envious that she got to flirt with the sommelier and I didn't. The thought of having a four-way wasn't a possibility, because of the whole brother/sister thing. We were unconventional, but we were not sickos. I had to live vicariously through Desiree as the sommelier persistently came on to her. I died for her inside.

The night couldn't go on forever. Tyler had a shoot the next morning without me. Desiree wanted to stay the night with the sommelier, even though she was still on her period. He'd invited her up to his downtown loft nearby.

"Please? Can I? I promise I'll be back early tomorrow morning. Please, Scooter?" She looked up at him with batting eyes and clasped her hands together, begging.

Tyler let her go.

"I can't believe you think it's okay for her to just go with some strange guy! We don't even know him. What if something happens to her?" I was shocked that he didn't worry at all. I didn't want to think of anything bad happening to her, but I couldn't help it. I'm a big worrier. At least Oliver was someone we knew.

"She's fine. You have *no idea*. Desiree is a smart girl. She can take care of herself better than most girls twice her age. She wants to go. It will make her happy. Don't worry so much," he shrugged.

"He doesn't know her real age." Visions of her never coming back flashed in my brain. The phone calls we would have to make to her mother.

We left The Standard without her.

Before seven in the morning the next day, she walked through our apartment door. She sat down on the corner of our bed and looked dreamily out the window.

Tyler and I were in a cab going to the airport. Our flight was leaving for Paris. We were going to make it with plenty of time to spare. It was crazy at LAX, ever since 9/11. I was so nervous. Someone asked us for our tickets and passports. Tyler reached into the shoulder bag I'd put all of our important documents in. Everything was supposed to be in the front pocket. "Ori, where are the tickets?" He moved things around in the bag.

"With the passports. Right in there," I said and pointed to where his hands were.

"No, Ori! This is just the itinerary, not our actual tickets. Where are the tickets?"

"What? What do you mean? I didn't bring the tickets?" I began bawling loudly. "I thought that's what I packed! I thought I had them. What are we going to do?" Everything went nebular, I couldn't see. There were too many tears in my eyes. A wave of bad heat brushed through my body. I nearly fainted.

The man at the ticket counter was stern, but trying to be helpful. "You need the hard copy of the tickets to get on this flight. We can't let you on unless we get that. You've got some time. Is there anyone at home that can drive the tickets here in the next forty-five minutes?"

I fell to the ground, paralyzed and reduced to a puddle of sobs on the linoleum. The distress was too much for me to handle. I didn't know how to fix this. Tyler tried to think fast and pulled himself together for both of us.

"Oliver!" he shouted. "Oliver next door! Our neighbor Oliver!" Tyler sprang into action and called. "Hey man! I need you to break into our apartment...We forgot the tickets...Yes, the tickets... Just use a credit card and swipe it through the door lock, I've done it tons of times. We never lock the deadbolt... Just like Ernesto... Okay, you in? Great!... Where?... I don't know where they are exactly... Just look, look everywhere! By the computer, or in the kitchen, by the bed, in those drawers by the window...

You have them? Ori! He has them! Great, man! I love you, man!
We owe you our lives. Thank you. Yeah...We're at Air France/Air
Tahiti Nui. Thank you, so much. See you, bye."

To buy some time, the man at the ticket counter made it
possible for Tyler and me to start pre-boarding while we waited
for Oliver. The airport security escorted us through the lines
quickly, as we were holding up the flight. We were last to get on
the plane. But we made it. Good ol' Oliver—the rapist of a minor
in the eyes of California state law—was our savior.

CHAPTER TWENTY

CLUSTERFUCK

THREE days after we returned from Europe, Tyler had a shoot without me—a gang bang with seven other men—and I was relieved to drop him off in Sunland. I had sworn off gang bangs. He was doing two scenes for Roach. I had the entire day off to get a manicure and pedicure. My nails were white trash. I'd painted them a dark red while in Spain. Now, back in the USA, they were chipped, faded, and uneven from biting them on the plane. I'd been exhausted since our month in Europe. The very day we got back, I had a shoot. I was so upset. I was crying on the phone to my agent—Nelson. He booked this scene without telling me about it. While Tyler and I were still in Paris, I called Nelson back. I begged him to reschedule it. I felt like a slave. Ironically, the shoot was for a movie called *Slave Dolls*. The morning of, I showed up not having slept at all, jetlagged and miserable. Nelson picked me up from my apartment and drove me to the location. He knew I wouldn't have shown up otherwise. When we knocked on the door at the house a little girl answered.

"Um, hi. Is your mommy home?" Nelson asked the seven year old. This was not good. A kid was not supposed to be there.

"She's not here," the child answered. She was in a big tee shirt and her hair was a scraggly mess. It was seven-thirty in the morning.

The director pulled up and took over. Nelson left me there. This guy Jackal and I walked into the house. He was really nice and excited about the shoot. His energy lightened me up considerably. The girl's mother walked through the open front door. She was an older porn star named Priscilla, and Priscilla was spun out of her mind on meth. She started wiping down her filthy kitchen countertops while smoking a long tweaker cigarette. The little girl was sent to a neighbor's house while another tweaker lady started sweeping the floor. The place was a pigsty and a crack house. A perfect porn location, I guessed.

The scene took the entire day. It was another rough anal three-way. This time, there was a girl in it to dominate me, too. I was fucked in the ass by a guy who had a huge uncut cock, one of the thickest cocks I'd ever been fucked by. It was like a barrel used to store hazardous materials. The whole time, I was in submission to a man and a woman.

It was special enough to stand out in my memory from the blur of most of the other stuff I've done. I'm glad I did it. But I was so fucking tired. I needed at least a couple days to gather myself. Plus, after Europe, my tan was nonexistent. All of my clothes were still packed in a suitcase. I couldn't remember what bills needed to be paid. Things were in disorder.

Thirty minutes after I'd dumped him off in Sunland, Tyler called my cell. "Ori! Hey baby, what are you doing? Can you come back here? Roach wants to talk to you."

Then he just handed the phone to someone else, putting me on the spot, right as I was saying, "No, Tyler! I don't want to talk to him right now. Don't." Roach was a nice enough director and always had an earful of compliments for me, but I didn't care what he had to say at that moment. Every time I got on the phone with him he talked for an hour, and I knew it would be about work.

"Hello, Ori?" It was Nelson. "Ori, can you come back to the Tuxford House? Andromeda has cancelled at the last minute. She's come down with gonorrhea this morning and can't do it. It's putting Roach in a very difficult position. He'll lose a lot of money if we have to kill this next scene. All of the guys are here, doing the first scene. Can you please come and do it, Ori? We *need* you to come and do the second scene."

Tears filled my eyes. "I can't. I can't just come back and do it last minute. I don't want to do any more gang bangs, at least for a while. I can't do it." I was panicking. I had to be strong. *Don't let them talk you into it*, I told myself.

"Ori, listen. I need you. We need you. You're the best—the scene will be better for it. All of the guys are here, all ready to go, and it won't be as long as your last one. We have two cameras, and Roach has promised to be very quick. Guinevere is doing her scene first. We can start right away on the next scene as soon as you get here, won't take long at all. It's a lot of money, Ori. You would really be saving the day."

Unfortunately, I wasn't a tough sell. My problem always lay in the inability to give a firm no for an answer. "I can't. I'm sorry. No," I sobbed. But my voice was weak. My weakness was no match. Nelson fed upon weakness to get to the top of our frail porno ecosystem's food chain.

"Ori. Please. I know you're capable of this. It would really help out Roach a lot. If we don't get someone, everything will be lost. None of us will get to do the second scene or get paid for it. It will cost Roach the location. It'll be a mess. Please, would you just do us this favor?"

"Ashley Blue!" Roach's voice boomed in my ear. "Ashley Blue, how are you? Nelson's told you already about Andromeda and our little situation here. It would mean so much to me if you could come here and take her place. You are an absolute star, and you can handle this no problem. I shoot fast. You know that. Well, I'll shoot doubly fast this time. There are two cameras here. All of the guys are here and they're all dudes you've worked with before. It would be a disaster if we can't get a girl to do this second scene. A *real* girl, like you. Guinevere, my wife the superstar, is in the other scene. If you could come back and be a part of this, we will have one incredible movie. Ashley Blue, there is no one else who can do this but you. Will you please say yes and be here by noon?"

It felt like I was already being gangbanged by the phone. Every man I trusted was talking me into doing this scene, acting like they were all trapped in a mine shaft and I was Lassie. Time to save the day, girl! Pull them out of their life-threatening plight by coming to their gang-bang rescue. How was I going to say no?

"Baby?" The phone had been passed back to Tyler. "You can do this, Ori. I know you can. We know everybody here. It'll be quicker than last time. You can literally save the day if you come here. It will mean so much to Roach. I'll take care of you. Don't worry. I love you, baby. Come on, please? Applesauce?" He hit below the belt with that one. He used the pet name he'd given me. I adored being called Applesauce.

I relented. "Fine. But I don't know how soon I can be there. I look like shit! My nails are fucked up and my life is fucked up," I screamed. "I'm not prepared at all! I'm fucking hungry, Tyler! I wanted to eat today!" I punched the seat of my car. That was something I picked up from Tyler.

"Baby," he said softly, sweetly. "You look great. You're beautiful no matter what. Just throw some heels and stuff in a bag and come down here. You can eat later, when we're done. We can eat whatever you want. Just go see Ernesto before you come here. I love you, Applesauce. We'll see you in a little while. Bye." *Why can't I just say no to people?* I beat myself up about it, crying on the floor in my apartment when I was supposed to be getting ready for my gang bang. I had some coke, but not enough to put me into a euphoric mental state. I wanted to be drunk, but I didn't have any more vodka. Tyler had put an empty bottle back in the freezer. I went to drink from it, and there wasn't even a shot left. I viciously and dearly hated him for it. I was actually scared to do this scene.

I'd done a gang bang earlier that year, in the summer. I'd never fucked so many guys at once. Up until then the most guys I'd fucked in a scene were four, for *Down the Hatch 9*, not necessarily a gang bang in the world of porn. I was excited about it. I'd worked with the director, B-Bone, on *Service Animals 10*. I was so cocky and sure of myself that I could handle it, no problem. This was B-Bone's first time directing a gang bang. How could it be much different from any other type of scene? I was into hardcore, anal and double penetrations. This was the next step, I thought, naturally.

The movie was called *7 The Hard Way*. The scene started with me in a wheelbarrow. Seven large guys surrounded me. Each one slapped me and grabbed my face. They spit on me and pulled my hair. It seemed like they were all trying to outdo each other, to prove who could rough me up the most. I smiled and went along with the action. I did my best not to break down. Breaking down, crying, or complaining was a no-no. Plus, I wanted them all to see how hardcore I was. They throat-fucked me hard and I tried my best to enjoy it. My drool was all over the floor and dripping from each guy's cock. They pounded my ass and puss at the same time. My ass was fucked with two dicks at once. It went on for hours. B-Bone seemed unsatisfied with the footage. We needed more. It wasn't enough. All seven guys kept fucking me until I could no longer go on.

B-Bone finally directed us into the pop-shot position. Five hours after the scene started, I was hardly able to move. My holes were stretched and swollen from the constant cock rubbing and ramming. There were several rips in my throat and cuts in my mouth. My ass had blood on it when I wiped it with a baby wipe, but I was used to that. Assholes always bleed during anal scenes. My head was sore where my hair had been ripped out. The guys didn't mean to pull out my hair, but it got caught on their fingers when they yanked me around. It was a tangled disaster from being shoved onto so many different cocks. Tears stained my cheeks. I could hardly lift my arms, they were so sore from being held up in so many standing DPs.

The seven men dumped their loads into my mouth one by one. B-Bone wanted me to hold all of it in my mouth until each guy had finished cumming. I just stared into the camera, my mouth full of seven different kinds of sperm. It was horrific. B-Bone ordered me to swallow after I held it there for about a minute. It felt like I'd been waiting forever. It hurt just to swallow at all. As soon as it went down my enflamed throat, I showed the camera. Then I ran to the bathroom and vomited.

That shoot made me ill. I'd been completely worn down, physically. I developed a high fever. Tyler didn't know what to do, so he took me to Whole Foods to get some organic food. He thought I needed nutrients, but what I really needed was a doctor. I almost fainted in the store. Tyler grabbed a Whole Foods fair-trade Alpaca sweater off a shelf and wrapped me in it. I don't remember what happened afterwards. I blacked out.

We went to the doctor the next morning, the same one who prescribed Tyler Viagra and Xanax. It was too shameful to explain to any respected physician that I was sick from a gang bang. Pornography was too socially demoralizing for me to seek out better care for my body. I believed that any good doctor would tell me to quit doing porn, that I was hurting myself. A smart doctor would be able to tell that I was a drug addict, too. I had to stay away from this kind of advice.

What I had was strep throat and exhaustion. Surprisingly, I didn't catch gonorrhea or chlamydia. I did develop a very painful yeast infection. It was from having way too many different men's bacteria inside my vagina. I was better in a couple weeks, but I learned a valuable lesson: Gang bangs were too much for me. It was my first limit. I'd found something in porno that I was not good at. I swore them off forever. Tyler supported me at the time. Until, that is, Roach and Nelson brought it up, and Tyler was one of the bangers. I didn't stand a chance.

I had to do my own makeup for this shit, too, which pissed me off. I was doing everyone a huge favor by filling in on such short notice, and they couldn't even provide a makeup artist? Roach wanted it heavy. Well, too bad. I didn't know how to do heavy makeup, and I wasn't about to try. I'd lost my entire makeup collection in France a couple weeks before. All I'd bought since was a grey eye shadow, blush, and mascara. What did it matter how I looked? Anybody who was going to be watching this movie wouldn't care what my makeup looked like. Gang bangs aren't exactly about the girl's glamour. They are about brutality, getting ravaged. The girl always looks fucked up the whole time. The gang bang is slightly more than the video sequence of a rape fantasy. Whose rape fantasy? I suppose it could be anyone's. It could be the guys' or the girl's.

My hooker heels got thrown against the wall a couple times before I stuck them in a bag. I did as much coke as I could and took the rest with me in the car. I did get a hold of Ernesto before I left for the scene. I was visibly upset. I think he felt sorry for me. He sold me drugs and wished me luck.

The Tuxford house is the ugliest location to shoot porn. It's also the cheapest place you can rent that's big enough to film an entire movie in one day. It's over an acre of property, but it's trashed. The walls are dilapidated. The plumbing is constantly backed up. Hundreds of beers have been spilled on its carpets. Its pool houses as much piss and vomit as it does water. The man who owns it is a very kind old pervert, but he's too old to stop his house from being destroyed. Cum, cooze, spit, shit, and lube cover the walls of this four-bedroom, Southern Californian home. Once a nice place, with a tennis court, poolroom, gym, billiard room, and horses' stable, it's drenched in human DNA now.

I walked through the front door, where Guinevere's scene was taking place. The sight of her left me in awe. She was taking on the same eight guys I was going to. She looked like she was in total control of them. Even though she was outnumbered, she moved from position to position on her own. They didn't tug at her or toss her around. She was taking double vaginal and double anal penetration like it felt good. It was hard sex, but they weren't being rough. No one was acting like a tough guy. There wasn't any spit on her face or bruises on her arms. Maybe I would do fine, like they said. If it was easy-looking for Guinevere, then I could probably handle it myself.

I was worried about my bowels. For a month straight, Tyler and I did nothing but eat cheese and cured meats in Europe. How much of it was left to come out of my intestines was unknown. I hadn't shit during a scene since the infamous *Barely Legal* shoot. I usually had more time to prepare. I liked to starve for at least twenty-four hours and do fifteen to twenty enemas. I enjoy cleaning my ass out. It's a therapeutic exercise. I had to be totally empty in order to accommodate a gang bang. I could be getting ass-fucked for five hours again. I prayed my butt would stay clean for the whole scene.

I wore the same dress I'd worn two days prior in *Slave Dolls*. We began the scene with me on my knees. All of the men stood over me in a circle, surrounding me. I was in a hollowed-out portion of the brick floor in the poolroom. The walls were made of see-through plastic. At least they put some pillows down for my knees. All of the cocks came out of the pants. They circled around my face. The aerial view must have looked like some kind of prehistoric penis flower. The cocks smacked and rubbed against my face. The men started calling me whore and commanding me to suck their cocks. "Yeah, get down on it! Swallow it. Suck my balls! You fucking whore! Is this what you want? Yeah, take it. Take it all the way down."

My face was grabbed and passed around from cock to cock. It wasn't smooth and controlled like Guinevere's scene. It was a free-for-all. I was manhandled and shoved onto different bodies. There wasn't a second for me to breathe in between chokes. I couldn't see anything but dicks. Ball-sweat and spit covered my face. I wanted to cry, but I couldn't get enough air to make a sob. I heaved and cowered from the cocks. I had to stop. Tyler and Roach pulled me out of the brick hole. Tyler held me while I cried. I knew I couldn't stop now. If I'd just ran away, I'd have to face everyone later. They all wanted me to finish, so I did.

"I'm all right now. It's okay. Just don't be as rough," I sucked it up and got into it as much as I could possible feign.

Roach put his arm around me and led me into the living room for a pep talk. This was his specialty. He could talk at length and with great intensity about anything. He made me forget my fear and misery about what we were doing. "Ashley Blue," he said, looking deep into my eyes and handing me a lit smoke, "you are doing great. This is incredible. You are a star and you will be just as big a star as Guinevere. Are you all right? Do you need anything else? Some water? Let's get going so we can wrap this up and go home. We've got two cameras on you this time. So, let's go!"

Everyone kept telling me about the two cameras ever since I picked up the phone that morning. What exactly did it mean to me during the scene? Absolutely nothing. It was supposed to make me think it was going to be easier and go faster than a normal gang bang, but nothing makes fucking eight guys at once easy. Especially when it's all hardcore double penetrations. I did double vaginal and double anal. Every time I was penetrated, single or double, there was at least one cock in my mouth, throat-fucking me.

For hours, we stopped and started. All of the guys had wood, no problem. They all liked me. I was usually a great scene. They could do anything they wanted with my body. But I was crying most of the time during this one. I wasn't ready for another gang bang, not that day. I was still sore from a couple days earlier. Roach just kept telling me to hang in there, like I was a boxer in a ring.

It was time to pop. It can't be any worse than the pop shot for *7 The Hard Way*, I thought. Wrong. This gang bang's cum ending had to top other gang bangs. Roach wanted his movie to stand out. I was handed a metal cereal spoon from the Tuxford house kitchen. It was all dinged up and bent. Roach directed the grand finale.

Each of the eight men fucked my ass, one at a time. One by one, they came on my ass cheeks and hole. After each guy shot his load, I scooped the cum out of my ass crack with the beat-up steel spoon. Then I spoon-fed myself. It smelled like bleach and blood. The taste was too awful to remember, but the texture was worse. When cum sits on any piece of cold metal, it coagulates. It had body when it entered my mouth and sat on my tongue. I swallowed every lump. I just wanted it to be over, and for the finale to be good. I suddenly felt like I had failed everyone, not just myself. I did another gang bang after I said I never would, then I cried all the way through it. The least I could do was swallow.

When all was finished, Tyler was treated like the real hero for getting me to fill in at the last minute for Andromeda. He was full of pride. He'd fucked in two gang bang scenes for Roach and received five hundred dollars for each. We now had separate bank accounts, but I still paid all the bills and bought him clothes, dinners, his gym membership, and his HIV testing. Everyone thought Tyler had it made. He had the hot, willing girlfriend who loved him. Things hadn't begun to get dark for Tyler and me yet—at least I hadn't been able to perceive them. The only publicly dark things about our lives were the circles that'd formed underneath Tyler's eyes. From the outside, our lives seemed to be really coming together. It would still be a while before the unraveling.

CHAPTER TWENTY-ONE

MY MOTHER

CHERYL and I made up on the phone. She left messages on Tyler's voicemail, crying and begging him to have me call her. I was fully prepared to never speak with her again. I can be cold in that way—if I feel like somebody is doing more damage to me than good, I cut them out of my life. You have to remove cancerous tumors.

Tyler had a plus-size heart when it came to family sympathies. He listened to Cheryl's pleas on the messages, and then argued with me about the situation. "She's your mother. You only get one in life. Call her. You can't go on like this."

I pointed out to Tyler that no matter how much he loved his mother, his own Cheryl, he still lied to her about his occupation. His mother was flawed, but Tyler was forgiving. She'd lied to Tyler about who his real father was and chose her lovers over her children—just like my mother. It's eerie how similar they are, in name and manner. Tyler forgave his mother for all of it. They even did coke together.

I had called my mother from Paris. It was an expensive call. It was our last night before we left for home. In such a romantic, inspiring place, where it feels like anything is possible, I thought maybe I could change and somehow grow to be a more compassionate woman by reaching out to Cheryl. I needed her at the time. Just the thought of my family's reaction to my porn career made me cringe, and I hoped Cheryl would be a gateway to get through to them. No one would be happy for me. My family always praised me for having a sharp mind. Now, to them, I would be wasting my gifts and exploiting my body. Everyone in my family is extremely modest about sex, except for Cheryl. She taught me everything I know about wearing provocative clothing. At a very young age, she would embarrass me by wearing see-through tops and shorts that revealed her butt cheeks. I guess at some point I took after her.

My mom was so happy I called. She regretted how we ended the last call. I didn't remind her that she'd hung up on me. I tried my best not to be snotty. Both of us shed tears and choruses of "I love you." Cheryl can always get me to feel sorry for her. She makes poor decisions in the moment. But she's instinctively manipulative.

Cheryl and her new live-in boyfriend, Leon, invited Tyler and me over to their home for a visit when we returned. Cheryl couldn't go five minutes without a man. This one, she claimed, like the rest, was The One. I was well aware of her codependency. All I knew about this guy was that he used to have a parrot named Shithead. He was also fresh out of prison. Not jail, but prison. He did ten years of hard time for selling cocaine. He was supposedly clean now, or else he would be in violation of his parole.

Cheryl certainly was not clean. She still took a fair share of sedatives and methadone. She also smoked pot all the time because of its medicinal value. Her body was a wreck from various ailments. As a kid, it used to frighten me that she was such a mess. It didn't matter to me what she was taking anymore. I had my own drug issues.

Leon was overly friendly. Tyler and I had met him a few brief times before, but now that Leon knew about us doing porno, he was extra-delighted to have us over. With relish he wanted to know about our involvement in the porn business. How much money did we make? How many scenes did we do? Who did we work for? What were the people really like? Was it easy for us to get started?

Hesitantly, we answered all of his questions. My mom didn't get into the conversation at all. She just sat there, quietly, letting Leon do all the talking. I wondered why she quietly accepted her boyfriend virtually getting off on talking about porn with me. I just tried to be polite and not look offended.

Leon led us all into his office. He had saved everything he could find about me and Tyler in a folder on the desktop of his computer. Images of me naked, sucking cock, and Tyler fucking my ass popped up on the screen. It was too bizarre to be real, yet was all too real. Leon was all jacked up about showing us. He was so proud of his collection of my porn clips. My mom never looked me in the eye the entire time. I ducked out of the room and walked down the hall.

"Ori, hey," Leon called out. He came down the hall after me. "I just wanted to ask you and Tyler if you could put in a good word for me, you know, in the porn business. I was wondering if they need any guys who are in their 40s, like me? I think I can measure up. Ask your mom."

I looked at Cheryl. She looked back at me, smiling. She nodded and said, "Do you think you could help him get in? He really wants to try doing porno movies. I don't mind."

They both hung on me for an answer. I turned to Tyler, who had a hopeful look on his face. I was the only one who thought this was wrong.

The corners of my mouth turned down as I spoke, "I don't know." It made me sick to even open my mouth.

"You two don't have to tell anyone I'm with your mom. Just say I'm a friend."

I wanted to kick his teeth in.

Tyler stepped in, but instead of siding with me, he sided with Leon. "Well, maybe, Ori. There's always Jim. He hires anyone. You don't have to do a scene with him. Let's just see."

I looked at Tyler with fractured eyes. The discussion was over. I was ready to puke. I didn't even want a stepdaughter's relationship with Leon, let alone a professional one. "We have to go home. I'm really uncomfortable that you guys asked me this. I don't know what to say."

Leon's feathers got ruffled. He stiffened up and acted put out. My mom acted like nothing was wrong. Tyler and I hugged her and said goodbye. None of the other men she'd been involved with over the years ever acted perverted toward me.

In the car, Tyler wanted to continue the discussion. "It would help them out with money. Your mom said she didn't care if he did scenes. I think he's disappointed that you said no, just like that."

"We are not going to do anything to help that man. This is unthinkable. It's almost incest. I don't care if his feelings are hurt."

If we would have gotten Leon into porn, directors would have worked the incest angle to no end—or at least marketed him and me in the same films—and that was downright disgusting, even for me. How my mother could sit there blankly smiling, a doped-up specter, I could barely fathom.

I shouldn't have expected much from a woman who basically never had a chance to learn how to be a mother. Her own mother gave her and her twin up for adoption when they were newborns. Life had dealt Cheryl a sad hand from the start. At fifteen, she got pregnant by a guy named Chuckie, my sister's dad. When my mother got to the hospital to deliver, one of the nurses called out, "Here comes another baby havin' a baby!"

Cheryl was wild, too. She started smoking cigarettes and pot in elementary school. She repeatedly got into fights in junior high and high school, resulting in expulsion. As a teen mother, she was already married and divorced by the age of eighteen. Chuckie taught my sister a nursery rhyme that went something like, "Two Englishmen, two Englishmen digging a ditch, one called the other a son of a bitch... And if you ever get hit with a bucket of shit, be sure and shut your eyes."

Cheryl and I once had a close relationship. She called me her best friend. When I was a child, she would let me get out of bed late at night and play gin rummy. At thirteen, I was old enough to smoke cigarettes with her. I admired the way she could blow enormous smoke rings. I don't remember an age that she didn't allow me to drink alcohol. There was always a bottle of vodka in the freezer. Cheryl never cared if I drank from it, just so long as I left some in there for her. She would even order margaritas and kamikazes for me at restaurants when I was underage. She was into really good, racy literature. Of course I thought she was cool at the time. Being a cool mom was the top priority for her. Never mind that she forgot to pay electricity bills and spent all the grocery money on perfume and boots.

I learned the difference between being drunk and buzzed by watching my mother. A few drinks meant she was buzzed. Her complexion would get a little flushed. Laughter would come easily, and loudly. She'd start singing and dancing, full of joy. Drunk Cheryl, on the other hand, was nasty. Fights would break out. She always fell to the ground in some way, usually on her ass. Once, she was severely drunk at my cousin's tenth birthday party.

Our extended family went to Roller Gardens. The Wagon Wheel Bowling Alley was next door. My mom and her brothers got shit-faced at the bowling alley before joining the kids for some skating. Cheryl laced up her roller skates and barreled out into the rink. Halfway around the lap, she fell on her ass. She was just lying on her back, in the middle of the polished floor, kicking her legs in the air while sprawled out, slurring and unable to get up.

Still, there was more love than hate most of the time, at least when I was young—just enough. And I admired Cheryl's brash fuck-off attitude, though her unpredictable and out-of-control behavior caused me to develop into a worrier. She might crash her car on her way home, drunk. My dad, Gary, might catch her in a lie about where she'd been. She could lose her job because of her bad temper. The cops might come and take her to jail for smoking pot or fighting with my dad. Etc.

When she had self-esteem, she was lively and unstoppable. She was the life of the party. My mom was the funniest person on Earth, always cussing and making me laugh. Her sense of humor was mean. The outgoing message on our answering machine said, "Leave a message...and fuck you." My friends all thought it was hilarious and envied me.

I don't remember her ever telling me not to do drugs. Throughout my childhood, both of my parents smoked pot. Cheryl openly admitted that she smoked weed while pregnant with me. I think she was proud of it. My parents sniffed speed, too. I think their drug use is the reason why my parents split up. All the fighting and lying was amplified on drugs. They stayed out all night sometimes, doing speed and drinking. All I could think about was them ending up in jail, until I became an adolescent and began to think about exercising all the freedom their behavior provided me. At age thirteen I got picked up by the police while I was riding around in my neighbor's van. I was drunk with some other thirteen year old girls, high on oregano. The cops dropped us back at my house and we never got into trouble for it because my mom and dad weren't home.

Cheryl constantly cheated on Gary. It began when I was a toddler. She abandoned my sister and me with my dad while she ran off to Nebraska with her lover. Gary took her back a few months later, but she never stopped screwing around with other men. She brought me out on her dates sometimes, while my dad was at work. One of her boyfriends took us to Catalina Island for the day when I was seven years old. She told me never to tell my dad who we were with or where we went. I followed her instructions carefully. I was her little sidekick, her accomplice.

My parents started abusing speed when I was around eleven or twelve. By my fourteenth birthday, they were out of their minds on it. I'd become bulimic and started having sex. Then my dad and I left my mom. We moved to Texas.

Cheryl went to live with some other guy. She started using heroin with this other guy, so he became her boyfriend. She went from using speed with my dad to shooting heroin and speed with her new boyfriend. I loathed this man. I came to live with them when I returned to California. I couldn't stand Texas for very long. My father made it clear that I was choosing my mom over him. He was hurt. It ended our relationship. Gary no longer wanted to be my dad after I returned to Cheryl.

The plumbing her and her boyfriend's house was a mess. The only thing that worked in that house was sadness. I wanted to run away, but I didn't want to be a loser. I needed to finish high school. I made the best of this gloomy life. My mom was always passed out from drugs. She could barely speak half of the time. She would go crazy and fight with her loser boyfriend every few days. She had a gun and would threaten to end her life with it. She held the gun in her mouth and to her head, in front of me, many times. I would cry and tell her not to do it.

I wanted to kill myself, too. A few times, I came close. I wanted to electrocute myself by tossing my radio into the bathtub with me. Thankfully, the thought of dying in the presence of my junky mother and her equally despicable boyfriend prevented me from trying. I lived through my depressing teen years. I smoked a little pot and tried speed, but I didn't want to be like my mom and dad.

As much as my real parents fought and did drugs, it was nothing compared to how much worse things became after they separated. Both my mom and her boyfriend contracted hepatitis C. They got it from used heroin needles. It didn't stop their drug abuse. They would often pass out with lit cigarettes dangling from their mouths. As early as six or seven in the evening, they would be smacked out of consciousness. I would peek into their bedroom and glare at the two lifeless bodies on the waterbed. My heart would fill with darkness. The ash would fall and smolder on the blanket, never turning to flame.

At fourteen, my sister—who lived with her father and stepmother—took me to live with her for six months. The living conditions in our home had become unsuitable. There were needles lying around the entire house, with two other junkies living there. The house was full of cigarette smoke and ashes. The carpet had too many burn holes to count. There were broken windows with tape on them. Until Cheryl could provide me a real bedroom and clean up the rest of the house, I would live with my sister.

My mom was in and out of mental health facilities as well. She had to find ways to get prescriptions for downers. Because she was so fucked up all the time, my mom couldn't work. Her job became a full-time effort to find ways *not* to work. She compelled countless doctors and psychologists to deem her crazy and disabled. Her liver and thyroid were legitimately shot. The valium, Vicodin, Percocet, methadone, and codeine pills she was taking made her incoherent enough to be viewed as mentally incapable. She collected worker's compensation and disability. She qualified for welfare until I turned eighteen. After she could no longer claim benefits in the name of her child, she began making a case for social security.

The fact that I returned to and graduated high school (not on "independent study") was miraculous. My mom never made me go to school. I ditched all the time. She was so out of it she never even knew when I was in the house. She let me get tattooed at fifteen. I got picked up by the cops pretty regularly for alcohol and curfew violations. I chain-smoked and drank hard alcohol until I was sick. I came and went with my friends as I pleased. It wasn't a real home for me. Just a place I had to live.

My mother always had an excuse, a reason, for poisoning herself in all of these ways: to deal with the pain of being alive.

No matter how much I tried to assert my individuality, I ended up being like her. I was a rebel *like* her. I started to take drugs. They started out as something fun, just like they probably had for Cheryl. Then I turned to them when everything was going wrong. My mother ruined her life because she never stopped using.

Now, Cheryl lives just down the street from my sister. When we talk about it all, my sister, with an even, noble tone, suggests, "Just wait until you have kids, Ori. You will understand how much it hurts when a child turns their shoulder to their mother."

Each day I get older and closer to understanding my own mortality, I think of my mother's life. She was a vibrant person once.

When I was a child I often wondered, *If I am unable to take care of myself when I grow up, will all I need to do is shack up with some asshole and get wasted to survive?* But I never fully fed into the legacy. Tyler had his faults, and we had our chemical fun, but the reciprocity of love was more than maybe even I give it credit. I do, however, think my mom definitely contributed to my drug addiction. She and I did drugs together until I stopped.

But only her good characteristics influenced me—gave me the balls, so to speak—to get into porn. She showed me D. H. Lawrence, Henry Miller, and Anaïs Nin when I was a kid, and my sexual life, for pleasure and for work, has been its own poetry. My mother was open about sex, positively. And she was the life of the party. In her better days, she taught me a fun way of being, by example. Her FUCK YOU, DONT TELL ME WHAT TO DO attitude built me to be bold enough to start doing porn, and I thank her for that.

CHAPTER TWENTY-TWO

CHRISTMAS VACATION

TYLER and I flew to Houston for Christmas. I didn't want to stay long, maybe just a few days. He threw a tantrum when I said this, so we booked a trip for ten days. Ten days is a very long time to spend in Texas. It becomes eternal when you have to lie about the fact that you're doing porno—and perhaps extends somewhere beyond eternity when it's an open secret.

Tyler's mother, Cheryl, picked us up from the airport. From the backseat, on the way to her house, Tyler could no longer stand the secrecy. We'd only been with his mom for ten minutes, and he had to spill it to her, a nice little speech.

"I have a little confession to make," he blurted, smiling. "I haven't been selling cars. Ori and I have been doing some adult movies. But don't you worry. We really like it and we're doing well in it. Best jobs we ever had. So, please, don't be mad or anything. I love you."

I cowered in my shell like a tortoise. As bad as the lies were, I preferred them to bearing the consequences of the truth.

Tyler's mother listened calmly from behind the driver's seat, eyes succinctly on the road ahead. There was a little silence as we waited for her verbal response. She sighed and said, "I know. I've known for a little while. Desiree told me."

Tyler wasn't angry, maybe a little shocked. But I was angry. "Well, what do you think about it?" Tyler said. He was looking for some approval from his mother. I could understand that. No matter how shitty parents might be, you still want them to love and accept you.

"Scooter, I don't really like it. You're an adult, and you make your own decisions. But if you're happy, then I'm happy."

He was relieved. Her voice was ill-equipped for strong, maternal guidance. She just answered flatly. She wasn't upset at us. That was all Tyler needed. But we soon found out that nearly everyone in Tyler's family knew about it. All his cousins, aunts, and uncles. They all agreed not to tell his grandparents or littlest sister.

Tyler's mother acted as though she didn't want to get her hands dirty by talking about it, this pornography business we'd gotten into. She'd had no problem asking us for two thousand dollars just a couple months prior. While Desiree was staying with us on her last visit, Cheryl called Tyler in a panic. She was going to lose her house and needed two grand right away. Tyler told me to give it to him. I hesitated, but I gave him the money, and Tyler sent Desiree home with a check. She said she'd pay it back but so far hadn't mentioned it at all. When Cheryl told us in the car that she'd known about the porn for a "little while," it dawned on me. She'd already known how we made our money when she asked for the loan. Not repaying it was her way of maintaining a twisted moral high ground, taking a fucked-up ethical stance. She ended up ripping us off. She ripped me off, and I couldn't get it out of my head.

Desiree apologized for outing our secret. It was okay. She was just a kid. There were no hard feelings between us. She was having a rough time. Since we last saw her she'd put on twenty pounds. On her last visit to LA, she'd filled out and looked great. Now her depression and withdrawal were showing. Meth had screwed her up, and now its absence screwed her up even more. If she couldn't get high, all she wanted to do was eat. Eating made her fat, which only led to more sadness. The obsession I have with my own eating issues heightened my empathy for Desiree. Tyler and I wanted to help her. We took her out with us and offered to pay for a gym membership for her. We both felt guilty about her condition.

Tyler and I only stayed with his mom, sisters, and stepdad the first night of our trip. The rest of the time, we were at his grandparents' house. We golfed with granddad Emmett, went Christmas shopping with grandmom Naomi, and to a holiday dinner at his aunt's house. By day, we did all of the normal stuff people do when they go home to visit for the holidays.

By night, we made ourselves at home in Texas as much as we could. We'd bought even more coke and ecstasy than usual to stay in the Christmas spirit. Tyler and I went out into Houston every night with some of his hometown friends. Tyler's grandparents lived in a suburb twenty minutes outside of the city. One of our many destinations was JR's, a gay country-western bar. The first night, I didn't have an ID with me, but since I was a woman they let me in after I paid a sixty dollar cover charge. Tyler bought pills off some dude in the bathroom. All of us swallowed a couple, and I don't remember much from that point on. The nights in Houston blended together into one bandaged-up sock monkey.

The order isn't clear, but all of these things did happen during our nights in Houston: A drag queen karaoke contest going on in the back room of JR's. Tyler almost getting into a fight outside the club. A lot of driving around high with a lot of people. A foursome that included a crazy stripper who bit me on the neck and shoulders, leaving nasty purple and red bruises on my skin. A trip to a stranger's house to buy some more drugs.

One night ended when we bought a couple shitty eight balls of coke from a sketchy bar dude. It was probably ninety-nine percent baby laxative. We couldn't keep going on it. Life was troubling when it was morning at Tyler's grandparents' house and we were on ecstasy and had been on it all night and were supposed to be bright and shiny people at breakfast.

"Hey, do you want to smoke this crap?" Tyler asked.

"What, like crack? How do you do that if it's powder?"

"I know how to make it. I learned it from the *Anarchist Cookbook*. All we need is some baking soda."

We got up and floated to the pantry. "Grandmom? Where's the baking soda?"

"It's on the shelf, next to the rice, baby." Tyler's grandmother was such a lovely southern lady.

Tyler grabbed a candle from his great-grandmother's bathroom. He mixed the coke and baking soda together in a spoon and held it over the flame to cook. We were making crack cocaine as if it were some children's science experiment. But we did not yield rocks. Our crack balls were lumpy and wet. We sucked at the simple chemistry it supposedly takes to make crack out of baby-shit powder, and it was too goddamned funny.

Desiree showed up. "What are you doing?" The coke was out and she saw that we were cooking something on a spoon.

"Making crack," I laughed hysterically. "Here, you try it!" I handed her the spoon with our works on it. She enthusiastically took the utensil and started her own batch of crack balls. They were supposed to be rocks, but every single one of ours were balls. They wouldn't dry properly, probably because of our shitty coke.

"Let's smoke them!" Desiree said.

"Out of what? How can we make a crack pipe?" I asked.

"Out of an antenna," Tyler said.

"Or, with this," Desiree said. She unscrewed a lightbulb. "I've smoked crystal out of lightbulbs lots of times." She broke off the metal part very carefully. "Scooter, go get me some salt." She poured salt into the bulb to clean off the white tint that was on the inside. When it was all clear, she dropped one of the crack balls into the broken bulb. She rolled up a dollar bill and stuck it in her mouth for a straw as she lit the bottom of her new pipe with a lighter. The crack was supposed to cook and smoke inside, but it wouldn't. The plan was a failure.

If we hadn't been high on ecstasy, we would have never even thought to smoke crack, let alone try to make it. But crack had been in our minds since we'd visited Tyler's biological father the day before. His name was Eddie and he'd just gotten out of prison for using heroin. Eddie was a very sweet, dear man. He looked exactly like Tyler in the face. He was much shorter than Tyler, though. I think being in a Texas prison for ten years probably shrunk him. Eddie was a sad guy.

Until the age of eighteen, Tyler didn't know that Eddie was his real father. The man who'd raised Tyler as his son, and even given him his same name, disowned him when he found out the results of a DNA test. The test was done without Tyler's knowledge. One day, his father asked him to swab his cheek with a Q-Tip for medical insurance purposes. Days later, Tyler was told that he wasn't his father's son. His mother had lied to him for his entire eighteen years. Eddie was in prison when Tyler first found out. So, during that ten-day stay in Texas, we met up with Eddie at a billiard bar. We drank Coors Lights while Tyler tried to get to know his dad. They did their best to bond in this short amount of time. Tyler asked Eddie if we could get some coke, so we could do lines and talk over at his place. Eddie couldn't get coke. He could get some crack. We settled for two twenty-dollar bags of crack. Each had two rocks in it.

Eddie rented a room at his mother's house in Houston. He had to live with her because of his parole. Eddie had been in and out of prison for over twenty years. I thought he was too good-natured to deserve prison for his weaknesses.

I'd never bought or smoked crack before. I was freaking out. "Tyler, I don't feel comfortable. Crack is bad. I don't want to be here doing this." I was scared to be in this strange house and doing drugs with a repeat offender, no matter how endearing.

"Ori. He's my dad! I just want to spend time with him. If he wants to smoke crack, we'll smoke crack. Don't be so fucking selfish."

Eddie was getting his crack pipe from its hiding place. It was a glass tube with a piece of steel wool stuck in the end. He pushed in the crack rock and lit it up. Tyler and his dad took turns passing the pipe back and forth. I gave in and took a couple hits. I felt scummy. And it didn't even get me high.

Tyler and I cried when we were done visiting Eddie. We lay down in his twin bed at his grandparents' house and sobbed ourselves to sleep. I cried for Tyler and Eddie. I also cried for my own mother and myself. Having an addict for a parent hurts all the time, but it's mostly a silent pain, a pain similar to carbon monoxide poisoning. It's colorless, odorless, and can quietly fill the air around you and make you sick, gradually. We try to put it out of our minds and carry on independently, but it never stops seeping in.

We had a few days to go before we could finally leave Texas. It was New Year's Eve. Tyler took me out to a charming French bistro in Houston. The menu was superb. Tyler was in an especially lavish mood and explained to me in detail about all the different dishes. I had grilled fish and Tyler had a steak. We drowned ourselves in red wine. At the end of the meal, Tyler ordered champagne, two flutes of the finest the waiter could muster. A candle lit up our faces in the dark of the table.

Then Tyler pulled out a little black fuzzy box.

"Ori, will you marry me?" he asked, on one knee, in the middle of the room. There were tears in his eyes, and hope.

I nodded, "Yes." Tyler picked me up and hugged me as the restaurant cheered us on. It was a proud moment for Tyler and a spectacle for me. The little platinum diamond ring slid onto my finger. It was a perfect fit.

Right away, Tyler called his family. "She said yes!" he shouted on several different phone calls. I watched him and cried with a smile. However, I wasn't completely sure about it. To be honest, I had dreaded the day Tyler would do this. I didn't want to get married to him. I didn't have the faith in our relationship he seemed to have, even though I loved him desperately.

Both of us agreed we wouldn't get married for a while. I wanted to put it off as long as possible. We both needed time to grow up before doing such an adult thing like getting married.

I was afraid of marrying Tyler because he had fallen behind me in terms of maturity. When we first met, I looked up to him. Now all I did was take care of him. He didn't take care of me enough, and I did not think he ever would. It was wrong of me not to have had the balls to tell him this when he proposed. But we were in his hometown and staying with his family; if I'd said no, it would have been a huge drama. I knew the ring came from his grandmother. There was no way I could disappoint them all. I'll wait until later to tell him, I thought. There was no right later time to tell him I didn't want to get married. We returned to

LA and had to pack up again to go to Las Vegas. The big porno convention was held there every year, and I was asked to attend.

After a week in Vegas, we came home only to start packing again, but not for a trip. We said goodbye to our old Hollywood studio apartment and the neighborhood streetwalkers and relocated to Tarzana.

For a mere fifteen hundred a month, Pro Trusion offered to rent us the same townhouse he'd choked me in. Tyler insisted we take it. I went along, once again.

CHAPTER TWENTY-THREE

KRIS AND RANDA

I had already met Kris. Kris was a photographer for hardcore sex shots and porno girls' glamour photos. He did the stills for some teen movie I was in. He'd asked me for my phone number, and I told him I had a boyfriend. He wanted it anyway, to hire me for something to be shot for his website. I gave him the number and thought nothing more about it. Later that day, Kris called my cell while I was with Tyler.

His voice was happy and nonthreatening. "I want to shoot you for this side project I'm doing. It's for my website and it's a POV blowjob scene, with me. We can do it at my house later tonight, if you can make it. I pay cash, two hundred bucks, same day."

My face must have gone from pleasant to disgust right away. Tyler watched me and wondered who I was talking to. "Kris? Hold on a second," I said and clasped my hand over the receiver.

"Who is that?" Tyler's face was serious and his back straightened up. He was being jealous and protective, and I loved it.

"It's this guy that I gave my number to for work. He said he wants to shoot me tonight at his house, for a POV blowjob. He said he'd pay me in cash."

"Tell him no. I don't want some guy we don't even know having you come to his house and blow him. No way!"

Inside my chest, my heart was melting from Tyler's show of dominance. He'd almost always had a change of heart when cash was mentioned.

"Hello, Kris? I'm sorry. I can't. I don't do POV scenes anymore. It's too weird. If there's anything else in the future, give me a call. Alright, take care. Bye."

When Tyler met Kris for himself, his tune changed. Kris was shooting stills on a set where Tyler had a gig fucking. They hit it off big time. Tyler had a new male crush. Every chance he had, Tyler would call him up to hang out or just chat. Tyler was no longer concerned about me doing a POV with Kris.

Tyler and I stayed in a motel room with Kris and his girlfriend, Randa, when we met up to go to Coachella again. This time it was without Desiree, who stayed home in Houston. Everyone would be too fucked up to drive the three hours back to Los Angeles, so we crashed in Palm Springs for the night. At the show, we did some ecstasy and coke together in one of the electronic music tents, where Kris introduced us to Randa. She was really skinny, but not in a fashionable way. There was nothing fashionable about her. She had on baggy nylon ski pants and a tank top. Her sandals were more mountain-climber than cute. This chick did not seem like Kris's type at all.

Kris was six foot four and very fair. His shoulders were broad and he had long limbs. His size made him attractive. Everything on him was gigantic to me. His eyes were an arctic blue. I kept my distance. I stayed close to Tyler at all times.

After the show, Tyler and I followed Kris's directions to their motel on a drunk-driving journey down Highway 111. Thank god for the cocaine. The motel was called the Hotel California. It was a grimy, rundown, Spanish-style parking lot-villa that had its charm at two in the morning. Tyler was thrilled to be there with people doing drugs, people like us. Kris and Randa were older than Tyler and me. They did more drugs than even we did. Randa held out a little bullet vial and offered it to Tyler. It was Special K. We had never done that stuff. Ketamine. But we didn't hesitate to try it.

Kris and Randa preached the gospel of Special K. I thought it was just used as a cat tranquilizer, but they informed me differently. It was used in hospitals, on babies, to soothe them, as well as grown people. I soaked up all of their bullshit as fast as they could dish it. We stayed up all night in that motel room in Palm Springs. The next morning, the four of us checked out, but the party wasn't over. Randa wanted to go to a spa. She'd looked it up online at home and had the directions with her. No one objected.

Tyler and I jumped in his new car, a brand new V8 black convertible Mustang, his dream machine. I put up most of the down payment for him, five thousand dollars. He promised he would make the monthly payments on it. I wasn't stupid enough to cosign. Tyler was still Tyler, no matter how much porno money we made.

Kris took a nap at the spa. He'd rented a room for half the day. He was cranky and needed to rest. He got mad at Randa for staying up and doing coke and K instead of sleeping with him. I wanted to leave as soon as possible, but Tyler was out of his mind and wanted to bond with Randa over the Ketamine. It was uncomfortable to be there as Kris's mood deteriorated. He sulked, saturating the room with his misery. He and Randa began yelling. It was loud and clear that they had problems. Tyler and I could relate.

After Coachella, Tyler couldn't get enough of Kris, his new number-one guy. The three of us went to dinner and to the

Zwan concert at the Wiltern. Then we stayed up and did cocaine and Special K at another friend's house. There wasn't a time we socialized without drugs. It was a given that we would at least be doing coke, if not more than that.

Kris, Tyler and I took a separate trip to Palm Springs one weekend. Kris didn't tell Randa about it at all. It wasn't shocking. Ever since we got to know Kris, he told us about how unhappy he was in his relationship. Kris complained about Randa constantly. She didn't work. She didn't clean. She did too many drugs. She stole his drugs. She was a liar. She was too skinny. She went out without him. She did speed. She didn't contribute. They had been living together for six years and were tentatively engaged. There wasn't a date set for a wedding, because he had serious doubts. It was all too familiar to me. I still hadn't told Tyler of my mixed feelings about our own engagement. Randa was making an attempt to become a television actress. The only effort she seemed to be making was by asking Kris for headshots. When Kris vented about Randa, his face got dark.

The most disturbing thing Kris told us was that Randa accused him of physical abuse. Kris told us first, before Randa could spin it her way. He wanted to defend himself and explain the situation. She made him so angry that Kris pushed Randa and shoved her into a wall during a rage. He didn't hit her, but she called it abuse. I didn't know what to say or think of all this. It was their relationship, not mine. I barely knew them. I didn't want to know their secrets.

I couldn't worry about Kris and Randa. I had my own issues with Tyler's growing temper. He'd started taking steroids. At first, it was just pills. A fellow porno actor hooked him up with Winstrol, a horse growth hormone. Then another colleague sold him Deca. It came in little vials from Mexico and Brazil. Tyler used a hypodermic needle to inject the Deca into his leg. He didn't ask me to do it for him because he still didn't trust me with sharp objects. Sometimes a male friend would come over and shoot him in the butt with the juice.

Tyler didn't need steroids. He was fit and muscular and went to the gym. He ate whatever he wanted and never gained unsightly weight. Tyler had a great body and sex drive. His wood problems came from cocaine. He wanted to be just as virile as the health fanatics yet party every night. Steroids became the answer to his prayers, just like Viagra. All the porno dudes shot steroids. They did it to get big muscles because they thought it looked good on camera. It also served as a shortcut, a cheater way to a get that teenage rage of hormones, and another way to get high.

I was against the steroid use, but I didn't have the backbone to stop him. He said they made him feel better. Cigarettes made him feel amazing, too. Really, I had no idea what the proper thing was for a human body anymore. My head was full of excuses for doing porn and coke. We drank to get drunk. That's the point of it, right? I still had an eating disorder. Tyler took vitamins. Both of us went to the gym. We liked Special K. We convinced ourselves that it didn't matter. *Whatever we do to our bodies will not harm us right now.* We were still young, resilient, and beautiful.

Not even a week after he started using them regularly, Tyler had all the stereotypical side effects from shooting 'roids. He flew off the handle at the slightest irritation. He picked fights with men he didn't know. Back acne showed up, right on schedule. He wanted to fuck everything that moved. One morning, during a screaming match in our bathroom, he broke the door off one of the hinges. Tyler was violent, but he never scared me, which probably egged him on even more. He felt like a moron.

Maybe I should have taken it more seriously at the time, but it seemed ridiculous. Tyler, the tough, steroid guy, was not a scary dude. I still kind of liked it when he got physical. It was sexy when it happened only occasionally. When he started shooting steroids the macho act got old fast.

The weekend Kris, Tyler, and I stayed in Palm Springs was fun. We ended up having a threesome on coke and ecstasy. Kris brought Special K for us. Tyler was the one who planned and pushed for us to fuck. As with his other dude-crushes, he thought the ultimate way to bond with Kris was to share me in bed. Tyler gave the gift of girlfriend ass. I was used to it. This was how we'd always been and I'd liked it in the past, but I was growing increasingly disinterested in it. Tyler was always pushing me into threesomes for fraternal reasons and not for our mutual sexual satisfaction. Or he would use it as an excuse to conquer other women with my consent.

At first I didn't mind us having an open relationship because it wasn't wide open. We were a team and everyone else was an outsider to an extent. I felt more secure with Tyler in the beginning, but as time went on I didn't feel like number one. That's the most important thing when it comes to love. We have to feel like we're the most important person to the ones we love.

I can blame it on the steroids, or the porno. Nonetheless, Tyler didn't have me at the top of his list anymore. He slacked off when it came to putting me first. His friends and other girls were out there to fuck and do drugs with. He took me for granted now. We'd been doing porn for over a year. People had been telling us that sooner or later the business would break us up. We weren't paying any attention to the warning signs. I wasn't happy. The most attention Tyler paid me was in an argument, or in tears.

Our friends were "there" for us. Kris, Tyler's favorite friend at the time, was there for me when I needed a hug or someone to make me laugh. Right in front of my boyfriend, who ignored me, I fell for his good friend. I always passed harsh judgment on girls that fucked their boyfriend's friends without consent. Girls who did that were awful, deceitful—especially in a porno world that depended so much on trust. Until it happened to me, I thought I was better than that.

You don't always plan to deceive or betray someone. I felt an attraction to Kris because he filled in a gap. He showered me with affection when Tyler had no interest in me except as a piece of property. Kris made me feel special again, and I fell for it. The big plan for male bonding out in Palm Springs had backfired right in Tyler's face. He was still too busy ignoring me to notice.

After our weekend together, we met up for dinner at Cobras and Matadors; this time Randa was included in the equation. She had no clue about my affair with Kris, but I knew she was suspicious of him. She was the one who initiated the outing to dinner. She wanted to hook up with Tyler something fierce. I don't know if it was because she simply found him sexy or if she wanted to get some kind of reaction out of Kris. But I didn't want to feel too much for her because of the crush that was going on between Kris and me. It was a bizarre love vortex.

I was on tons of coke and uncomfortable the whole time. Randa bugged the shit out of me. I hated the way she and Tyler flirted with each other. I didn't get it. I smoked my cigarette outside and watched them through the front window of the restaurant. How could he be attracted to her? She told us a story about how she broke her cherry with a shoehorn when she was ten. Everything about her repulsed me. We all went back to Kris and Randa's place after dinner. They lived in a guesthouse in a halfway decent neighborhood near Fountain and La Brea. Tyler dumped out a pile of cocaine on the glass coffee table. Randa made some cocktails and Kris went to the bathroom. He was sick from the food at Cobras. I felt sick, but not from what I ate. Randa's cheesy smile and nasally, Midwestern accent made me nauseous.

Kris came out of the bathroom with a sour look on his face. Without much small talk, Randa gave Kris a glance, as if seeking a sign of approval. Kris's body language said, "I don't care." Randa put her arms around Tyler. He looked into her eyes and started kissing her. She loved it. Tyler's hands came around her back and felt her ass. Then he looked over to Kris and me and smiled his dumb-guy "this is awesome" smile.

I remained sitting on the floor in front of the coke. Kris took a place next to me. Randa's tits came out and Tyler was slapping them. The living room was literally not big enough for me to be able to turn the other way. I did so mentally. I cut out two huge lines and snorted them. Kris did the same. I felt like an old bar hag, sitting belly-up at the local dive. I felt used, unwanted, and discarded. I was only twenty-two years old.

Tyler reached out for me while Randa was bent over, her panties off. It was clear that sex was going to happen. Tyler wanted to include me in his charade. I hated lesbian sex. I just don't like vaginas. The only one I'm interested in is my own. Tyler knew all of this but pulled my head over to Randa's cunt. She had big dangling labia, and Tyler wanted me to put my mouth on them.

I couldn't jump back and start screaming like I wanted to. That would have hurt Randa's feelings. Part of me did despise her, but still, I had manners. The color and texture of Randa's cunt made me cringe. My mouth rejects the metallic taste of pussy, no matter whose it is. I licked Randa's vagina for a few seconds, then I turned my head to Tyler's dick. All was forgotten about the puss-eating once he began gagging me with his cock.

Tyler grabbed Randa's head and shoved his cock in her mouth. We gave him a double blowjob for a minute, then I let her have the thing to herself. I felt no sexual stimulation from any of this. My heart was cold, wounded. All I felt was anger and frustration. I crawled on the floor over to Kris and the coke. We did another couple lines and I got on his lap. I straddled him and pressed myself against his big, elongated frame and we kissed deeply. Kris didn't care for what was happening between Tyler and Randa on the other side of the room. It annoyed him more than it hurt his feelings. He said that he was done with Randa and wanted her gone. He let Tyler fuck her because he said she didn't turn him on anymore.

Kris and I made out passionately on the floor. I pulled out his dick and licked it. I put it in my mouth, sucked it, and played with it in my hands. I wanted nothing more than for it to get hard so I could show Tyler how great I was. But Kris's dick would not get hard. It was the coke. His long penis was limp as a shoestring. It embarrassed him and he reassured me that it had nothing to do with me. Instead of letting Tyler and Randa steal my attention again, I put my ass in Kris's face and laid my face on the floor.

"Spank me. Hit me. Come on, I want you to," I said.

Kris's humungous hand made firm contact with my butt cheek.

"Harder! Do it harder!"

He reached back and got a full swing. Smack! It hurt, but it felt right. I needed it to hurt. He got excited and pulled my underwear down.

"Come on, give it to me harder. I need it!" I yelled. The blows came quickly and mercilessly. Both of us were getting off on the infliction, the punishment. It was an outlet for what was going on inside. Tyler and Randa were now fucking and making noises on the couch. I kept begging Kris to hit me more. He spanked my bare ass over and over. Finally, I couldn't take the pain anymore. My ass cheeks were turning a dark black and blue. Visually, it was exciting. Kris and I sprawled out on the carpet and continued to kiss. When Tyler and Randa finished fucking, we all came back to the pile of coke. Everyone forgot what'd happened for a while. Kris put on music and we drank some more booze. Tyler and I planned to stay the night, since it was already nearly four in the morning.

Kris and I went into the bedroom and fell asleep in his bed. Tyler and Randa weren't ready to retire. They didn't go to sleep. Instead, they did more coke and Special K before leaving to the neighbor's house to fuck some more. Both of them were out of their minds. I don't think there was a lot of premeditation put into their plan. Before they left, Tyler pulled me out of the bed. He got angry with me for cuddling up to Kris. I slept on the floor after that.

Daylight and yelling woke me up. The guesthouse was empty except for me. The front door was wide open and there was some kind of screaming match going on in the yard. I got up and scurried outside. Good thing I slept in my clothes all night.

"Hey man, just cool it. Calm down! We weren't doing anything!" Tyler shouted at Kris.

"Look, don't tell me shit right now! I saw you coming back from the neighbor's house! What the fuck is going on?" Kris stood tall over Tyler and Randa. He had his fist cocked, ready to hit someone.

"Kris, it's not what you think. We just wanted to party a little and we didn't want to keep you up. I'm sorry. I didn't know you'd be upset." Randa looked creepy with her sunglasses on and her skinny body squirming around as she tried to explain herself. They looked caught to me. I didn't care, but Kris was filled with hatred, mad at them both.

"Kris, I'm sorry. Please don't make it such a big deal. We weren't doing anything, please trust me." Tyler's eyes were wide from being on drugs all night. He was lying, but he was so fucked up that he meant what he said.

Kris had to go to work soon. The rest of us had the day off. I think that's what pissed him off the most. We returned to the guesthouse, and Randa followed Kris into the bedroom, shutting the door.

I was ready to leave right then and there. Tyler said he was too fucked up to go anywhere. He put his arms around me and pulled me onto the floor with him. His eyes shut and he fell asleep. There was no reason for me to ask him what happened. Only lies would come out of his mouth. I didn't care too much. I gave up. His actions only made me resentful. The fun was over for me, with Tyler. He was off having it without me now.

IT didn't happen overnight, and it was messy. Our inevitable breakup exploded into reality. Tyler didn't see it coming. He wanted to stay together forever, but he didn't show me that he cared anymore. He said he loved me, over and over, but he couldn't prove it. All of his actions spoke more than a thousand words which ultimately spelled out IT'S OVER. He even forgot my birthday. The more he told me "I love you," the more I resented him. By now I felt more like his parent and guardian than his girlfriend.

Our demise began shortly after the introduction of Kris. Kris remained a steadfast pal to my boyfriend after the fateful night between Tyler and Randa. They worked together, drank, and hung out. And they talked. Tyler confided in Kris about the many girls he was fucking on the side, girls I didn't know about. He was giving them rides in the car that I put the down payment on and fucking them in the backseat. Sometimes he did it in our garage in Tarzana, while I was upstairs clueless. Even open relationships require honesty. I'd let Tyler have sex with whomever he wanted for work, or in our private life, as long as I knew about it. I tolerated so much, there was no reason for him to be unfaithful behind my back.

Kris also lent his sympathetic ears to me when I cried about Tyler's thoughtlessness. Kris complained about his own cheating girlfriend and encouraged me to stand up to Tyler's behavior. I trusted Kris. He cared about me, deeply, or so I thought. When Tyler had his back turned, Kris told me, showed me, that I was special. I fell hook, line and sinker for the seduction. Kris knew exactly what to say to make me feel better. I felt justified indulging in the emotions I suddenly felt for another man. I wasn't cheating on Tyler because he was cheating on me. I was taking care of myself. I was falling in love with Kris.

Tyler had met a skinny Canadian girl on one of his sets. Her name was Trixy. She had dishwater hair, blue eyes, and a knobby body. He brought her to our home one afternoon after they had both fucked in a scene. I thought nothing of it. Tyler was casual about it when he said he was going to drive Trixy home. I said, "It was nice to meet you, Trixy." I kissed Tyler goodbye. I never thought he would take hours and hours to return. I never thought he would come back an emotional wreck. Tyler had a painful expression on his face when I asked him where he'd been.

"Ori, I think I just need a vacation. I need to take a break from all this." He held me by both of my hands, desperate to get the words out.

"Sure! We can go anywhere we want. Let's go on a vacation. Why are you so sad?"

"Baby, I don't know how I can tell you this."

"Tell me? I don't understand you. If you want to go on a vacation, we'll go," I said.

"No, Ori. *I* want to go on vacation. Not us. I want to go by myself."

"What do you mean? A vacation by yourself? Why? How could you go on a vacation without me?"

"No, don't cry. Just listen."

He put his arms around me. But he couldn't properly explain himself. It crushed me. Couples that live together, especially with our freedoms, do not go on separate vacations. I could understand if I was a frigid and uptight chick that never let him go out, but we did porn and drugs and had a very exciting life together. The confusion and argument and tears went on all night, until I finally cried myself to sleep. Tyler tried to cuddle up next to me in bed, but I wasn't responsive. He'd finally broken my heart. The next day, we talked about his trip. He was going no matter what and wanted my blessing. Five days in Miami.

I said, "Have a good time."

Less than a week before Tyler was to leave I learned that he was taking the Canadian porno chick with him. Tyler and Trixy had made the plans even before he brought her over to meet me. Tyler slipped up and mentioned her name on the phone while we discussed the money I was loaning him for the trip. I never knew it was possible to feel such hatred, such rage. It filled up my whole head, up through my chest, choking me. I couldn't breathe. Tyler bought Trixy her airline ticket. He borrowed five hundred dollars from me to pay for their hotel room. I was going to stay home and shoot anal scenes to pay the bills and the rent. Was this a joke? No, no joke was this funny. I was the fucking joke. Tyler was going to leave with this whore in a couple of days, and I was staying home to cry about it. This was not how I had envisioned our lives only six months after he'd given me an engagement ring.

After Tyler left, Kris soothed me as I sobbed over my life and the dire situation my relationship was in. I felt like an ugly, useless, non-sexual slave.

"Don't say that," Kris said, calming me. "You're gorgeous and sexy. Tyler's a chump for treating you like this. Let him go off with that ugly whore. He's the one missing out. You don't have to stay home and think about him if you don't want to."

"What can I do, I'm not the one on vacation. He is. I wasn't invited."

"Come with me to Vegas! I want to take you to see Duran Duran! I got tickets for this weekend. They're my favorite band. What do you say?"

"I don't know. I mean, Tyler will get mad if I go with you. He'll be jealous."

"Fuck him! Look at what he's doing to you right now. He should be jealous. You don't need to worry about him. He's on vacation with someone else. You just worry about *you* right now. Say yes, come on."

"Okay."

I called Tyler and told him about the plan. He hesitated, then said, "I'm sure you'll have a good time. Kris's a really great guy. I'm happy for you." Nothing in his response was heartfelt. He sounded sad but resigned. I yearned for him to fill with jealousy and beg me not to go, crying that he still loved me, that he was a fool to leave me and that he was coming home immediately, but it didn't happen. There was no way Tyler would tell me not to go with Kris—he wouldn't cancel his own affair.

At the time all I wanted to do was numb the pain. I loved Tyler, and it hurt to have us end up like this. Jealousy was new to me, and it consumed me. I was sick from it. Jealousy flu. A fever that I couldn't bring down, and it was cooking up my brain. It poisoned me, deep in my soul. I couldn't get rid of it. Every time Tyler came into my thoughts, the jealousy rolled into my head in a toxic smog.

I called Tyler in Florida again from the Las Vegas hotel room. Kris and I were already doing coke not two minutes after we set our bags down. I told Tyler I was happy and to have a good time with his tramp without me. I told him Kris was taking *really good* care of me. My anger was so deep that it seeped out of my every word. No amount of drugs could mask my true feelings about what was happening.

Kris had had the trip planned for weeks. I don't think he ever had a doubt in his mind that I would be coming with him. We went out to clubs, the Duran Duran concert, restaurants. He gave me money to gamble with and let me try GHB. We sniffed cocaine all weekend and had terrific sex. Kris swept me up and away. By the end of the three days, I was in love with him. He was in love with me, too. His sensitivity was electric compared to Tyler's disconnection. Far away from my crumbling, heartbreaking relationship, high in a fancy hotel room in the desert paradise, Kris was a new Prince Charming. My old one was a toad fucking some frog on my dime somewhere in Miami.

Things were tense when Tyler and I returned home from our separate vacations. He started staying out all night without calling me. There were more girls like Trixy. He went on actual romantic dates with other porno girls, while still calling me his girlfriend. I was his girlfriend, but he dated anyway, regardless of how I felt about it. He took a known industry prostitute to dinner for her birthday.

"Her real name's Billie Rae, and she's really cool," he told me. He stayed out doing coke with her all night. I tried to remain calm. "She and I totally started talking about our childhoods. I told her about my mom and real dad. She opened up to me about her father. He used to force her to have sex with him."

"Tyler, why are you telling me all of this?"

"You know how everyone starts talking about deep stuff as soon as you do a couple lines. I feel like you would like her. We really connected." This is how Tyler justified taking this girl to the Water Grill, for her birthday, just days before my own.

Shortly after my twenty-second birthday—which he forgot—I told Tyler to move out. He'd stayed out doing speed with some whore named Lucky and didn't come home all night. It was the final straw. I couldn't take being so insignificant any longer. Tyler fell apart, crying and yelling, "We're going to be together forever, and get married! Ori, please! Don't do this! We can work it out! Say that you love me!"

We bawled and fought all night over breaking up. He didn't want to, and I did. Tyler was convinced that if he got in my face every second that went by it would convince me to change my mind. Every move I made, he was there, holding me by the shoulders and forcing me to face him and look him in the eye. I still loved him, but I couldn't forgive him. We fell asleep on the floor of our bedroom, exhausted. When we woke up the next morning, Tyler got up and went looking for an apartment. I loaned him eight hundred dollars to make the deposit on his own place. I thought, *now* he can date all these other whores and not have to parade it in front of my face. I was happy for him. I was free to see other guys. This was a huge benchmark in my adult life.

I put some tacky blonde highlights in my hair to signify a new beginning. My porno career was flying. A company paid me to shoot in Prague that summer. I bought some fancy new luggage and flew to the Czech Republic, all on my own. I felt like the most independent and successful young woman alive. It just so happened that Kris was shooting there, too, on a different assignment during the same week. I stayed in Prague for seven days. Kris picked me up at my chaperone's house and we roamed the city. We went to the opera and did sightseeing. Like cinematic lovers, we held hands and kissed in the middle of the cobblestone streets. The time we spent in Prague shooting porno movies felt more like the workings of a romance novel. It felt like Kris and I were just meant to be, that circumstance brought us together for a reason. It felt like fate.

It was easy for me to read too much into it. I didn't look at the whole picture. I fell in love with Kris too quickly. Tyler was still a fresh, deep wound. I didn't have a clear enough head to accurately evaluate my feelings for Kris. I see it all now, as it really was, years later. Kris was Tyler's friend. Kris cheated on his own girlfriend to be with me. I chose not to see that Kris was a cheater—or that I was, too. Kris and I justified it by kidding ourselves that Tyler was the only one who did wrong. I feel ashamed now, but at the time it made sense.

I returned from Prague only to go on a jaunt to Mexico with Kris, strictly a romantic getaway, not intended for work or revenge. The whole time, we condemned Tyler for being such a liar. I was too caught up feeling sorry for myself to realize how hypocritical this point of view was. Kris officially asked me to be his girlfriend on his thirty-eighth birthday. We had just returned from Mexico and were having dinner at the Water Grill. I was doing to Tyler exactly what he'd done to me. I'd convinced myself that Kris and I were different. We were actually falling in love. It was real and dreamlike at once. Kris was decadent and wooed me, showering me with attention and affection. I saw no flaws in him—then.

Tyler started doing heroin. Getting his own place turned out to be the exact point at which his life started to go rapidly downhill. Drugs had already been a daily staple, like water and air; as a couple, we functioned a little better on them. Without me to care for him, Tyler was too fucked up all the time. I'd always made sure the bills got paid, the clothes were washed, the toilet paper bought, etc., and Tyler could not fend for himself. None of his new girlfriends took care of him like I did.

I was, and am, very scared of heroin. I've never done it. Because my mom's a junky, I've always been afraid that if I do it one time, I'll be hooked. There's too much risk of addiction in my DNA to play around with heroin.

Tyler started with Vicodin and OxyContin before turning to heroin. Over the course of a couple months his new apartment transformed into a junky hangout. He dated a few druggie porn chicks before settling with one main one. They got a dog, which they never took care of. They let it piss and shit all over the floors, let it eat garbage. Heroin makes you cease to care about anything except getting a fix. It's not like speed or coke—it doesn't make you want to get up and clean things and be proactive.

Fulton, Tyler's downstairs neighbor and a mutual friend of ours, called me up and told me about Tyler's new habit. Fulton had had his own drug problems. He told me he saw Tyler using needles.

"Are you sure they weren't for steroids?"

"No, he's shooting H. He's a mess."

"Well, what am I supposed to do?" I wept. This wasn't what I wanted for Tyler, no matter how bitter I was.

"You should talk to him. He'll listen to you. He still loves you. Just come over, now."

The neighbor let me in the locked gate to the apartment complex. I was nervous. I didn't want to be there, near Tyler's new whore or anyone else who might be living in his apartment. I knocked, and Tyler opened the door. He was shirtless as usual and in designer jeans. Smoke billowed out of the open door. He was surprised and smiled at me. It wasn't Tyler's normal, gleaming Colgate smile. His eyes were only half open and his face was pale and saggy.

"I need to talk to you. Come here. Come outside with me." I was stern, but I could not stop the tears that welled up in my eyes.

It was like he was sleepwalking. "I just got up," he said. It was past four in the afternoon.

"Tyler, what are you doing?"

"I was partying last night and I couldn't wake up this morning. What's the big deal? Don't act so perfect. You do the same thing."

Yes, but I wasn't the one looking like a malnourished albino. Tyler had lost at least fifteen pounds since I last saw him. He looked like he hadn't seen daylight or a tanning bed in months. However, he did have a nice haircut. At least there was one thing I never had to worry over with Tyler. His hair always looked perfect.

"Tyler, are you doing heroin? Because if you are, I am really, really fucking mad at you. You know your real father and my mom are junkies. Their lives are fucked up because of it! Please, Tyler, don't do it." My screaming voice bounced off of the sides of the buildings in the middle of his apartment complex.

"Shhh! I'm not! I'm okay, please. Don't worry. I am partying a little too much, but I'm fine. I'm working and I'm trying to get my shit together. Please."

"Do you promise me?"

"Yes. I'm fine. I miss you. A lot."

"I miss you, too."

We stammered on and on with half-hearted sentiments: I wasn't happy, and neither was Tyler, since we'd split. We were happier together. Maybe we could have worked it out. Maybe

Tyler just needed to get his whoring out of his system. I just couldn't say the truth. I was a jealous bitch who would never be able to get past his indiscretions. The reality was that I had a new boyfriend and was way too involved with him to turn back. Tyler looked at me with sad, tired brown eyes. He still made my heart sink when I looked up at them.

I asked, "Do you have any of the money you said you would pay me back?"

"Oh, yeah. I wanted to pay you a big chunk of it, but I just haven't been able to. I don't have it right now. I'm going to pay you, though. I mean it."

He may have meant what he said, but he didn't act on it. The longer he took, the angrier I grew. The money was important to me now. I was still spending at least a thousand a week on coke, just for myself. All of my spending habits had gotten out of hand since we'd broken up. I went out every night and shopping every day. After Prague, my porno work started slowing down. I started to panic about how I was going to keep it all up.

Kris and I were in my bedroom, sitting on the floor. We had the coke plate lying on the carpet with us. I did line after line, trying to figure out how I was going to pay Tyler's five hundred dollar phone bill, which was in my name.

"What can I do? There's no way for me to make him pay it. He shouldn't just be able to get away with it." I wiped some excess powder off the end of my nose and reached for my vodka tonic.

Kris said, "You should file small claims against him. My friend did it and she got a judge to order payment for her case. It was easy. You just go down and file. And it's cheap, too." I took his advice and filed a small claims suit against Tyler. All it required was thirteen dollars and a drive to the Van Nuys Courthouse. Another friend suggested I contact Judge Judy. I went to the website but didn't find any information about how to contact the show. It seemed too far-fetched anyway.

Then, two days after I filed the claim, I picked up the phone at home and it was a producer for the *Judge Mathis Show* in Chicago. She somehow knew I had recently filed a suit and asked if I would like to come on the show for a ruling. I couldn't believe it. The producer said that she could have me on in a month. When I told her that Tyler and I were porn stars, she told me she could book us in a week.

The producers took the courtesy of calling Tyler and telling him that he was being sued. He would never have consented to going on television to air his dirty laundry if they hadn't mentioned they would pay the settlement of the case. If he lost, the money wouldn't come out of his pocket. He was sold because he knew he would lose.

The *Judge Mathis Show* flew us out in less than a week. I was almost flat broke. My porno dollars were being spent as fast as I could fuck for them. It wasn't just the principle I was after now, it was cash. My landlord, Pro Trusion, was kicking me out of the condo. He callously delivered the notice, giving me thirty days to get out. It was early November. Porno was shutting down for the holidays. I was screwed.

Thank god for this show, I thought, for saving my ass. Not only was I suing Tyler for the phone bills and the loan for his apartment deposit, but for another unpaid loan: the two thousand dollars his dishonest mother, Cheryl, had borrowed. Because Tyler had told me to give her the money or it meant I didn't love him, it was emotional ransom. It turns out that the money didn't even go to Cheryl's mortgage. She used it to buy expensive gifts for her daughters and herself. I held Tyler responsible.

On the day of the show, I sat in a greenroom for the plaintiffs. Tyler was in another one designated for defendants. There was a swarm of young, talkative, attractive producers who gathered information from us. It was their job to get our stories and twist them into entertaining TV. They gossiped back and forth, telling me what Tyler was saying about me in the other room. By the time it was our turn to go on air I was exceedingly fired up and pissed off.

When I watch the tape of the show now, it's silly. At the time, I was so angry I couldn't see straight. I was hot, ready to take the legal system by storm. My hair was freshly dyed black to get rid of those awful blond streaks. My makeup was perfect and my outfit was a new cream-colored suit jacket and miniskirt from Bebe. I thought I was something else. Tyler surprised me by wearing slacks and a slightly wrinkled jacket. I expected a dirty tee shirt and jeans. His eyes were barely open. There were soot-colored circles underneath them.

Tyler had brought his new junky girlfriend as a character witness for the show. It was the first time I ever saw her. She was a mess. Her hair was clipped cheaply in a bun and had obviously not been brushed for days. She wore a baggy hooded sweatshirt and jean skirt. The outfit was not what you should show up to court in unless you wanted to say, "I don't really give a fuck about anything."

Tyler and I both had a chance to plead our stories to the Honorable Judge Mathis, who started the proceeding by asking, "You all real freaks, or do you just play the role?"

"He started to fall in love with girls that he would do scenes with!"

"We did stuff off camera, before we even started. We were crazy!"

"In our business, you have the opportunity to make a lot of money. And he chooses to spend it on drugs instead!"

"She partied her ass off, too! Oh, sorry, Your Honor. She partied a lot."

The porno, the women, the parties, and the love story, all summed up for the man before he deliberated. It was a joke. Everyone looked foolish. Fortunately, I was used to doing way more outrageous things on camera for money. Being on a mainstream television program yelling at my ex-boyfriend is actually one of the tamest moments in my video history.

The ruling was in my favor. I was awarded the sum I'd loaned Tyler, plus what he owed for the phone bill, but not the two thousand dollars I loaned to his mother. Mathis said I had to sue Cheryl directly to get that back. Fat chance. She lived in Texas, and I was never going to go back there. I didn't see Tyler or his girlfriend after our appearance. It was several months before I saw him on a set, then years went by before I saw him again.

The last time I saw Tyler was at a bukkake shoot in 2006. I was there to mix up a bowl of cum in a blender for another girl to drink. I didn't even touch a cock that day, just mixed the seed feed. Tyler was one of the sixty guys present to jack off into the bowl. There is no lower you can go in porn than bukkake guy. I was shocked to see the person I used to be in love with look so terrible. He was weathered, the constant drugs and hard living having caught up to him. It was extremely sad. I was high on coke and drunk when I got to the scene. When I saw him, I was too numb to feel what I truly felt for Tyler. I was sorry for my own share of the dealings when we broke up. Perhaps I hadn't acted as compassionately as I could have because I was in my own downward spiral. We were still a lot alike, but somehow I was getting away with it. Tyler had begun to pay the price. My penance was still on its way.

CHAPTER TWENTY-FIVE

ASS CREAM PIE

AFTER my appearance on the *Judge Mathis Show*, I moved out of the condo in Tarzana. I found another apartment in Hollywood, right at the bottom of the hills. Technically, it was in Hollywood Hills. I was going to be much happier there, living alone, but it would take some time. Until then, I'd never lived alone in my life. I looked at Pro Trusion's sudden eviction as a blessing in disguise. Living in the place that Tyler and I once shared was too painful, even after I'd taken in a roommate. It was time to move on, geographically and otherwise.

But moving couldn't have come at a worse time. I was on the latter half of my second year in porn and the job offers had come to a halt. I'd left Nelson and Hannah's agency, and things were slow. It was the holiday season and nobody was shooting. I could barely pay my new rent and deposit. The savings account I'd started for my porno money was empty. In addition to the rent, I had to buy Christmas gifts. Car payments and insurance didn't go away either just because the porn industry gets slow. Soliciting myself to directors and producers was never my best quality. I'd had Nelson to do that for me for over a year. Then we had a final argument on the phone and came to the conclusion that I would move forward alone. I was happy about it. Nelson, already a tyrant, was turning into a cold-hearted pimp. I couldn't handle fighting with him anymore, especially over the people I would fuck, and for how much.

My self-esteem was burning low. I was desperate for someone to care about me for something other than my place in a sex scene. I thought that person was Kris, but I didn't even know who I was anymore. In less than two years, I'd done over a hundred scenes. Tyler was gone from my life. I thought I'd be happier without him. Then it all started to sink in. Everything about my life before I got into the business was gone. Where were the traces of Oriana Rene Small outside of porn? I didn't draw or paint anymore, just covered myself in cocaine and makeup.

That December, a director from Anabolic named Marco called me. He'd called three times over the course of a few months about the same thing: He wanted me to be in his movie called *Ass Cream Pies*. It was a series he directed. I'd steadily declined. It was an anal movie where the girl gets fucked really hard in the butt, followed by a cum shot in the ass that she has to push out for the camera. At the very end, the guys throw cream pies in her face. The offer hadn't been appealing to me when I had other work. Now I had nothing else. The scene paid twelve hundred dollars. When Marco called that third time, it was like he was psychic. Of course I said yes.

I was deeply ashamed of myself for doing this movie. The shame was related to my desperation for money.

Where had the money gone? I'd been making several thousand dollars a week, but I hadn't saved any of it. I was a total failure with my finances. I always thought the good times would never end.

People had warned me about getting "shot out," meaning that everyone had shot me already and I had become old news. I routinely performed the most hardcore scenes, so no one was waiting anxiously for me to do my next anal movie as if it were a rarity. I was becoming yesterday's porno girl. My motto getting into porn was, "I don't care about this business or my life, it's fucked up anyway." That attitude helped put me where I was. I'd imagined dying young and burning out before my time, a tragic hero, a mystery. That dream never came true because I wasn't being honest with myself. I didn't really want to die. I did care about my life. *I am fucked up, but I will probably live through it,* I thought. This is what doing *Ass Cream Pies* was trying to tell me. If I don't do a better job of watching out for myself, I will end up doing worse and more desperate things to survive.

Instead of taking the job as a clear warning sign toward future disappointment, I wallowed in self-pity. The night before my shoot, I drank and did several grams of cocaine. Same old story. I blamed the porno business for tossing me aside. I'd become the jaded twenty-two year old porno star that the business had used and then tragically forgotten. That's why I have to resort to doing such a degrading scene, I told myself. My drug-and-alcohol abuse wasn't the problem, because it got me through such difficult times. Right.

I showed up at the Anabolic office for makeup at 8:00 a.m. All of my coke was gone and I hadn't slept, so I was falling asleep in the makeup chair. My nose was a crusty, red scab. I reeked of cigarettes. All of my limbs were stiff. That's what these people deserve, I thought, a total mess. I hated the idea of this movie, so why not come to set as a zombie.

As ridiculous as it seems to me now, the real reason I was so against *Ass Cream Pies* was because of the actual pies, the dessert food. Marco was a nice enough director. He always gave me compliments. The two men doing the double penetration were decent. I was used to the rough scenes that Anabolic commanded in their movies. Even the double internal pop shot was fine with me. I never thought about diseases. I didn't worry about catching

AIDS because everyone was tested. There's a certain amount of blindness you absolutely must develop when you perform sex for a living. I'd honed that skill after doing two gang bangs with multiple guys cumming inside my ass and in my mouth. It was just a bad time for me to get pies thrown in my face. If my sense of worth had been a little higher, I would have had the humility to be able to laugh at myself. Humility and humiliation are two very different things. I didn't see myself as human. I was a porn star. I was supposed to be sexy, period. That had become my entire identity. The crazy fun was fading and things were feeling serious. Jokes in sex scenes confused me. I felt like everyone would laugh at me and look down on me for getting pies thrown in my face, like some clown. As an object, I would decrease in value to men. I couldn't have that happen. My value to men was everything.

Part of the destruction of my self-esteem was slowly resulting from my relationship with Kris. He'd become my full-time boyfriend and we spent every night together at one of our apartments. Like most courtships, when we first got together I only saw his good side. We went on trips together to Cancun, Miami, and Chicago. Then, when it came time for me to get back to doing my scenes in the real world of porn, Kris showed his oppressive side. We would get all coked out the night before I had to perform, and he'd spend hours saying things like, "I just wish you didn't have to do this. I love you. I want you to be with me, and me only. I don't know if I can deal with this for much longer. I love you and I want you to quit, but I know you can't. It sucks. This is hard for me. I can't stand seeing you fuck these other disgusting porno dudes. It kills me. When are you going to start making plans? You can't do this forever. I can't do this. I don't know. You've got to do something else soon. I can't take it."

It sounds sweet, but it's a two-way street: Kris wanted me all to himself while maintaining the right to fuck whoever he wanted on camera. Hypocritical possessiveness. Kris worked in porno, I had met him in porno, the first conversation we'd ever had was about him hiring me to suck his cock on camera. He was making me feel there was something terribly wrong with me for doing porn, a new reason to hate myself, even though it was fine for him to do so. Doing scenes started to make me sad, like I was a horrible person who couldn't get my life together, hurting the one person who truly loved me.

Kris wasn't exactly trying to help me for me, or solely for our romance. He had after all hired me to fuck other guys in his own movies. But suddenly "he cared about me too much to see me do this" because of his own insecurity. Kris is one of the most insecure people I've ever known, and if he couldn't get his self-esteem up, he'd whittle mine down to his level. Early in our relationship, I exuded confidence, even after Tyler had neglected me. Kris must have been attracted to that, but he somehow turned jealous along the way, and the pressure wore me down.

I didn't tell Kris that the scene I was going to do was for a movie called *Ass Cream Pies*. He would have made me feel awful about it. No way would he have found it humorous. I was too depressed about my life at the time to see the humor in any of it, but I find it funny now.

Marco and the two male performers didn't mind that I was wasted. Marco just laughed at me. He took the glamour stills and had to coax me into opening my eyes the whole time. He was kind. I was so out of it I couldn't hold in my stomach or smile without grimacing. The dilapidated house we shot at belonged to Voltron, my old acquaintance from the *Pissmops* and *Meatholes* days. Voltron was drunk at 10:00 a.m., same as me. As soon as I walked in the door he handed me a Bud Light. I cracked it open with my weak, shaky fingers and chugged it down. I asked for two more cans before I went into the bathroom to do my enema.

I hadn't eaten in at least twenty-four hours, so I wasn't expecting much to come out of my intestines. The bathroom was filthy. I didn't want to spend more time in there than I needed to. There was toilet paper all over the floor. It was dark and the light bulb was yellowing, about to burn out. I didn't see any shit on the floor, but maybe only because the light was dim. It smelled like dirty, stagnant creek water and mold. There was a disturbing absence of soap. When soap isn't available, people who use the toilet are not washing their hands.

Voltron owned a nicely built, Spanish-style home. He'd destroyed it. The walls were smeared with grime. The lawn was overgrown, garbage in it. The white driveway had a couple of beaten-up cars and was covered in oil stains. None of the windows were broken, nor the doors, but they had to be next. Or maybe they were replacements. In the corners of the living room, where we were shooting, were piles of old used baby wipes. The hardwood floors had a layer of dirt evenly distributed throughout every room. I didn't go in the kitchen because I didn't need to. The beer I was drinking was warm and sitting next to the front door.

My scene started as if someone had pulled the trigger to sound a race. I was getting face-fucked by my two male counterparts, and they had a standard to keep for their company. Anabolic movies continued to have the hardest fucking known to woman. I was just a piece of warm flesh for them to pummel with their cocks. I knew the role. I was good at this.

I have to say, when the sex was happening, I felt better. I forgot all of the cry-baby shit. Getting pounded in the ass is very empirical. I was in that moment and nowhere else. Worrying about paying my next GapCard bill was no longer necessary. All I had to do was get my brains and ass fucked out. The sex itself wasn't what dehumanized me. It actually made me feel more of a human being, while simultaneously connecting me deeply to an animal world. The dehumanizing happened outside of the scene, at home, in the hands of the ones I loved.

Therapeutic is not the right word—I don't want to sugarcoat it—but it did sober me up. The men grabbed me by the hair and yanked me around during the scene. One fucked like a robot. The other actually had some talent. When I say talent, I mean that he was spontaneous. I think porno performers have talent when they bring something unique to the sex scene rather than memorizing some moves that got positive reactions in the past and doing nothing more than employing them over and over again. To be captivating isn't a formula. You either have it or you don't. No one can teach you how to be a standout porno star. It is way different than being good in bed. They are two completely different forms of sex.

Marco couldn't wait for the pies to get thrown. If I were in his position, I guess I would have been just as antsy. Voltron handed me a beer and I downed it. It wasn't bad at all. The buildup to being made fun of was the worst part—not the fucking, but the anticipation of humiliation. I left that day with my rent money but without my dignity. I started to feel really bad when I thought about how Kris would respond to the scene. The movie would come out later, so I put off telling him about it. I would deal with his criticism then.

You cannot hide from what you do when you're doing porn. What I've done is out there for the world to view. Porno is a brutally honest job.

CHAPTER TWENTY-SIX

PERFORMER OF THE YEAR

JANUARY of 2004 brought me back to Las Vegas for the big porn convention and awards show. JM Productions, who'd asked me to sign autographs at their booth the year before, wanted me again. The company was run by a husband and wife team named Jeff and Sandy. I starred in several of their videos, in a series called *Girlvert*. I had a recurring role as the Girlvert character, an angry, abusive, young girl who forces other girls into rough sex. It's the best work I have done in my porno career.

Girlvert won for best continuing series at the awards show. Then, I won porno's highest honor: The Female Performer of the Year Award. I did not expect it whatsoever. I always thought that if I ever won anything, it would have been a newcomer trophy. Instead, I beat all of the best girls in the business. I cried at the podium and couldn't think of anything profound to say. Despite being rewarded for so ridiculous a thing—fucking—my emotions ran surprisingly high. At one time I'd been choked out, but now I was purely choked up. It was my moment for it all to seem worth it. I was the best girl in porn.

Afterward, Sandy, Jeff, Kris, and I rushed up to our hotel rooms at the Venetian. We toasted to my enormous achievement. Kris popped open two bottles of champagne that were waiting in our room on ice. They'd all had faith I would win something, but our expectations had been blown away. However, my bright minute in the big porno sun was soon blackened. The champagne had barely made it into my glass when two friends, Fulton and Shasta, showed up at the hotel room door. They hadn't made it to the awards show to see my big moment. They were too cracked out. Shasta was actually one of the girls I was up against for Performer of the Year.

Here I was, trying to celebrate, and these two ghouls came haunting. Fulton always looked like he was going to die at any second. He was corpse-like, grey and clammy. The bones on his face stuck out and his eyes were sunk in. His nose ran with snot and a tint of blood. Only his unshaven stubble gave contrast to his gaunt complexion. Shasta was hanging on Fulton, barely able to stand up on her own. Black eyeliner and mascara caked her wrecked cheeks. Her nose was a bright red target in the middle of her pale white face.

"We need to get her to the hospital! She's really sick. I'm going to take her or call the ambulance. Can we come in and call the front desk?" Fulton was stuttering as he helped Shasta into the room.

I took a drink of my champagne. "Sure. Take her to the hospital. I hope you're okay." Pissed off, I was flat when I spoke. My lack of sympathy was fueled by my inflated ego from winning the industry's highest honor, and I wanted to bask in it for a while. They needed to get out of my hotel room if they weren't going to participate in the celebration.

Shasta went into the bathroom and partially shut the door. Kris and I just looked at each other. He smiled at me and I rolled my eyes. We heard a nose honk and blow out some snot. Then Shasta's loud and obnoxious voice shrieked, "Oh shit! Dog, I'm fuckin' bleeding! Do you have something?"

I may have been annoyed, but I wasn't heartless. I went into the bathroom to help her. We applied a towel to her bleeding nose. She washed her hands and I brought her a sweatshirt. It was a cherished blue Rip Curl from my cousin. Every time I put it on, I had good vibes. I wanted to send them on to Shasta so she could calm the fuck down. The night would soon be over, and all of the awards-show excitement, too.

A month before the convention, Shasta had announced her retirement. Another boyfriend of hers was a dealer, so she didn't need porn anymore. She and Fulton had borrowed five hundred dollars from Kris only a week before driving to Vegas. Their big scheme was to buy a kilo of cocaine and sell it to all of our friends at the different parties. They came to Vegas a few days before anyone attending the convention had arrived. Shasta thought that one of her sugar daddies had booked a room for her at Mandalay Bay. It was supposed to be "a fuckin' penthouse suite or the presidential, dog..." She must have been delusional because no one booked anything for her. She and Fulton stayed in some economy roach motel until Kris and I arrived. In the meantime, the kilo was diminishing like sand through the hourglass. For five days straight, they consumed day and night. It was nasty shit, too, really low-grade stuff that smelled like kerosene.

Turns out that Shasta blew out her nose. In non-druggie terms, it means her nose was terminally stuffed up, and her sinuses were infected. She also had a horrendously swollen throat. Fulton had to resort to blowing the stuff up Shasta's asshole to get her high. Her asshole was the only unblocked passageway into her body.

Kris let the two stay in his room. It soon smelled like a dirty hippie's sleeping bag. Cigarette and pot smoke coated every upholstered surface in the room. Kris had to move his clothes out just to keep them from getting a contact reek.

Upon my return to LA, I was contacted by a couple of porno columnists about my big win. One guy paid me five hundred dollars to endorse his porn star vacation package on Howard Stern. I still needed money, desperately, so I flew to New York with him. We arrived at the radio station before dawn. It was the coldest January day that New York City had seen in seventy years, and I forgot to bring a jacket. I wore lingerie under my jeans and sweatshirt. I was dead certain Howard Stern would not like my body because I wasn't super skinny or big-busted. My figure was even on the chubby side, for me. The holidays had just passed, and I had some winter blubber to work off. What a relief it was when I didn't get ridiculed on the air. I was quiet as possible so it wouldn't take too long. It was being taped for the E! Channel as well. I just wanted to get out of there as quickly as I could. I wasn't really Howard's guest; I was just this porno girl who was supposed to talk about some special trip. Nobody acted like I was important because of the award. It was a self-contained credential, relevant only in porno circles.

I was still broke, shot out, and uncertain about what the future held. The only difference is that I had a brand new big plastic bookend that read "Female Performer of the Year."

Becoming a contract girl was the highest standing for a porno girl. "Contract Girl" is a title given to performers who are exclusive with one company. No one else can have you. You're taken. That company becomes your husband or daddy, and your ass belongs to him. Contract girls are the stars of their movies. They're on the front of the cases for all of their films and get to do all the promotional appearances. Most importantly, they don't have to worry about where the next gig is going to come from or if there will be enough money to pay the rent. Contracted means guaranteed. You are set. Other porno girls envy you and try to emulate you in the hopes of getting a contract for themselves. Everyone in the industry admires the contract girls.

After Vegas, Jeff and Sandy asked me to be the contract girl for JM Productions. There was no actual written document, but we had a verbal agreement that I would perform in no less than one and no more than three scenes per month. Their company would pay me a $5,500 monthly salary. They also financed a new car for me, and paid the five hundred dollar monthly installments. The car was the most exciting thing for me at the time, a blue BMW, a sports car! It's cheesy, but I felt like I had it all. My life was the best it had ever been. I lived all by myself in my Hollywood Hills apartment. I was the best performer in pornographic movies. I was driving a BMW. I was a contract girl.

I always wanted more than what was offered. My entire motivation in life was based on my incapability to be satisfied. I wanted more money, more attention, more praise, and more love. With Kris, I had a constant source of longing. Kris simply replaced Tyler. Everything in my life seemed like a shallow replacement for a sense of contentment that I had never achieved. None of it made me happy, just temporarily high. Kris fell into this category, too. My little successes made Kris bitter and jealous. Because I was young and drugged out, I blamed myself for his insecurities. Even with my newfound success, I felt worthless.

CHAPTER TWENTY-SEVEN

HIV BREAKS OUT

APRIL of 2004 was the beginning of a terrible panic in the porn industry. Three girls and one guy contracted HIV while doing scenes. The guy caught it first while filming in Brazil and then transmitted it to the girls back in California. His name was Daryl and I'd done one of my first scenes with him. The testing in Brazil is sketchy at best. Producers go down there to shoot because the girls will do scenes for bargain basement prices. The cost is dirt cheap because the talent pool there is dirty and cheap, but with much bigger risks.

Daryl gave HIV to the three girls unknowingly. When he'd returned from Brazil he still had a clean AIM test, good for thirty days. Because he only spent half the month shooting in Brazil, he went to work right away doing scenes back at home. There was now a hole in the system.

My contract agreement with JM Productions was finalized mere weeks before the HIV crisis. It was scary, and I felt lucky. I could have easily been one of those girls. They were infected doing the kind of hardcore sex scenes I was known for, anal and ass creampies. Just a few months earlier, two other guys had shot their loads up my ass. I'd needed the money, badly. If I hadn't since come under contract, and someone had asked me to do one of those scenes with Daryl, I would have.

All of the producers, directors, and performers had to halt production for a few weeks while a quarantine list was put together. Some companies took the moral high ground and said that they would no longer put internal creampies in their movies. Everyone who wanted to be viewed as an important player in porno made the declaration that anyone who shot during this time was an immoral criminal. A few others announced that they would produce condom-only films from then on. In my opinion, it was quite lame the way so many voices wanted to be heard on record about their "safety." I don't advocate sleaziness or those who disregard the health of others by any means, but some of these people said and did things just to make themselves look better. If we all really cared about the health of porno actors, then why would we shoot in Brazil in the first place? Or be allowed more than one scene per HIV test?

My contract company wanted me to shoot regardless. Kris freaked out. He was supposed to be shooting his first movie for Vice Seraph Productions, but was postponing it because of the scare. It was important to Kris to do everything that Vice Seraph told him to. It was his equivalent of winning the Lotto. His dream job was to produce porno movies with this company. He hoped to get rich and famous with the new deal. Vice Seraph had quickly become more important to him than me.

I called Jeff and told him I was too scared to shoot any scenes.

"Look, no one in the movie is on the quarantine list. You've got to get this movie done by the end of the month, or it will screw things up for us. I can't tell you what to do, but you will be fine. Trust me. We've dealt with this before." He'd been in porn a lot longer than me, and it had happened before. Two girls who were popular in the 1990s caught HIV from a male performer in 1998. That incident is what prompted mandatory PCR DNA HIV testing for performers.

I could not stop thinking that it could have been me. Over the two years I'd been performing in sex scenes, I came down with chlamydia and gonorrhea six times. Not to mention the herpes and bacterial vaginitis infections I was constantly plagued with. My body was an STD cesspool, exploding at times with outbreaks. If I had kept up my usual number of scenes around the time of the HIV outbreak, there was a strong chance I would have been infected. I signed the contract in the nick of time. I felt saved by JM, in a way.

I had to face the fact that what I did for a living was dangerous. Thus far I'd chosen not to think about the risk and consequences of catching something terminal like HIV. All of the STDs I'd come down with were fixed with a dose of antibiotics. Just because we tested did not mean we were fully protected.

"Okay. I'll shoot it next week," I finally agreed. I talked to Sandy about it afterward. She was the kind one at JM. I could always talk to her, and she never got frustrated and pissed off like Jeff did. Sandy was also friends with, and former employer of, one of the girls who'd contracted HIV back in 1998, a hardcore anal girl. As their contract girl she was the star of many JM movies. Sandy explained to me in detail about what happened and about the business itself, and how now JM took extra precautions to make sure no one on the current quarantine list was linked to anyone I would be working with. But porno isn't any safer than the last person you fucked.

I had to live up to my obligation if I wanted to stay on as the JM contract girl. All four scenes were shot in one day, and it was a blast. I was supposed to be the director, but I didn't really have any responsibility. My directing consisted of being disruptive and laughing so hard during the sex that I was asked to leave the room. I didn't take it seriously at all. Porno movies as entertainment really shouldn't be taken seriously.

A lot of people do take them seriously.

Kris was one of those people. Ever since he became the newest director for Vice Seraph, he started taking himself most, most seriously. He insulted the movies I did for JM, calling them garbage and bottom-of-the-barrel. I tried to let it roll off, but it hurt. When he put down the work I was doing, he was putting me down. Kris certainly succeeded in making me feel like less of a person. The *Ass Cream Pies* movie I did for Anabolic back in December became a huge issue.

"You lied to me," he said. "You never told me it was an internal pop! I have a right to know these things, since we're together. Aren't we?"

"Yes, of course we're together! I'm sorry, I just didn't think to tell you all the details. You hate hearing about them!" The internal ass cum shots became a safety issue. It was accepted as the likeliest method of contracting HIV. Nobody was concerned about this six months before, including me. None of us had any fear of ass creampies.

"Well, I just can't stand secrets, Ori!"

I groveled to him. I knew I could spread a disease to him. It was a horrible guilt to live with everyday. He didn't do scenes like my scenes. I was the dirty one. It would be my fault if we got sick from HIV, or any other STD.

It's not like STDs suddenly sprung from nowhere. They had always been present, and we had elected to ignore them. And anyway, I could as easily catch them from him as he from me. Kris could be so condescending that it was almost like I had to keep reminding myself—and him—that he worked in porno, too.

Right around the time of the *Ass Cream Pies* argument, Kris had moved into my apartment for a month. He'd rented a big expensive downtown loft to live in, but it wasn't ready. I offered my home as a temporary arrangement, and it was a temporary hell for us both. Kris was always cranky and spiteful toward me. My attitude was still immature and babyish. I was still only twenty-two. We weren't getting along at all.

Stress brought on a massive herpes outbreak to Kris's genital region. We went to see a doctor together. He said that he'd never had herpes before and that he must have gotten it from me. I assumed responsibility. I'd been tested, and I did have it. I apologized over and over for it. Kris accepted and allowed me to comfort and care for him. I held his hand dotingly even as the doctor took one look at the big red blisters on his private area and said, "Oh, no. This isn't your first outbreak! You've had this before."

I did love being the JM contract girl. I cannot stress it enough: That contract probably saved me from catching HIV. I was damn grateful I was one of the chosen few deemed special enough for a contract. I only had to perform in three scenes, at the most, per month. One of the reasons I wanted to be exclusive with JM was to not have to work as much. I thought it would improve my relationship with Kris. It didn't. He refused to see what I had as something special. Though only a few each month, I was still doing scenes, and he was still insecure if I did even one. He didn't want me to talk about my scenes, though it's natural for couples to talk about work at the end of the day.

I wanted to talk about my JM scenes. The people I worked with were all crazy and something always went wrong. I was proud. I got used to the feeling from being with Tyler. He'd always bragged about my scenes and loved to dish about the craziness on set. Tyler encouraged me to do porn, almost too much. He only made me feel bad about it when he couldn't perform with me.

As far as I was concerned, the only person who'd earned the right to be morally conflicted about my work was me. I couldn't explain this to Kris. His ego was pushing so hard. He was changing from a party guy in his thirties into this electro-hip suave porno mogul. It was a sham. Kris wasn't satisfied with being Kris anymore. He had to be *Kriss*. He started wearing AG jeans and buying tee shirts from Barney's. *Kriss* was somebody. *Kriss* was a big-time porno producer. He was doing his best to reinvent himself, but I wouldn't buy it. I'm all for people making money and buying nice things, but not for building up phony personas. I hated the image Kris/Kriss was creating. It was dishonest. I couldn't stand the way he kissed the Vice Seraph people's asses. When I called him out on his identity crisis, he would get defensive and withdrawn.

According to the new Kriss, I did the kind of porn that only low kinds of people do. *Trash*. It affected my enthusiasm for my scenes. Before Kris and I started dating, I was a confident and willing little chick. Now, I was insecure and depressed, hindered by my guilt. Kris didn't like it when I fucked other guys, so I better not be into it. That would hurt his feelings, so I told myself I really wasn't into it anymore.

I began to hate the sex. I dreaded the days I would have to shoot. The job that had given me such freedom to do what I wanted in life had turned ugly. I would still go to the gym, but it wasn't for any reason but to keep my weight under control. Adding Xanax to my cocaine diet, I stayed in this debasing relationship and continued to wallow. I was miserable most of the time. I couldn't tell what I hated more—myself or sex. These two hatreds fed one another.

CHAPTER TWENTY-EIGHT

WHITE TRASH WHORE

DURING the summer of my first year on contract with JM, we shot *White Trash Whore 30*. When I say we, I mean the director, Jim, and the production manager, the still photographer, and the gaffer. I worked with the same crew on every movie I shot with JM, over a hundred scenes altogether. Originally, I was asked to star in the lead role as the main White Trash Whore. Sadly, I could not handle the detail. I quit doing gang bangs the year before. The White Trash Whore is required to do an all African-American, six-guy gang bang, no matter what. I stood my ground. I would not do another gang bang. My craving for giant cocks was at an all-time low. Jeff was disappointed. I was given the supporting role as the White Trash Whore's sister instead.

We met at a liquor store off the freeway. Fitting for a White Trash Whore, I thought. I had to take the I-5 almost all the way to Valencia. It was rural. There were cows in the distance feeding off endless hills of grass. As I got off at the instructed exit, I saw a sign on the off-ramp that read "STATE CORRECTIONAL FACILITY AND DETENTION CENTER." JM had gone to junkyards, deserted trailers in the desert, garages, farms, and tweaker houses to shoot these films. There are plenty such locations available in the San Fernando Valley. In some neighborhoods it's all you can find. A tweaker house is perfect for shooting a white trash movie. The set's already decorated to exact detail. Sometimes the tweakers who live there will play extras for you in the movie.

I pulled into the driveway of a strip mall parking lot. I saw the crew talking to some perfectly trashy girl getting out of her car. The star of the movie. I got out and walked over to them. "Hi Ashley, glad you could make it on time today. This is Sissie."

Sissie was loveable. Her face was quite pretty. She had bleached-blonde, shoulder length hair. She had on white sweat-pants and a cutoff white wife-beater tank top. Sissie had a giant all-natural DD rack. Her tits were showing proudly through her shirt. She looked like she was ready to shoot some porno.

I, on the other hand, wasn't. It had recently been established to everyone that I hated sex. I liked everything up until the actual intercourse. Everything about the fucking grossed me out. It was a phase I was going through. The smell of balls and sweat from a man's ass was repellent to me. When my hair would get stuck to my cheek because my face was sticky from a blowjob, I gagged. Not only was I burned out from doing the same old routine, I was grossed out because Kris told me repeatedly how disgusting these other guys were. He did his best to drive it into my brain, over and over, that I was doing seriously repulsive work. I was young and in love, so I believed him. All I could think about were his insulting words when I fucked these other guys on camera.

I would make excuses when I couldn't fuck certain people that Kris despised. Before, I would have done anything that JM asked me to. I wanted to please Kris and JM both. There seemed to be no happy medium. Whatever I did would not be good enough for one or the other.

I did not feel this way when Tyler and I did porno together. Each of us fucked gnarly strangers—there was equality. Tyler may have been a manipulator, but he wasn't an insecure one. Whatever quality I was grasping so desperately for at the end of Tyler's and my relationship was not what Kris possessed. Kris couldn't love or accept himself. How was he ever going to accept me?

When the rest of the crew and talent arrived, we caravanned to the feeder road on the side of the freeway. For a couple of miles we headed toward the correctional facility, then took a turn into the hills. A winding road, nothing but trees and cows to look at. The grass was yellow and the trees were giant oaks. It was a beautiful chaparral landscape.

We pulled to a stop in front of a big iron roadblock. There was a redneck guy in a pick up truck waiting for us. He was a big man with a stained white tee shirt and a beer gut. The director, Jim, waved his arm out the window to signal all of the cars to follow. The redneck unlocked the big chain holding the blockade and opened the gate. On the other side was a private road. He got back into his truck and onto this road, his huge Rottweiler in the bed of the truck grinning maniacally.

It was a dirt road covered in potholes and sharp rocks. I was furious that I had to drive my beautiful new car on this shit. I was a prima donna because I was the contract girl. Besides being late, hating sex, and whining, I was also consistently rude, only because I knew I could be. Being civil had been left behind at the liquor store. Trailers lay tucked in between giant oaks, and broken-down cars were scattered throughout the scenery. The place was reminiscent of a polygamist compound, but without the pioneer women. Colorado City with dirt bikes and beer.

Jim was always cheerful. Every day was a new and exciting day to shoot pornography. Nothing ever got him in a downer mood. Shooting for Jim felt like day camp. We were all here to do some nasty sex scenes and have a good time. He kept morale up and made me laugh at myself, which was crucial since I'd been feeling alienated from everything. If it weren't for Jim, I would have hated every single thing about my job.

I followed Jim up the gravel driveway. Our *White Trash Whore* house was a pink crumbling mountain shack, a three-room dwelling made out of rotting wood. Random machine parts lay strewn around the sides of the house. Chickens wandered around the property, in and out of the house. An old, sick cat drank out of a moss-covered bowl. The smell of sulfur was strong, almost unbearable. An old, dirty trailer sat next to the back door of the house, along with more broken things. It was perfect.

The makeup artist went to work on Sissie right away. Sissie had to do the scene before mine, and the one after. First two white guys in a DP, then five black dudes in a gang bang. We had to get moving, as Jim would say. Sissie was covered in blue eye shadow and pink lipstick while I rifled through the home's belongings.

Jim said, "What are you doing going through this poor woman's possessions?"

"A woman lives here?" I asked. I'd found a pile of old photographs lying in the bedroom. "Whoa! Look at this!" I held up a photo of a dead skunk. There were dozens of photos of a mountain lady holding her rifle and the dead animals she shot. There were skunks, deer, raccoons, squirrels, and coyotes.

"Ashley, the woman who lived here died a few days ago. Her son is the one renting this place to us. This house is set to be demolished in a few days." He held up a necklace made out of snake rattlers.

I dug out a tiny confederate hat and a coonskin cap. This dead woman's things were going to become our white trash props for the day.

Sissie emerged from makeup. Her blonde hair was curled and her big boobs shone. Jim asked her if she was all right to do some dialogue.

"Oh yeah, I can act. I've been studying drama for seven years. I did it all through high school. I just have to smoke beforehand." She reached into her purse and pulled out her bag of weed and a glass pipe. This is a ritual that almost all porno actors must go through before attempting to act.

"Why do you need to smoke, Sissie? Because it makes you smarter?" Jim asked, both sweetly and sarcastically.

"I smoke it because I think too much. I've been tested and I actually have a really high IQ and an overactive brain. When I smoke, I can focus better on one thing. I can be normal."

"So, you just smoke it to be normal because you're too smart otherwise?"

"Yep," she replied. Her voice was distorted from holding in the smoke.

"Well, I'm glad you've found marijuana to help dumb you down to a normal level," Jim said. He had a way of never making you feel bad when he was poking fun.

Sissie exhaled, finally. Part of me wanted to hate her because of the rumors I'd heard. She was supposedly seeing Tyler. I know I dumped Tyler, but I couldn't help but feel the jealousy. Sissie was just an eighteen year old kid. It wasn't her fault that I wasn't over him. I don't know if every ex-girlfriend in the world is like me, but I know I'm not alone when I still feel ownership over the ex-boyfriend. It takes about a year for me to stop hating other girls who date the ex.

Makeup was applied to my face while Sissie fucked her two white men. I had to do my enema in the only bathroom. It was dark and damp. I was just thankful that the plumbing worked. A

strong smell of sulfur overpowered everything else in the house.
We must have been sitting on an abandoned mine or something.
That, or one of the skunks that had been shot in those pictures
lay buried under the floor.

My scene was with two performers I'd worked with before.
One of them, Whippet, was in my last gang bang and had also
recently fucked me while I was covered head to toe in peanut
butter for one of Jim's movies. I played the role of a girl who
masturbates with peanut butter and then gets fucked in the ass.
Whippet was one of the most annoying porno dudes in history.
His voice sounds like a banjo being picked. Every one of his
sentences contains a double negative and he rambles nonstop.
He isn't a mean guy, but fucking him is a form of punishment.

After Sissie completed her DP and swallowed both loads, she
and I did some dialogue together for the movie's opening scene.

SISSIE: Get out! Get out! Go! Get out of this house. Fuckin'
chickens, get out. I said get out! Fuckin' chickens! You, too, get
out! I told you chickens to stay out. Go! Now!

ASHLEY: Sissie! Those are my pets!

SISSIE: They were shittin' all over the fuckin' house!

ASHLEY: Now they're gonna get eaten by coyotes.

SISSIE: That fuckin' chicken shit on my bed! How the fuck
am I gonna get a man with a fuckin' chicken shittin' on my bed?

ASHLEY: Now I have to go out and fucking shoo them into
the pen.

SISSIE: After you're done with that, make sure you pick up
Grandma's social security from the mailbox.

Sissie ate a couple of McDonald's cheeseburgers, and it was my
turn to do a DP. Whippet and the other dude put on the coonskin

and confederate hats. Whippet's head was so small that he fit into the tiny cap like a glove. He seemed inbred. You've got to hand it to those inbreeders: They had big dicks. Otherwise, there was nothing appealing about him. He weighed only ninety-five pounds. I felt like a fat toad getting on top of him. His whole body felt encased in my crack as soon as I lowered myself onto his cock.

My sex scene started out back, next to the trailer. I lay down on my back atop a broken-down washer. Whippet fucked me missionary style, while the other guy straddled my head and fucked my mouth. My holes were tight.

I wasn't having much intercourse at the time. Kris and I were too busy doing drugs. We hardly ever fucked. He was almost forty and a complete cocaine addict. The sex drive was low for both of us. Usually, I would just blow Kris or jerk him off into my mouth. If a woman's mind is her largest sex organ, it's no wonder Kris seldom turned me on. Sex wasn't making me happy anymore anyway. It was all so confusing—every instance felt like work. Having an orgasm wasn't my main concern. Reconnecting with Kris on the level we had been at in the beginning was impossible. It was easier to just let him cum on me. Sucking dick was my specialty.

The upside-down, gag, spit, drool, throw-up blowjob was referred to as a "Gag Factor," named after the JM movie series of rough oral sex. Jim would only have to call out to the boys to "Go ahead and Gag Factor her," and everyone knew what to do. The point of it all is to make the girl's face into a slimy mess. Blowjobs in this fashion are not always the best feeling, but the visual effect is most stimulating.

Flies were swarming around and sticking to the talents' balls while I choked and gagged on cock and my own saliva. All of a sudden, I felt a sharp and intense pain in my inner thigh. A cock was still in my mouth as I shrieked. "It stings! Get it out! Get it out!"

One of the hundreds of insects landing on us had stuck its black, sharp, poisoned stinger into the flesh of my leg. I squeezed and pulled the little stinger out. My whole thigh was burning. I jumped up off the washer. I stomped around on the dirt, wailing about how much it hurt. The gaffer tried to help me walk. I hated the location, I hated Whippet, I hated porno. My leg was red and swelling up fast.

Jim said, "Ashley, we've got to finish the scene!"

It was too late for some other girl to come and fill my spot. I had to be in the movie. Back at JM HQ, Jeff would be enraged if he found out I left the set because of a bee sting. I hadn't been stung by a bee in ten years.

"We've got to get the DP, Ashley. You guys have barely shot anything," Jim had a single-minded tone. The gaffer brought me some ice. The welt was now golf-ball-sized.

"Jim, I am not going to fuck outside anymore!"

"I think you killed that bee. They die when their stingers come out," he said. "Let's just do the rest of the scene on the steps of the trailer. You'll be mostly inside that way."

Whippet got on his back on the steps of the trailer and propped his boner up. I sat my fat ass on top of his greyhound-like body. He told me to go ahead and lie back, but I couldn't trust his brittle frame to hold my weight. My mood was as foul as the sulfur that surrounded us. The other guy crammed his thick penis into me while Whippet's was shoved snugly in my butthole. We did our best to get through the DP and cum shots so I could leave as soon as possible. The affected area of the sting was puffy and hard, full of fluid and really itchy.

I had to wait for the redneck to come back to the house and lead me off of the property. The gate was locked, so no one could get in or out. The talent for the next scene, the black guys, began to arrive in their cars. One of them drove right into a ditch and got stuck. Everyone had to help push it out, including Jim. I hauled ass back to Hollywood to see a doctor about the sting. By then, my thigh had swollen to twice its normal size.

CHAPTER TWENTY-NINE

CHANNELING THE INNER GIRLVERT

I began starring in the *Girlvert* movies in the summer of 2002, before I was a contract girl. The first one I starred in was actually the second volume in the series. Another girl had the role before me. She and Sandy were best friends until Sandy found out that her husband was having an ongoing affair with the girl. Jeff had to sever all ties to the actress if he wanted to keep his marriage intact. I was still fully involved with Tyler at the time. The first time Sandy ever saw me was on the internet, being choked to death by Pro Trusion. She said she would never forget how Tyler reacted to me getting strangled: When I came to, after passing out, he said to me, "Okay, are you ready to do the scene?"

Sandy hated Tyler. Jeff liked Tyler. Not because he saw something good in him, like I did, but for all of his flaws. In Jeff's eyes, Tyler got me to do gang bangs, fuck lots of different men, do interracial, get slapped around and choked—all greatly appreciated qualities from a porno producer's point of view. My non-protective boyfriend was as valuable on the porno circuit as a life coach can be in other professional lives.

I had to prepare to play the Girlvert. The character was a mean teenaged girl that forced other girls to have anal sex. Tyler was going to help me rough the girls up by degrading them. I'd never been dominant. I was used to being the one who got slapped and sodomized. I was afraid to be in charge and get rough on the other talent. The power was more intimidating than playing the victim.

Jim was constantly telling me, "Be mean, Ashley! Slap her around! She can take it. Don't be afraid to really go wild!" Even though it had been done hundreds of times to me in the past, I didn't know the first thing about inflicting pain on someone. It seemed unfeminine, and it wasn't natural for me at first. The only thing I was good at was the spitting. Thank god for Tyler. He taught me everything I needed to know about rough sex.

I relied on Tyler a lot for encouragement when we did these movies. My heart wasn't completely in the first *Girlvert* movies. My hair was in pigtails, and I had almost no makeup. The outfit was cartoonish—white knee socks, pulled all the way up, with Mary-Jane type doll shoes. I felt like a lunatic, acting angry and stomping around in my scenes.

It wasn't until Tyler and I broke up that I really started to understand anger. All of the rage I felt from my demented relationship started to work itself into the *Girlvert* role. At the end of our relationship, Tyler was scheduled to star in the fourth movie, but he didn't wake up early enough to shoot. The girl I had to work with was absolutely out of her mind on crystal meth. Speed sweat covered her entire body. This chick also threatened to kick my ass. But I was too angry myself. Instead of watching Tyler torture the girls in my scenes for *Girlvert*, all I had to do now was let thoughts of him roll into my mind. Thinking of him made me so insane with rage that I had no problem going ballistic on the other girls. I shouted at them, pulled their hair, shoved giant toys in their butts, and stepped on their heads. I really felt all of that negative energy pulse through my veins. Jim rarely had to tell me to be harder with them afterward. *Girlvert 4* was the first one I truly loved. After that, I owned it.

All of the physical and mental agony I had endured in porno had been building up into a combustive fury. In the beginning, I was this open-minded girl who was getting into the adult business for money and sexual exploration. A couple years later, I was still doing it for the money, but there was nothing left to explore. I was jaded and cynical. I felt like my plan had backfired. Porno wasn't the temporary summer job I had intended it to be.

Not only did I lose Tyler, but I'd sent myself far away from my sister and her family, too. Before porno, I was close with them all. Now, I couldn't face them. I couldn't look them in the eye. My sister found out I'd been doing it from the extended family. Some of them had seen my appearance on *Judge Mathis*. Because I'd distanced myself from her, my sister resorted to driving to my apartment, with her husband and three kids in tow, all the way from Ojai.

"Are you okay?" She sobbed. My sister is a motherly woman. She'd cared for me when our own mother was completely incapable.

"I'm fine," I wept. "I didn't mean for you to worry. I just thought I would stay away."

"Ori, don't be ridiculous. I love you, and my kids love you. Don't just disappear." She cried and hugged me. She had no idea what trouble I had put myself in. My sister has been married to her first love since she was twenty-three. She has three children and a respectable accounting job. Our lives have gone in completely opposite directions. She was still my sister, and she worried about me. She came into my apartment so her daughter could use the bathroom. I was happy to show her that my place was nice. I had white couches, a big flat-screen television, and a spacious back deck. I was on my own in a clean and lovely apartment. Part of me wanted to be proud of all of the little successes I'd had in my porno career. I had two separate people doing documentaries on me at the time. In addition to my Performer of the Year trophy and the six others I'd won, I was working on television for Spice Channel and Playboy TV. I had traveled the entire country and across the world due to my popularity in porn.

But porn was still porn. It's a disgrace to outsiders. It revolved around fucking and indecency. I come from a totally dysfunctional family, full of druggies and jailbirds. None of them are very comfortable with sex, though. My sister sends her kids to Catholic school. Her husband was raised in the Catholic Church. Even though I was making lots of money, it was still not okay. She took her disappointment with her back to Ojai.

The *Girlvert* series became an ongoing saga. As JM's contract girl, I turned it into a full-on mockery of whatever was going on in my life. There was always a story to go along with the scenes. Despite its classification as gonzo porn, it had storylines, and I felt like it was a sicker version of the story of my life. The series included flashbacks to when the Girlvert was a little girl, at her mom's creepy boyfriend's house, or getting teased at school—experiences similar to my own. All of my problems with Kris and Tyler were incorporated into the storylines. Some of the scenarios are entirely fictitious, though, like when the Girlvert burns her mom's house down, or when "Uncle Harry" molests the young Girlvert as a child.

I was no longer breaking down and crying during my scenes. Instead, I made other girls break down. I got to become a different person as Girlvert. I was in charge. Jim and I controlled everything. The series brought me the praise and power I craved from everyone except Kris, who continued to put down all of my efforts. *Girlvert* installments were relatively inexpensive to make. Kris referred to them as cheap garbage even though

I loved them. He was jealous of all the attention my "crappy, low-budget shit" received. I just threw myself into making the storylines even more bizarre. I felt like I had a purpose when we shot *Girlvert*. These movies were the most important thing in my life at that time.

Sometimes, though, Jim pushed me to do things I didn't want to do. He wanted me to put a candy bar in my asshole and shit it out on a girl's face. Things like that.

Jim said, "Jeff will love it. He told me you have to do it!" That's all he had to say. I was scared of Jeff. When Jeff wasn't happy, nobody could be happy. I didn't want to get fired. I didn't want to lose my contract. Jeff could threaten me with that at any time.

In some of the shots, Jim needed me to walk around in public wearing a backpack stuffed with giant dildos. They were hanging out in an array of rainbow-colored cocks.

"Ashley, no one will notice you. No one will care anyway. It will be classic. Don't worry about it. I've just got to shoot you walking around in front of cars and stuff."

Jim pushed me on in his usual non-threatening way. He was slick at persuasion without seeming aggressive. I gave in and walked around Northridge in my outfit. He was right. It is classic on video. I have to admit that some of the things I was uncomfortable with doing at the time proved to be unforgettable moments in the movies, like walking down Reseda Boulevard wearing a backpack full of dildos and flipping off cars. We went through the drive-thru at Wienerschnitzel and I shoved my hand down my throat at the window. We had a group of girls throw bloody tampons at me. I walked in front of high schools and on community college campuses dressed in schoolgirl outfits with my ass hanging out of my skirt. Most of the *Girlvert* scenes were extremely embarrassing, but that is what makes them superb. There was nothing typical or boring about them whatsoever. They are simply outrageous.

As I grew, the Girlvert grew. My weight went up and down, and so did my spirit. I made a concerted effort to not be fucked up on coke or Xanax during the tapings of *Girlvert* movies. My head had to be sharp enough to think of dialogue for the role. I had to be clever for the character to work. I tried my best to make them as humorous as possible. I would get totally drunk, though. I felt even more comfortable when everyone drank lots of beer on set. The girls would feel more relaxed, and the guys would be a little more comfortable being a bit rougher during the sex. We all relied on the beer. It kept up the morale for Jim, too.

Despite the ups and downs, even the darkest points of my career, these movies have remained consistent. I will never be able to show them to my sister, but I still see them as some of my greatest achievements. I feel lucky to have been part of such a unique project. Yes, these are triple-X-rated videos, but they are more than that. Those who are open-minded will get it. They are performance art.

CHAPTER THIRTY

DISAPPOINTMENT

ANOTHER year had quickly gone by. It was already 2005, and Kris and I were in Vegas yet again for the big annual porno convention. It feels like a little reward for all of the hard work everyone puts in all year, an excuse to party together. No one knows how to party like a bunch of slacker porno people.

I was signing in the JM booth with Sissie. She and I had separate hotel rooms that shared an optional adjoining door. We kept that door open most of the time because Sissie's male companion (no longer Tyler, thank goodness) was a coke dealer. He told me I could have as much as I wanted, and I sure did. I was high the entire week. It was a good thing he was Sissie's boyfriend and not mine. Part of my subconscious has kept me from falling for a drug dealer. If I had, I fear my life would have come to a tragic ending.

Kris and I drove to Vegas in my beautiful BMW. He loved my car but couldn't stand it at the same time. Kris was frustrated because he wasn't making money yet off of the movies he was producing for Vice Seraph. It takes time for anything worthwhile to see success, but that's not how it happened for me. I was a porno girl, and everything was instant. Kris could hardly bear to ride in my new car when all he could think about was what he didn't have. Kris wasn't green with envy, he was chartreuse. When we settled into the hotel room, Kris got on the phone immediately to call his friends. It wasn't about us anymore. I had to sign autographs all day, every day of the convention. So he would go out without me.

I wanted my depressing relationship to work out. Kris was just going through a rough time, and I wanted to stick by him. He'll snap out of it, I thought. Things can't be good or bad all the time. Emotions fluctuate. I wanted to show him that I was truly in love with him. I would be there for him when he didn't make much money. I wouldn't just give up on the love we had. I tried to appease him as much as I could.

While Kris went out all night, I stayed at the Venetian with Jeff and Sandy. Sandy hated Kris just as much as she hated Tyler. Jeff didn't like Kris at all. They saw Kris as a whiner and a source of torment in my life. They knew I was doing a lot of drugs, and they blamed that on my relationship with him.

The convention lasted every day from 10:00 a.m. to 6:00 p.m., Wednesday until Sunday. All day I slaved, strung out on coke, signing posters and taking photos with all of the fans. My forehead was an oil slick and my nerves were a mess from all of the excitement. All we could focus on was getting through the days so we could drink and party at night.

Saturday was the night of the awards show. The entire thing is ridiculous, but I love it. The porno industry gets to act like the Academy of Motion Picture Arts and Sciences on Oscar night. It was a surreal event for me. The massive attention and illusion of glamour somehow made what I did for a living a respectable facet of the entertainment profession. There were cameras and fans everywhere. All the porno girls felt like Cinderella. On that one special evening we pretended to be bona fide film stars rather than glorified hookers.

It was such a thrill for all of us to gather downstairs, dressed up in sparkly outfits, and go to an event where our work was honored. I cared about what my peers thought of me. I wanted to win and make all of the other girls jealous. My self-esteem was a garbage can that could be filled with the envy of the rest of the porno girls until it shone like a pot of gold by winning those damn awards.

Sandy, Jeff, Sissie, the coke dealer, and I sat at the JM table. Kris—Kriss—didn't want to sit at our table with me. He was my boyfriend and my date, but he refused to sit with us. He sat at the Vice Seraph table. I was an important part of JM, but my value there meant absolutely nothing to him.

I was nominated in a few different categories. JM won for some of them, and I forgot all about Kriss. I presented an award on the stage and accepted another on someone else's behalf. Then I won Best Supporting Actress. I was all over that awards show. And again, as cheesy as it is to be awarded for your contribution to pornography, the feeling was genuinely joyous. Then, *Girlvert* won the award for Best Continuing Series again. I was so happy. It was *my* series. I ran over to Kriss, at the Vice Seraph table.

"Can you believe it?" I was beaming from ear to ear.

"I lost, Ori!" Kris sobbed and reached for me and buried his head in my stomach and chest. "I lost. So don't rub it in my face. I even lost to you, Ori!"

Those words have stuck in my ears for years. They've left a skid mark because it was such a shitty thing to say. He was supposed to be my lover, not my competitor. That's all it had been for all these months, some sick and cruel competition. If he had won something, I would have been sharing his joy even if I'd lost to him. Didn't Kris remember how I'd won the biggest award possible the year before, and how little it'd mattered after? Kriss was devastated by the industry's lack of recognition for his self-proclaimed greatness.

"It's okay," I stammered. He clung to my blue sequin dress and bawled his heart out. I was mortified at his public display of self-pity. He had no shame. It certainly embarrassed me to be holding my big, old, bawling baby of a boyfriend. I did my best to avoid eye contact with the rest of the people at his table. He was acting like an idiot in front of his company. I pulled at him to get up and walk with me to the restroom. We needed drinks. As we walked, he said hello to other porno girls and congratulated them on their wins.

We went up to the hotel room and Kris got on his cell phone. He was going out to a club to see some of his "real friends." He wanted to be as far from porno people as he could. Before he left, he said, "I'm going out to this club. You're welcome to come with, if you want, but I don't want to hear any shit out of you, if you don't like the music, or if it's too loud. I am not in the mood. I just want to get wasted and forget this night ever happened."

With an invitation like that, how could I refuse? Well, I refused. Kris left and I went into Sissie's room to do some coke. The night, spectacular in the beginning, was ending sour. Sissie was having a temper tantrum, screaming about not winning Best New Starlet. She thought she was a shoo-in because she fucked one of the guys on the awards committee. She was also livid about something her coke-dealer boyfriend had done. Who the hell knows what she was mad about? She threw all of his clothes into the hallway and proceeded to knock over the furniture in her room. I didn't want security to come and ask me to help get her under control, so I went to the bar downstairs.

Everyone I passed congratulated me, but the only praise I wanted was Kris's praise. Lacking that, I wanted more cocaine. I bumped into a guy who owed me payment for when I hosted one of his parties. I told him to just pay me in coke, and he did.

I spotted Kris walking through the casino. He was with a group of other old wasted adults. He was smiling and carrying on. I joined the group for some more coke and booze. We moved to the room of a guy I'd done coke with all night a couple of times without Kris, back in LA. He'd asked me to fuck him about twenty times, but I always refused. I said it would be a conflict of interest, since he was the editor of the magazine that handed out the awards. Sissie had fucked him under false pretenses. I sure as hell was not going to. I didn't need to fuck anyone to win an award for fucking.

Up in the room, several men and women in their thirties, forties, and fifties were doing coke and ecstasy. I just sniffed the lines of coke. I couldn't do enough of it that night. My misery wouldn't numb, no matter how much I put up my nose. Kris ignored me like I was a moldy heel of bread. I sat solemnly in the room while everyone else partied. At six in the morning, as the sun was starting to peek up over the desert, I left the room.

I called Sandy when I got back to my room. "What am I doing?" I cried. I was laying in the bed with my pajamas on, thrashing around like a dying fish.

"Kris is a jerk. You should tell him to get out of your room and find somewhere else to stay," she calmly replied.

"I'm just going to leave him here. Right now. I'm packing up and getting the fuck out of here. I don't care what happens to his bags either! When he finally decides to come back to my room, his key won't work anymore. Fuck him!"

"You can't drive back by yourself. It's too dangerous. Let me see if someone can go with you. Please don't take off yet," Sandy said. She knew I was out of my mind on coke and hadn't slept at all.

I packed up my things in minutes. I was dumping Kris, literally, in the middle of the desert like a dead carcass. He could find a new ride home and a new, young girlfriend to talk down to. I was through with him. I called a couple of friends to tell them what I was doing. I hoped that the maids would just throw his bags in the garbage. I should have done it myself, I thought, as I strode down the hallway of the Venetian to the elevator. I'd thrown Tyler's clothes in the trash when we were breaking up. Not all of them, just the ones I'd bought for him.

Wyatt, the sales guy for JM Productions, agreed to ride home with me, bless his soul. He was very brave to do so. It was raining, and I was ranting. The road was practically invisible the whole way home from Nevada. The rain kept coming down harder and harder. My driving was the worst it had ever been. I felt like I'd sobered from the coke, but I hadn't. Wyatt listened to me yap and tried to warn me about watching the road. I thought the car was the only thing I had under control. I wasn't worried about the pouring rain. My life was much stormier. We hydroplaned several times. I could have killed us. I drove my little blue sports car way too fast. I am an LA driver. I don't know how to drive in the rain. It was heavy all the way to Hollywood.

Ditching Kris in Las Vegas, as it turned out, was merely the first of several break-ups to come. It did empower me, though. Maybe it didn't turn me into an assertive, independent woman overnight, but it made a rip in the wool Kris had pulled over my eyes.

On Valentine's Day, he gave me a half-assed marriage proposal. His attitude about it was that I seemed to want it more than him. We had discussed getting married many times during the course of our relationship. He said he wanted to marry me. I didn't put any pressure on him, but Kris gave the impression that I'd been hounding him for this ring—a beautiful diamond on a platinum band. It was prettier than the one Tyler'd given to me, which I lost as soon as we broke up.

Kris acted somewhat excited to give it to me, but ultimately dismissive, like, "Okay, so now you have my ring, does this make you happy?" I felt like the ring already represented an unwanted union, and it scared me. We didn't have anything in common anymore except what we watched on TV. A marriage cannot be held together by episodes of *South Park*.

I again had a ring on my finger, and again it meant nothing.

CHAPTER THIRTY-ONE

ATTENTION WHORE

MY engagement to and entire relationship with Kris was off again for the tenth time. It left me with a vacancy for a trip to Jamaica. While Kris and I were having a good week, I'd booked a stay at Hedonism III, a "pleasure-seekers" sex vacation in Runaway Bay, Jamaica. The airline ticket I purchased for Kris was a wash. It was a small price to pay for the way I felt about him now. I called all of my friends to join me, but to no avail. My best friend, Hannah, was still an illegal immigrant at the time and couldn't leave the country. The others I asked couldn't take time off work. I found it hard to believe because they were all porno people or drug dealers.

I'd started starring in a show for Playboy TV called *Night Calls Hotline*. The gist of the show is that people called in to have phone sex with real porn stars. My producer, Derek, called and said, "Al will go with you."

"No, he wouldn't. I'm such a pain in the ass to him." I couldn't fathom the production assistant I never responded to on a routine basis wanting to join me for a week's vacation. I'd been rude to him. I was known at Playboy for being a little abrasive. I didn't mean to be inconsiderate, but I was sort of an angry, conceited, and self-centered brat. My head was huge now that I had my own show on TV. Still, Al agreed to come with me. The morning of our flight, I drunk-drove to his house. We left my car there and Al's stepdad drove us to the airport.

"*Modern Drummer?* What is that? Are you a modern drummer?" I mocked Al, regarding his magazine.

"Yeah, actually. I play the drums." He handed me the mag. I couldn't stop sticking my foot in my mouth with this guy. I was trying to act like a normal girl, but the Girlvert in me just took over.

We landed in Miami for a layover. We'd drunk vodka sodas and Jack Daniel's the whole flight. Al had me in tears when he told me about his Mormon grandma. Al was chasing the dream, the cliché, in Hollywood—to make it big in the movies. He wanted to finish a documentary on Thor: The Rock Warrior. It was in process and had a lot of promise.

For the next plane, I popped a Xanax and offered one to Al. He'd never done Xanax, or any other drug. He had only smoked one cigarette in his life, on a dare. We were having such a good time. We each took a pill. Then we blacked out.

Hedonism III is a swingers' resort. I knew that when I booked the trip. I only wanted to go because coworkers from Playboy TV were going. Two women who were the most established hosts at the channel were going, and I looked up to them. Everyone knew me as a classless girl. I wanted to be perceived as having some kind of intelligence and charm, as these two were. Other than a few familiar Playboy TV faces, the people at Hedonism were all cruising for sex. I didn't know that it would be so blatant. It was definitely a *Real Sex* crowd, but they were all fans of Playboy TV. I was sort of a small-time celebrity there. Everyone knew Ashley.

I have a tendency to underestimate the amount of exposure I've had because of porn. I never think people will recognize me. I always believe I'm under the radar. From the first scene, I've believed this and never stopped. I'm not a porno-looking girl. On the surface, I'm normal. *I'm the exception to every rule*—another ridiculous motto I've lived my life by. Because of this motto, I've made mistakes that could have been avoided by common sense. Because I thought I was so different, I believed that Al wouldn't go for me. We got wasted on rum and whiskey on our first night at the resort. We clung to each other for protection. Everywhere we turned, there were couples scanning us up and down, waiting to get us in bed. In the room we shared, on the king-size bed, we passed out in our clothes. In the middle of the night, I awoke and curled up to Al. Half-asleep, I started making out with him. Then I reached into his boxers to grab his dick. I was surprised to feel how big it was. He's a short guy, but his cock was huge. I went for it like a drunken college girl.

We had sex that night. We had sex day and night the entire stay in Jamaica. We acted like best friends, always joking around and making fun of each other. I pushed him around but held hands with him at the same time. One day, by the pool, I ordered him, "You know what? I don't like your name. I don't want to keep calling you 'Al.' It sounds awful. From now on, I'm only going to call you by your full name, Alan."

Alan didn't mind. He didn't mind any of the insane, pushy things I did or said to him. Alan liked me. For so long, I'd had the mentality that I was damaged goods and not good enough. I was convinced that no normal guy would want anything from me other than a blowjob. Alan was happy to be with me. He didn't demand a condom, either. He fucked me with the risk of catching all my diseases, no questions asked. He was proud to be strolling around side by side with me. I felt confident.

I did do a substantial amount of cocaine while in Jamaica. Here we were, on a hot, beautiful, Caribbean Isle, and I couldn't go one day without coke. As soon as I got there I asked around. I asked the men selling knickknacks on the beach. Alan escorted me to the spot where I bought the drugs. I paid a hundred dollars for two grams. I also purchased a large branch of marijuana for some of the other guests I'd befriended. The Jamaican drug lord didn't have a bag for the weed bush, so I just dropped the whole thing in my purse. It was hanging out of my bag as we walked back to the resort.

The humidity was so extreme that I couldn't cut up my lines fast enough. The coke kept getting wet from the air, even with the swamp cooler blaring in the room. I was frustrated, but managed to shovel the damp white substance into my nostrils. The stuff was good. It was really pure. I can still remember how it tasted. It wasn't like the turpentine mixture I usually got at home. It was more organic. It got me feeling high and blissful, not paranoid and tense.

"Have you ever seen a girl do as many drugs?" I turned to Alan. The last line was still trickling down the back of my throat. "And you love me for it, don't you," I laughed. My ego was soaring. I could do anything and he would like it.

We continued our casual fling and friendship all the way home to LA Alan was the first guy to make me laugh in a long time. He was twenty-eight, a bit of a late-bloomer. He looked like a teenage boy. He was a pretty, wholesome, small-town boy from the state of Washington who played jazz drums. I teased him about how many girls he'd had sex with. He'd only done it with six. I was his seventh. He also revealed to me that the girls he'd been with were a little "sporty"—the term he used for girls who had a few extra pounds on them.

My self-esteem was still bruised from Kris, who'd always made sure to tell me how beautiful every other girl he shot was. I tried not to overanalyze it too much. Alan could take me as is—a drug-using, foul-mouthed, loud, careless, conceited porno chick. I was constantly smashing up my car and losing my belongings.

All of my money was drained from my bank account. I had no sense of consequence. I had become my own version of Tyler.

On our way home, we again had to change planes at the Miami Airport. I wasn't dumb enough to bring any coke back with me. Alan asked me five different times to make sure I wasn't carrying any. The drug-sniffing German shepherd at the entrance to our connecting terminal lunged forward and barked as I walked by. "I don't know what that dog thinks it can smell. I don't have anything on me. You can check." I was annoyed that this service animal was making a stir. The cop holding the leash was a woman. I rolled my eyes at her and looked at Alan

The policewoman said, "Ma'am. Excuse me? I'm going to have to search your belongings." I handed her my purse and she looked through it carefully. There wasn't anything in there, but it was the same purse I'd been toting grams of coke and bushels of weed in. When she was finished, the policewoman said, "Go, on. Have a nice day." The dog had obviously smelled the remnants.

Just in case we might feel differently when reality truly set in, Alan and I fucked once more in his bedroom before I went home. We both knew that the odds for us to try to make it as a couple were risky.

No matter what he thought of me at the time, he could have done a lot better. Though I'd returned my ring to Kris, we were still engaged. I never told Alan. I dated both of them simultaneously because I was too selfish to let either one of them go. I strung each along, telling both how madly in love I was and that I wanted to be together forever. I was so scared of losing affection from men. Breaking my own protocol, I'd even fucked my drug dealer so he would still hang out with me and like me. When my platonic male friend and old neighbor Oliver came on to me, I gave in and made out with him. I needed him to love me, too.

He was married and I felt like a total whore, so I tried to keep it to a minimum. We kissed only a few times late at night, drunk and on coke. He wanted more, I could tell. I'm sure Oliver would have loved one of my sloppy porno blowjobs from the movies, but the most I did was grab his cock outside of his pants.

It hurt to realize that the men around me were only after sex. I should have been happy about it, right? I chose to be a porn star. My entire livelihood counted on how much men wanted to bang me.

I remember being on the kitchen telephone when I was thirteen. I was talking to my friend, and I said, "When I grow up, I want to be a porn star!" I did it to get a reaction out of my dad, who was sitting nearby. He turned around and looked at me and shook his head.

"Ori, don't say that. It hurts me to hear such vile things come out of your pretty face."

As a teenager, I knew that my life was going to be a lonely and desperate struggle to survive. By the time I was fifteen, I lost all communication with my dad, and my mom was a complete junky. I was never abused physically or sexually as a child or teenager. The abuse I received was in the form of neglect. I sought attention very negatively. I could easily find boys and men to have sex with. I was shrewd and put all of my energy into meeting the opposite sex. Why should I do that well in school? I thought. My mom didn't deserve to put my A+ papers on the refrigerator. I missed my dad's love. I needed him around, but I told myself that I didn't. I told myself it didn't matter that my own father decided to cut out. I must have slept with at least thirty guys by the age of eighteen. None of them were my true boyfriends. I told them all that they were, and that I loved them. I couldn't stay infatuated with one boy for longer than a week or two after I'd slept with him. Enduring relationships seemed very trivial. Sex gave me a sense of empowerment. I started having it when my parents began to fail me. I got the love and attention I craved from sex. It was a solution to some of the confidence I'd lost.

So now I'd gotten what I wished for. I became the porn star that I'd always wanted to be. All the attention I could possibly ask for was mine. I could have sex with anyone and they would definitely remember me. Well, it didn't fulfill me. Admiration is like empty calories. With Kris, Alan, and the other men around, I was starving for affection. I was too busy being a selfish pig to see that it didn't fill me up. The life I'd created for myself was just a trough for me to gorge in. I couldn't get enough.

CHAPTER THIRTY-TWO

AT THE RITZ

HANNAH came over one night before I was to leave for Hawaii. Kris was at my place, too. He and I were all packed and prepped to spend a week at a resort on Kauai. Hannah said she'd house-sit, make sure my kitty had some company. Kris was sweeping me away on this luxurious vacation to win me back from Alan.

The whole thing reeked of misgivings. I wasn't sure about getting back with Kris. He still wanted to marry me, but he remained as condescending as ever. He brought the ring to put back on my finger. It was too hard to let go of Kris no matter how ominous it all felt, and, worse, to let go of Alan. I was going to leave on this trip and deal with Alan's feelings when I got home. If there were a more selfish way to go, believe me, I would have found it.

Kris kept saying rude things to Hannah. He told her that her middle name, Claire, was a "fat girl's name." I realized that he was trying to make a *Breakfast Club* reference, but Hannah had never seen it. She was struggling with her weight at the time, so it was clearly a hurtful thing to say. Kris put me down in front of Hannah, too. He was listing off things that I couldn't do well and arguing with me about them. I was a bad cook, bad driver, bad pet owner, and a legendary gossiper. He went on and on. I would look over at my best friend during his tirades, and she stared back at me. Hannah and I wedged ourselves into my big, white couch. Kris went to bed, finally. He expected me to go and cuddle with him. If he hadn't offered to take me on a trip to Hawaii, I would have told him to get lost. He was just another bad addiction for me. He gave me a brief high, but the comedown was not worth it.

"What am I going to do?" I whispered to Hannah.

"Babe, you don't have to go on this trip if you don't want to. You don't have to marry him." Tears were in her eyes. No one else had the sympathy for me that Hannah did.

We smoked and drank vodka until the sun came up. Kris began stirring at six. He walked out of my bedroom and I told him I wasn't going to Hawaii.

"You *are* going with me."

"I'm sorry. I can't go with you. I can't marry you. Please just leave, Kris."

"Fine! That's just fine, Ori. You'll never have someone as good as me, or who will love you as much as I do. Good luck in life, Ori. Have fun finding someone who will take care of you! Give me back my ring."

I threw the ring. Kris picked it up off the tile floor of my tiny kitchen. He had his hand on the front door when he bent down to get it. Before he flung it open to storm off, he shot off a menacing grin. Throwing the ring really pissed him off, but he knew he couldn't grab me and shake me in front of Hannah. I wasn't afraid. It was all over. All he could do was lift the cat litter box and dump it upside down on my kitchen floor. Then he reached into my purse and snatched two hundred dollars and the pair of Armani sunglasses he'd bought me.

The door slammed harder than it ever had before. I'm sure Kris was trying to break it. He was gone. There was a mess of clear crystal cat litter on my floor. My apartment was a wreck of empty beer bottles and coke plates, but there was peace.

"I did it," I breathed, happily.

"What should we do now?" Hannah said.

The only thing that made sense was to do some ecstasy.

Our friend Haywood came over. Haywood was a handsome friend of mine that we randomly called on to party. It was only eight in the morning, but Haywood was up for anything. We called a limo to pick us up. It drove us to a liquor store, then to the Ritz-Carlton in Marina Del Rey. I booked a room with an ocean view. I was determined not to be depressed over Kris. I'd met Haywood through Kris. We'd spent Thanksgiving at his house with another group of porno people, doing coke and cooking a turkey. Haywood was the source for any drug you could imagine. Kris envied him because of his connection with Hollywood celebrities. I had no interest in doing drugs with famous people.

On the way to the Ritz, Lindsay, another girl I knew from porn, called. She and I had met at a Hustler Casino bikini competition. She was a really pretty redhead with dangerous curves. Her curves actually got too dangerous. When I'd last seen her, at a bar in Venice, her hipbone was sticking out far enough to poke someone's spleen out. Skeletal skinny. Most hardcore tweakers pick their faces, but Lindsay's skin was flawless. Within a couple of hours we transformed a horrible morning into an upbeat party. Haywood brought a projector that spun a kaleidoscope of shapes and colors onto the ceiling. We drank champagne and ate ecstasy pills. There were a couple of huge mounds of cocaine sitting out on hotel plates. The music was good indie rock that I couldn't put a name on. The ocean breeze swept into our room through the open balcony door.

The pills I swallowed were beginning to take effect. I was in my blue Calvin Klein swimsuit I'd bought for Jamaica. It was a little past midday and the sky was a gorgeous blue. My phone rang. I didn't recognize the 818 number, so I picked it up joyfully. If it was Kris trying to sneak a call from someone else's phone, I wanted him to know I was having a fantastic time without him.

"Hello," I sang.

"Hi, Oriana. This is AIM Healthcare. I'm calling to let you know that your gonorrhea test came back and it's positive. Can you come in and get medicated today?"

"What? I'm positive for gonorrhea." I said it loud enough for my friends to hear. "But I haven't done any scenes this month..."

"I'm sorry. I don't know...but you've got to come in and get medicated. Can you come today?"

"No, I'll have to come in another day. Thank you." I hung up my phone.

"AIM?" Hannah sat down on one of the beds next to me and put her hand on my shoulder.

"I have gonorrhea. But the last scene I did was a month ago. The only person I've fucked is Kris." I'd contracted STDs plenty of times, but always from other performers. As far as I knew, I never caught a disease from a personal encounter. Kris had given it to me. He'd told me he wasn't fucking anyone else, including for work. We had a pact.

I was going to have to call Jeff at JM and tell him my scene for him that week would have to be postponed. Nothing could prepare me for how pissed off Jeff would get. He already had anger management problems.

He screamed at me on the phone. "What the fuck do you mean you have gonorrhea? I pay you six thousand dollars a month and you don't even do any fucking scenes for me! You're fired. I am so fucking angry I can barely talk right now." I could picture his eyes rattling in their red sockets.

"Kris gave it to me. I didn't do it on purpose."

Jeff breathed fire into the receiver. When I couldn't stop crying, he hung up.

Around this time, I'd also wrecked the BMW JM had paid for. I didn't tell Jeff, but I did tell Sandy. It was the second time I had done it, and it was my fault in both instances. I'd been driving a rental around for over a month because the whole front end of my car had to be rebuilt.

Jeff told me I'd better get to AIM and "take the fucking medicine" and get retested. As I put down my overworked cell phone, the sun was going down. We had a lovely sunset from our balcony at the Ritz-Carlton.

Alan had also been calling me. He knew I might have been in Hawaii with Kris and was overjoyed to discover that I hadn't gone. He wanted to see me. My friends sat around and tried to comfort me. The drugs were not working as well as they used to. I'd done a good job of surrounding myself with ways to ease my pain, but now it was all totally useless. Everything came from inside. There was no escape.

Back at my apartment, everything was exactly as we left it; empty bottles, cigarette butts on the tops of beer cans, magazines and papers strewn around on the carpet, the cat litter on the kitchen floor.

The movie I had to postpone was *Girlvert 10*. When the infection cleared up, I was freshly fueled to turn the plot of this porno into a full-on ex-boyfriend bashing. I renamed a character Krass and fucked him in the movie. At the end of the video the Girlvert finds out she has contracted gonorrhea from her boyfriend Krass.

CHAPTER THIRTY-THREE

OBSCENITY

I had learned nothing from my mistakes.

The same problems that I constantly had were still prevalent in 2006. It was my fourth year in the porno business, and I was stuck. The sinkhole was formed of my own muck. Cocaine use was still number one on my list of priorities. I spent all of my cash on my rent and coke. All of my credit cards were maxed out. I only made the minimum payments. I was making less money now that I was no longer featured on *Night Calls Hotline*. It was cancelled, and there was really no other spot on the network for me. After all of my effort to be thin enough and sexy enough, I was not chosen for a new show. JM paid me over six thousand dollars a month, and I was living paycheck to paycheck. I started stripping to pay for my constant auto repairs. I'd wrecked my silver BMW convertible for a third time. I paid the owner of the car I hit two thousand dollars so he wouldn't sue. I was drunk and driving down Sunset Boulevard in rush hour traffic.

The owner of the car said he smelled alcohol.

"Oh, no. I'm not drunk! What you're smelling is this," I smiled, reached into the door of my car, and pulled out a bottle of Dolce & Gabbana Light Blue perfume. "It's the fragrance I'm wearing. It smells like Absolut Citron. See?"

I sprayed it on my wrist and gave him a whiff. I was luckier than hell that he didn't call the cops. Later, he called me up and asked for money. I thought it would be easier to pay him off than to deal with my insurance again.

When it came time for my two-year anniversary with JM I debated asking for a raise. But my self-worth was yet again floating in the bottom of the toilet since leaving Playboy. I felt like all of my scenes sucked, that I was a washed-up, has-been performer. My lack of confidence in my efforts for the JM movies was like a layer of lead paint all over my body. I felt like box-cover poison. I did not feel hot anymore, I felt like a dinosaur, like my body was getting flabby. I needed to exercise more! Be more of a whore in the scenes! This is what I told myself in order to dodge the inevitable. Ever since the day I walked into World Modeling, people had told me there was going to come a time when I wasn't the hot, young thing anymore, and that I would have to accept it.

But it was more than all of this that had me down. I was also soon to be judged obscene by the state of Arizona and the federal government.

That summer, JM Productions was charged by a federal grand jury and indicted on four counts of obscenity. This wasn't the first time that the authorities went after JM. The City of Los Angeles had charged JM with obscenity before and lost. JM beat the local system in 2000. *Liquid Gold* (girls peeing) and *American Bukkake* (men ejaculating) would not be censored. This time, the charges were much more serious. Federal. Four different movies were accused of being too obscene for the public: *Gag Factor 18*, *Filthy Things 6*, *Gag Factor 15*, and *American Bukkake 13*. Jeff turned himself in so that he could be released on bail. He was indicted on behalf of JM for all counts. Jeff told me that sitting in federal jail is much different than county jail. In county jail, the guys talk a lot. Faced with federal charges, the inmates are silent. No one speaks a word about what they might have done. The attitude is much more somber.

Sandy had been telling me for months that some day the government would step in. I didn't know what she was talking about. Porno was legal. How could the government just come in and say that what we were making was obscene? The situation was scary. I was in *Gag Factor 15*. In my scene, I dressed up as an Iraqi soldier and we reenacted a situation at Abu Ghraib, only this time the Iraqi prisoners face-fucked me for revenge. Was I guilty of contributing to obscenity?

Everything seemed to be in jeopardy. Not just my job at JM, but the entire industry of porn as well. Was the federal government against the porn industry? The answer seemed to be yes. But there didn't seem to be a clear logical explanation for why these four JM movies in particular had been picked to be deemed obscene. I'd done much more violent and degrading sex scenes than the ones in *Gag Factor 15*. *Service Animals 10* was something I did in 2002. That movie was more abusive than a *Gag Factor* movie ever could be. So were *7 The Hard Way* and *Clusterfuck*.

What makes certain movies bad and others okay? Why just *American Bukkake 13*, and not the entire series? Why was JM Productions singled out? Their movies were comedies. Sure, all of them had little plots which centered around the degradation of women and hardcore sex, but the girls were paid and they weren't complaining. Jim made everyone laugh during the sex. We had fun making this stuff. Perceptive ability should tell you that these flicks were sex comedies. We were *actors*. The *Gag Factor* series is all about sloppy and rough blowjobs. The girls' heads are upside down while they are face-fucked. It's a fantasy sequence for men to get off on. You have to be really willing and able to want to do that—it's a *job*. I've done it many times. My face was covered in my own vomit, drool, and snot, and it was hard to just stay still and let it run down into my mouth and eyes. It's part of the effect, for the scene. It is a porno video and people are watching. It was my job to keep up the act, and that's exactly what it is, an act.

When I found out that Jeff was in trouble, I was worried. We had our differences, but I never wanted anything bad to happen to him. The thought of him picking up trash on the side of the freeway in an orange vest may have brought a peculiar little smile to my face, but I didn't want him to go to prison. The feds took his passport away, and he was told to not leave the city limits without verifying it with the police. When he spoke to me on the phone, his voice had electricity in it. He was high on the adrenaline. I can't imagine what was going through his head. He was still serving out a court order to attend anger management classes. He'd had legal problems since he'd smashed one of his customers' desks in with a baseball bat. He emitted negativity.

The reasons leading up to the indictment didn't seem adequate enough to put someone in prison for five years. JM had manufactured and sold their allegedly obscene material to a distributor named Five Star DVD. Five Star then sold the DVDs to a store in Arizona. The lawmakers in intolerant Arizona filed the charges. It was a federal case because the product had been shipped over state lines. Obscenity laws are not black-and-white. It is up to each and every community to decide what is or is not allowed. What is obscene in Los Angeles is not necessarily obscene in San Francisco. But everything is considered obscene in Arizona. The definition of the word obscenity includes: indecency, immorality, smut, lewdness, crudeness, vulgarity, dirtiness, dirt, filth, coarseness, crudity, profanity, eroticism. All open to interpretation.

Jeff faced the charges honorably. He may have been considered an asshole by most people, but he did deserve respect for what he stood for. It wasn't just Jeff going on trial. All of our porno lives were in jeopardy. If Jeff didn't fight the good fight, we all would lose. If his porn movies were deemed obscene, whose were going to be next? The censorship might not even stop at porn. Basic personal freedoms of speech and expression were at stake. Jeff was going to be pleading his case to defend the rights of us all.

We were just being creative, same as in other art forms. It's not right to censor artistic expression. An obscenity charge applied to pornography would inevitably spread to other forms of art. It terrified me to think of the government restricting my mind, my body, and my creativity. I can only speak from my own experiences. By no means am I an expert in obscenity laws, but vulgarity is not a universal concept. Obscenity is an opinion. It is as much of an opinion as gauging rudeness. What we think is taboo now will probably be in fashion in the near future anyway. A hundred years ago, women couldn't even show their ankles in public without being considered obscene. When it comes to pornography, it's fair to suggest that a viewer should know what to expect. If you don't want it, don't watch it. I don't know why anyone would find it necessary to protect the average pervert from a dirty movie.

CHAPTER THIRTY-FOUR

DAVE NAZ

I was introduced to photographer Dave Naz one night at a burlesque fashion show held at the club Dragonfly. I was trying to find some magazine modeling jobs. I was still having the worst time with my finances. Lindsay and I arrived late. I insisted that we take a cab because both of us had been doing speed for two days straight. We were late because we were having a crackhead argument about driving. She was accusing me of being paranoid and delusional because I didn't want her to drive and smoke speed at the same time. All I could focus on was our safety. It was taking the fun out of getting high on meth and going to a club.

Back at her hotel room the day before, Lindsay had just whipped out her glass pipe and declared, "Look. I have to smoke. I hope you don't have a problem with it. I don't do it around many people."

I was shocked when she flat out told me she was an addict. I appreciated her honesty, and she made it look tasty. I wanted to smoke it. She was resistant at first, but I said, "Lindsay, I've done speed before, even smoked it. That's not the drug I have a problem letting go of. Just give me the pipe. Please?"

We floated around the West LA Hyatt. Lindsay was a strange and pretty girl. She was a butch lesbian, despite the fact that she looked like a model for *Seventeen Magazine*. The only thing masculine about her was that she smoked crystal like she was huffing on the exhaust pipe of a dump truck. I think the meth made her slightly schizophrenic, too. Or it gave her some sort of Tourette's syndrome. Every so often she would criticize me out loud, just blurt rude things, like my name was unattractive or that my looks were not sexy.

She was staying at this hotel to see her clients. Lindsay had to quit doing porn because she said she couldn't handle it. Escorting was much more her thing. She bragged to me how much money she made. Fifteen hundred dollars in twenties sat on the bedside table. The safe in the room was stacked high with several more thousand. The clients were what she called "in-calls." She would chat with them online in various message boards and social network groups. An email relationship would evolve into an appointment. The men would come to her hotel, fuck her, and give her cash. She made it seem like it was the easiest, most killer job in the world. Despite getting pregnant from one of her johns and being addicted to speed, she made it sound appealing.

We finally got to the club via the most dangerous cab ride I've ever been on. Maybe the emotion was just heightened from being on drugs. Who knows, but we practically fell out onto the sidewalk and kissed the ground. Lindsay and I clung to each other's arms. All of the bickering was forgotten as soon as we entered the Dragonfly.

I was busy talking a mile a minute to every person who looked at me. Lindsay and I were at the same speed, on speed. I clutched a vodka soda in my hand tightly and walked over to Dave Naz. The amphetamines made me stiff and nervous. I was afraid of overdoing introductions. I didn't want to come off as too eager or a kiss ass. Dave Naz was the tallest man in the room. His eyes were big. That was the first thing I noticed. Dave had very big, kind eyes. We shook hands and smiled at each other

and that was the extent of it. I rattled on about possibly modeling for him. He just stood there, smiled, and listened. We would
be in touch. He would definitely shoot me.

I turned around to look for Lindsay, who had disappeared. I
couldn't focus on anything other than getting more drinks and taking a cab home. I lived just up the street on Cahuenga, so I bailed.

I next saw Dave at his house. He was shooting a friend and
I for a girl-on-girl set for *Taboo Magazine*. I was used to doing
grueling work for videos, so posing for still photography seemed
a little too easy. I brought my usual stash of booze in my porno
bag, just to loosen up in case I was uncomfortable.

Dave was cool and quietly sexy. He had true confidence, the
kind that doesn't jump out and shove you in the shoulder. He
wore a shirt that said "100% Dirty" on it, but was calm and
focused, genuinely professional. I couldn't get over the way he
remained detached from the anal beads or the girl-on-girl posing. I was automatically attracted to him. His non-reaction cast
a spell on me. The music he played was very interesting rock 'n'
roll that I'd never heard before. Dave was in a class above the rest
of the men I'd worked with over the years. He didn't have an act.
His was an effortlessly pleasant demeanor. I wanted him to be
turned on by me, but I just couldn't be sure if he was. He was so
different. I'd never met anyone like him.

I was loud and sassy during the shoot. When I get nervous
I put forth too much of my offensive charisma. The showoff
comes out. I couldn't tell at all what Dave was thinking, so I just
assumed he wasn't interested in me. No way would he ever go for
a basketcase like me, I thought. Besides, I had two boyfriends
already. Alan and Kris still hung peripherally in the picture, so
I was not really in any position to be looking for someone new.
But something undeniably real and magnetic was there with

Dave, something entirely positive in stark contrast to the negativity with which I lived my days.

Among the things that had been consistently going wrong in my life was a fix-it ticket I'd gotten in 2003 that came back to haunt me. The original reason I was pulled over was for speeding away from a porno shoot. I'd just finished and had the cum on my face to prove it. I was paid the same day, and I wanted to get my thousand bucks into the bank. The cop dismissed the speeding, but I had to get the address on my license fixed. Even though I'd been living in Tarzana and Hollywood, my driver's license still said Thousand Oaks.

I forgot all about the ticket. I was too busy partying to remember to go to the DMV. The term "fix-it" seemed like an optional kind of infraction anyway, so I ignored it. Ignoring the problem did not make it go away, as it rarely does with anything in life, other than maybe a pimple. The ticket caught all the way up to me one foggy afternoon in the summer of 2006. I was on the way home from a baby shower in Ventura. The California Highway Patrolman pulled me over for tailgating. He asked me for my license, but I didn't have it on me. It was in the pocket of a pair of pants lying on the floor of my bedroom, probably snug against a baggie of cocaine. I'd often used my driver's license to scoop the coke into my nose.

"I'm sorry. I can tell you the number," I said.

The cop took the number and walked back to his car to run it through his computer. When he came back he said, "I'm going to have to impound this vehicle."

"What? Impound? What do you mean?" I choked.

"You know why."

"I'm sorry. I don't."

"You don't know why you don't have your license?" He shook

his head at me and glared with dagger eyes through his sunglasses. "Your license is suspended. I could take you to jail right now, but I'm not going to. Just pick up your things and get out of the car. I'm going to have to get it towed. I'm writing you a ticket and you can clear this up in court."

We were on the side of the freeway in the town I grew up in. I asked the cop, "What am I supposed to do? Can you give me a ride?"

"No, I can't do that," he said. He handed me the ticket. The cop had no sympathy for a crying girl whose BMW was being impounded. "I can call you a cab."

I waited on the side of the 101 Freeway at the Reyes Adobe exit. The cab picked me up and drove me all the way to Hollywood. Alan met me at my apartment. He was always there when I was a mess, which was often.

It took me a day and a half of taking cabs around with Alan to retrieve my vehicle and renew my driving privileges. The whole thing cost me a thousand dollars in fees. While on the ride to the Moorpark Highway Patrol office, I thought about my life clearly for once. I was almost twenty-five years old and headed nowhere but the Simi Valley Court House. I was dragging the poor guy who was in love with me to the far corners of the county to pick up my impounded car. It'd come time to commit to change.

Many, many times I had said to myself, "Okay. That's it. I'm never going to drink or do drugs again. I've had it with all of this mess." However, I never had external forces to help impose these restrictions. I didn't go to rehab. I never got arrested. My job was never really in jeopardy for any of the partying. I could still pass as a recreational user. I didn't steal, or fuck anyone over in order to get high. The bottom of my existence never hit bedrock.

Dave Naz and I fell in love. It happened after our first real date. He took me out to dinner at Asia de Cuba on August 1st, the summer of 2006. From that night on, I decided to change my life. I'd been stringing Alan and Kris along, but when Dave and I got together, I decided to knock that shit off. The only reason I'd had more than one guy around was out of selfishness. I was greedy and couldn't stand letting my men move on to other girls. The time had come for me to stop being such a self-centered bitch, because it wasn't helping anyone, especially me. I didn't know what the future would hold for Dave and me, but it was time to start doing the right thing.

We'd flirted on the phone with each other since the day I first modeled for him. I would call him when I was fucked up on coke and alcohol. That's when I felt most confident. He didn't know that I was always like that. I didn't hide the fact that I was a partier, but I surely wasn't going to reveal how persistently.

I came home high after our first date, but not from drugs. It was the sex, the romance, everything about the high of falling in love. The moral conscience I'd chopped down long ago had grown into a little sapling overnight. I wanted to be an honest person. I broke things off with Alan and Kris immediately, and for good.

The next big revelation I had was to stop doing coke. There was just no room for anything else in my life if I was going to continue doing coke. It was time to retire it. If I wanted Dave in my life, the cocaine had to go. He deserved a better person to love. He was the perfect man, and this was my chance for redemption. Motivated by Dave, I could save myself from auto-destruction before my life got any worse. When I say I am lucky, words cannot explain my gratitude. Instead of getting strung out so bad that my life was ruined irrevocably, I turned my life around while it still had some potential left in it. I didn't want to end up like my parents, or so many of my friends, by letting drugs destroy important relationships. I didn't want my life to be mostly full of pain.

Dave helped me stay the course. I was in love with a man who didn't use drugs or abuse alcohol. I stopped picking up the phone when my drug dealer called. All of the friends I'd hung out and did coke with were eliminated from my social circle. It was as easy as not picking up the phone. I stayed away from the old bars and clubs. Los Angeles is a huge and exciting city, and I was rediscovering it all anew. With Dave, I was seriously happy.

Dave taught me about hip music like Paul Westerberg, Ryan Adams, and Sonic Youth. I wanted as much of him as I could get! Being a compulsive binge eater, to say that Dave was an endless buffet of comfort food is the highest compliment. I could be with him for the rest of my life, gorging myself on his love like shoveling in mashed potatoes. Only, most enlightening of all, I don't have to purge him out.

The absence of cocaine in my diet did, honestly, leave a big gap at first, which I filled with alcohol. I never realized that I drank so much. Maybe because I paired it with the drugs, it felt normal. Coke and booze are like an excellent wine and cheese pairing. I always drank to get drunk. No matter if it was to celebrate, get upset, cry, or out of boredom. Drinking filled up something inside of me that was vacant. I was addicted to it.

I moved in with Dave in June of 2007. We began living together happily, but I was far from being sober. I was still drunk every night. Although I'd quit the hard liquor for the most part, I'd graduated to consuming bottles of wine. Because it was wine, I felt like it was sophisticated. I wasn't fooling anyone except myself, and only for a short while. I got sick and tired of feeling embarrassed about what I said and did the night before. The apologies and the blackouts had to end. Dave never pushed me, but he was an influence on me to change. He loved me no matter what. I didn't want to exploit that. I do know that I loved to drink, and that I would crave it. As soon as I'd have one sip of something, a switch in my mind would go on. I would literally feel a click in my brain, and I would start to feel the high. And then the only thing I could focus on was staying high. I never wanted the sensation to end. I would drink as much as I could to maintain it, getting totally shitfaced in the process.

It became the norm for me to drink on every porn shoot. It was rare when I didn't get hammered with everyone on set. I even made beer bongs and brought them to the other talent as gifts. The last time I got incredibly drunk at a shoot, I'd been pounding wine and vodka all morning and was an utter mess by the time I had to leave. Before driving drunk as hell, I insisted on doing an enema in the bathtub, in the "pile driver" position. I don't even remeber this, but I've seen the footage to prove it.

When I got home, Dave was upset. He'd never been mad at me before and hasn't been since. It hurt him deeply that I drove home fucked up. I also passed out and couldn't be with him when he went to a business dinner that night. The kind of unhappiness, worry, and disappointment that my binge drinking had caused was finally, finally inexcusable.

I had to grow up and let it all go. It's not cute or excusable to be an aging druggie or an old drunk. The time had come for me to stop being a child and put the childish things aside. I'd found a man who was honest, kind, smart, and loved to watch me have sex with other guys on camera. It turned him on that I did porn. There weren't any issues of jealousy or insecurity to deal with when I did a scene. We agreed that anal was the best sex to watch, and the filthier the better. He praised my work (especially in the *Girlvert* series) as the performance art that it was. No one else has ever made me feel proud of myself for any of it. Dave always encouraged me as I fought to quit drugs and alcohol. Never once has Dave ever criticized me, condescended to me, or been cruel, because that's not what you do when you love someone. I have learned so much from him. I cannot say enough how lucky I am.

CHAPTER THIRTY-FIVE

BUKKAKE (DEATH) AND TAXES

SOME things in life are simply inescapable. There are famous sayings about these things. I'd heard the expression "death and taxes" before. I thought I could excuse myself from both while I was young.

The first couple of years, I did file my tax returns. I'd messed them up terribly in 2003 and received a letter of correction. The IRS told me to pay six thousand more dollars than the twenty-five hundred I'd wanted to pay. Keep in mind that I'd made over one hundred thousand dollars that year. I ignored the letter. I continued to ignore all of the letters that came to my apartment for the next three years. I had a special stack on my kitchen counter reserved for the Franchise Tax Board and the IRS. When the stacks would get too high and topple over, they were moved into a Nordstrom's bag in my closet.

When I moved in with Dave I finally dealt with my tax problem. I honestly thought that a miracle would occur and I would get lost in the system. I blame that kind of thinking on the influence of religion. Blind faith is not a good quality to apply to tax evasion.

Dave and I wanted to get married and we couldn't do it as long as my taxes were a threat. Marriage as my motivation, action was taken. The envelopes had to be opened—by an attorney.

It turned out that I had been audited in 2004. I had to go through every bank transaction for the past five years. There were so many cash withdrawals at two in the morning that we didn't even count them. Aside from sometimes spending a thousand dollars per week on coke, I paid for sailing lessons for Tyler. I bought Kris a thousand dollar Gucci watch. I took taxis and town cars everywhere. In one year, I spent eight thousand on car accidents. My phone bills were eight hundred dollars a month. Most of it went to things that I have nothing to show for now.

Dave and I read through my life in those bank statements. So much excess, I felt like a pig. I'd paid my friend and former neighbor Oliver nine thousand dollars to be my accountant. I gave him my checkbook and trusted him to mind my finances. He'd come to me asking for a bookkeeping job. I didn't think he was taking advantage of me when he wanted to be paid five hundred dollars a week, tax-free, for sticking paperclips on all of my utility bills and making files for them.

I'm sure there are others who have done well with all of their porn money, but in no way am I alone. I know girls who have never once paid their taxes or even opened one of their IRS envelopes. But they will. You must die first, or feed the monster.

I ended up owing twenty-six thousand dollars for three years of delinquency to the IRS and Franchise Tax Board. I remembered purposely not counting how much money I was making from all of my scenes. I didn't want to know. I was afraid of knowing. I don't know why I felt that way, because it could have been so easy for me to fix the taxes right as they happened.

Cleaning up the taxes wasn't the only thing I had to do. I had to come to terms with the aging process. It's different for a girl in the porno movies. You can be an old hag at twenty-three, just like in legit modeling. I'd stayed popular for many years by porno standards. The average girl's career is only two years. My span was pushing six.

Even if I didn't look that much different than my first day and first scene, I had definitely matured. My body wasn't a little girl's body anymore. Naturally, my bones had to grow and my hips and ass filled out. Thank god I didn't get fake tits or lips. Not to say that I enjoy gravity settling in, or the elasticity of my skin starting to loosen, but I still appreciate how my body turned out.

Most importantly, I no longer desperately required the approval of the variety of men who paid me to, or who watched me, fuck. The stability and happiness I found with Dave replaced the importance of being a contract girl with JM Productions. Sandy was happy for me when I got sober and found a partner in Dave. Jeff said he was happy for me, but I became less valuable to him as I became less of a disastrous porno star. I wasn't going to hang out with customers, party with them and let them jerk off on my back like I used to.

There was no doubt now that I would move on somewhat from porn and fill my days with other things. I was once so scared that porno would be the only thing I would do well or make money at. Now, I was growing stronger and could face down my demons, my fears.

When Jeff and I got into an argument over me refusing to do a bukkake, our contract was over. He screamed at me over the phone and I was physically shaken, as usual. This time though, I could see that it was ridiculous. I was a grown woman, not a frightened little girl. Jeff told me that I owed him a JM bukkake—a scene where sixty or so men jerk off onto a girl's face.

The guys that perform in these scenes are basically off of the street. JM puts an ad in the *LA Weekly* with a phone number to call if you want to "get into the porn business." They call it the Bukkake Hotline, a recording on Jim's answering machine that tells the guys where to get tested and when to show up. The end result is a collection of the rankest porno dudes that are ever caught on video. They define a whole genre of creep that still has yet to compare to anything I've experienced inside or outside of porn.

I knew about the bukkake series and made it clear that it was something I would never do. It's a fine idea as long as I'm not the one doing it. Nothing could sway me to get ejaculated on by the gnarly minions. Jeff sort of respected my decision over the years and didn't pressure me until now. He'd mention it from time to time, and tried to make me feel guilty for being his only contract girl that refused to star in the bestselling series. I'd been in a couple of the bukkake films, but only frying cum and putting it in a blender. I handled all of the grey, green, brownish, yellow loads. The consistency of bukkake cum is of infected phlegm. The stench of the room ends up reeking of unclean bleach. Infected bleach.

I thought we had a working compromise when I helped create the lesbian bukkake. Instead of a roomful of hideous men, I settled for fifty-five porno girls squirting on my face. Some of them pissed and the others squeezed ice-cold douche water up their cunts and sprayed it onto my half-naked body.

When Jeff called me up screaming, he was also pissed about the lesbian bukkakes because I had been standing out of the scenes for the last few movies. I was supposed to be one of the girls squirting. I thought he knew about it already because he watched every scene in every movie before it went to duplication. I wasn't trying to deceive him. The girls in these scenes were also not from the usual talent pool. They often had highly contagious staph infections. Staph goes around like wildfire in the porn business, and it leaves scars if you have to get it cut out. I was afraid of having contact with any of these women. I made an executive decision and took myself out of the scenes. I couldn't explain anything to Jeff. He said, "You're doing a bukkake or you're fired!"

It was shameful to let this man make me sick with fear. I couldn't bring this kind of conflict into my life now that I shared it with Dave. I had to have some respect for myself, and for the one I loved. I had been dependent on my salary from JM Productions for three years straight. Having that steady income and reliability was somewhat institutionalizing for me. I would have to go back into the general talent pool again and compete for DPs with girls five and six years younger than me. My ego was on the brink of suicide. *Don't do this! Everyone will call you a crackhead. You're not young anymore. Porn has used you up and is done with you. JM is all you've got.* The voice of doom wouldn't quit. I did it anyway. On February 13th, 2007, I called Jeff at JM and resigned. The conversation was short and polite, but I was lightheaded from it.

At first my split with JM Productions felt like a breakup with a long-term boyfriend. There were bitter feelings of betrayal on both sides. But it didn't last long. They were just growing pains. Jeff and Sandy turned out to be supportive of my decision to end my role as their contract girl. The Girlvert, however, would live on. I would continue the series as a free agent. On that common interest, we all saw eye to eye and it made for an amicable new working relationship.

JM Productions was dismissed of all the obscenity charges in November of 2007. Only one movie was deemed obscene by the city of Phoenix, Arizona. *Gag Factor 18*, starring an old pal of mine, Christie. The jury found this one movie to be too violent.

During the whole film, Christie is saying to the camera how she wishes she could be just like Ashley Blue.

AS I passed the six-year anniversary of my first porno scene, I was becoming what the business refers to as a lifer. It would have bothered me if someone had prophesized it years ago. My original intention was to just do a couple scenes to get me to a rock concert. I have gone so far with it, farther than I'd ever imagined.

Beyond six, seven, eight years, I don't feel damaged from my experiences in porn. I am at ease knowing that there are hundreds of videos with me naked and getting fucked. I don't have a problem with watching people in the nude having sex. It is a natural urge. The sex business has taught me compassion and tolerance, more than I believe I would have understood in an otherwise typical Southern California life.

The drugs were damaging. Drugs are for the young, and I got it out of my system at a good time. Older people look so stupid when they are fucked up and trying to hold on to something as intangible as youth. Youth can never be brought back, swallowed back, held back, or sold. I still worry about Tyler. Last I heard, he's in The Program. He may be surrounded by bible-thumpers, but I am happy to know that he's still alive. If Dave hadn't come along, I don't think I would have stopped in time to have any part of a brain left.

My experiences in porn have been so unique, and I cherish them. I have an appreciation for even the darkest hours. They contain for me a truth of existence that nobody can take away. Now that the pimply, eighteen year old razor-rash herpes-asses and the shit, piss, vomit, blood, gonorrhea, and cum-farts are gone, I can truly say I pushed myself into unknown passages—my senses, my body, and my mind worked out in extremes that are forever my own. I am obsessed with reduction. The definition of reduction to me is a large, mysterious mixture made smaller, concentrated, stronger, and containing the finality of truth.

If it weren't for porn, I would have never met Dave Naz, my husband. Our relationship is the most important thing that's happened in all of my years in porn.

I don't exactly know what I'm doing now. I have been put out to pasture, in a way. I am a married lady and a writer. I still do work sometimes, sometimes for other people, but mostly for Dave. Life after a six-year full-time porno career is not full of appetizing offers. Many fading starlets turn to high-priced escorting to make the same amount of money as they did in porn.

I am not nearly as busy as I used to be. That's just the way it goes with the nature of instant fame—poof! And then it wanes. It is somebody else's turn to reign in the spotlight. I'm happy for the new faces I see in the business. In them, I see myself. I want to warn them of all the things people warned me about, the things I myself had ignored. Don't do too much coke, and pay your taxes! They will find out on their own.

I am painting and drawing again. Just when I thought all of my natural talent had vanished from prolonged drug use, I found that it was only lying dormant. Since I have a clear mind, the more traditional visual artist in me has returned. The hardest part is remembering how to be free from character. Navigating the unknown is scary. There is no acting on the canvas. It's a different type of freedom, of reality. I used to have the honor of pretending to be someone else. Ashley Blue's scenes were demanding, but not as challenging as facing a blank canvas.

Is pornography art? It's something that is appealing or repelling just by looking at it, so I will say yes. Can a regular girl end up being in the sex business overnight? In my experience, the answer is yes. But can a porno girl ever become anything else in life but a warm hole? I want to say yes. I am trying to incorporate these two colliding worlds into a harmonious union. The pornography I've done, and periodically continue to do, will never go away. It's with me beyond forever, even after I'm dead. It is something that I will be remembered for. Porn is just a part of life. Then you move on because there are other things out there. I'm twenty-nine years old and fading out of porn gracefully. It will not be all that I am remembered for. There are other contributions I want to make to the world besides inciting orgasms, though I'm honored for the ability to do that, too.

This experience is my truth. I own it. I bear witness to my own life. I value this more than anything.

5 Guy Cream Pie 2, 2002
Assault That Ass #2, 2002
Barely Legal #27, 2002
Don't Tell Mommy! 2, 2002
Down The Hatch #9, 2002
Fast Times At Deep Crack High Vol. 8, 2002
Girlvert #2, 2002
Grrl Power! 11, 2002
More Dirty Debutantes Volume 227, 2002
School Bus Girls, 2002
Service Animals 10, 2002
7 The Hard Way, 2002
Spring Chickens, 2002
Straight To The A #2, 2002
Throat Gaggers #3, 2002
Young & Anal 2, 2002
18 & Ready To Fuck #2, 2003
18 Yr Old All-Star Whores, 2003
Ass Cream Pies 4, 2003
American Gunk, 2003
Ass Lickers Vol. 1, 2003
Best Butt In The West 6, 2003
Bitches Behind Bars, 2003
Black Up That White Ass, 2003
Bootylicious 41: Swirl, 2003
Glazed And Confused, 2003
I Fucked My High School Teacher 3, 2003
I Like It Black And Deep In My Ass 2, 2003
Internal Combustion, 2003
Italian Sausage, 2003
Little White Slave Girls 4, 2003
Loose Morals 2, 2003
The Most Beautiful Girl In The World, 2003
Pull My Hair And Call Me Stupid, 2003
Attention Whores, 2004
Bust My Hole, 2004
Cock Attack, 2004
Cum Buckets!, 2004
Cum Dumpsters, 2004
Dyke Club, 2004
Gag Factor 15, 2004

Guttermouths 26, 2004
Lesbian Bukkake, 2004
Liquid Gold 9, 2004
Oral Hygiene 3, 2004
White Trash Whore 30, 2004
American Bukkake Twenty-Six, 2005
Bootylicious: Slaves for the Black Man, 2005
Irritable Bowel Syndrome, 2005
Meatholes #3, 2005
Piss Mops #2, 2005
Anal Full Nelson, 2006
The Cream Team, 2006
Greatest Cum Sluts Ever!, 2006
Jam Packed Assholes, 2006
Reverse Bukkake, 2006
She Swallows Black Dick #2, 2006
Skater Girl Fever, 2006
Barely Legal Christmas, 2007
Bondage & Perversion In L.A., 2007
Clusterfuck, 2007
Crack Addict 7, 2007
I've Been Sodomized 4, 2007
Throated #11, 2007
White Wife Black Cock #8, 2007
4 in the Pink, Four in the Stink #3, 2008
Anal Beach Buns, 2008
Circa '82, 2008
Gapeman 2, 2008
It's A Secretary Thing!, 2008
L.A. Lust, 2008
Perverse, 2008
Slave Dolls Volume 3, 2008
Strap Attack 8, 2008
Sugar Town, 2008
Young Hollywood, 2008
Digging In The Gapes Vol. 3, 2009
L.A. Girls Love Big Cocks, 2009
Cheating Housewives, 2009
Pretty Sloppy 2, 2009
Make Them Gag, 2010
Turbo Rock, 2010

Thank you, Dave, the best husband ever, for encouraging every word. I hardly deserve all that you do for me.

A Barnacle Book and Rare Bird Lit for all of the work put into this! Tyson & Alex Cornell, Joseph Mattson, Devri Richmond, Julia Callahan, Aaron Petrovich, Charles Day, Tamra Rolf, Emi Kamei, Nick Cimiluca, Ray Hartman and Scott Rothstein.

Mike and Sandy Norton of JM Productions for sharing *Girlvert* with me.

Jim Lane, Ed Powers, Jim South, Mr. Marcus, Hannah Harper and Alan Higbee for permission to be part of my story.

Dennis McGrath for his beautiful and brutal documentary photographs.

Max Hardcore for being so hardcore.

Belladonna for being an idol.

Special thanks to: *AVN Magazine*, Howard Stern & Howard Stern TV, Playboy TV, *Howard Stern Show*, Hustler, Anabolic, Evil Angel, Elegant Angel, Sin City, Kick Ass, Red Light District, Judge Mathis, Topco, Dr. Rigg, AIM Healthcare, Corey Smith, James Frey, Katie Arnoldi, Ben Greenman, HarperCollins, Rachel Resnick, Rachel Kramer Bussel, Adrian Colesberry, Tesco Vee, Coco de Mer, Flanny and all at Largo.

All of my friends for their kindness and support: Dodd Bates, Lillian & Carlos Batts, Adrianna Suplick, Sarah Moraga, Eric Kroll, Ruth Waytz, Chris Cooper, Steve Diet Goedde, Cynthia Patterson, Victor & Susan Lightworship, Peter Kavadlo, Dawn Veronica Ciarlotta, Sarah Froelich, Don McCarthy, John Griffin, Josh Haden, Samantha Tradelius, Karry Brown, Michelle Salamaca, Valerie Beck, Ira Levine, Nina Hartley, Octavio Arizala, Hollie Stevens, Michael Daniels, David Hurles, Dian Hanson, Scott Fayner, Rich Brigham, Harold Loren, Enrique Machuca, Derek Harvie, Paul & Amanda Fishbein, Heidi Calvert, Rick Castro, Christopher Daniel Zeischegg, Eon McKai, Stacie & Bill Stevenson, Lincoln Camm, and Violet Blue.

My extended family. My mom especially. And my sister, Dawn. The Hernandez family. And the Smalls.

All fellow performers and directors that have enriched my life in their own unique ways: Missy Monroe, Cherry Poppens, Audrey Hollander, Johnny Thrust, Weed, Genesis Skye, Naughtia Sinn, Steven French, Gia Jordan, Brandon Iron, Hollie Stevens, Wesley Pipes, Joey Silvera, Nautica Thorn, Christie Lee, Brian Pumper, Katrina Kraven, Hershel Savage, Amber Wild, Dirty Harry, Otto Bauer, Brijaye Love, Desire Moore, Jasmine Lynn, Misti Mendez, Mark Davis, Billy Glide, Mark Ashley, Jay Ashley, Byron Long, Mike John, Tyla Wynn, Julie Night, Alec Knight, Lexi Love, Jake Malone, Eric Swiss, Kaci Starr, Scott Lyons, Mr. Pete, Arnold Schwartzenpecker, Veronica Jett, Buster Goode, Sledgehammer, Jiz Lee, Alex Devine, Ava Divine, Chelsea Rae, Alex Sanders, Julius Ceazher, Gorgus Drae, Michelle Avanti, Carly Parker, Cindy Crawford, Venus, Kat, Haley Scott, Dominique Swift, Rick Masters, Jenner, Skeeter & Brigette Kerkove, Ron Jeremy, Brett Rockman, Nikki Nite, Danni Woodward, Gia Paloma, Nadia Rio, Nadia Styles, Gauge, Taylor Mother-Fuckin' Rain, Arianna Jolie, Ken Wilkes, Colonel Rob, R. Dog, Catalina, Aurora Snow, Ginger Lynn, Sarah Shevon, Kristina Rose, Rio Mariah, Tiger, Sapphire Rae, Khan Tusion, David Stanley, Ben English, Jonni Darkko, and Trent Tesoro.

ABOUT THE AUTHOR

ORIANA SMALL is a writer and visual artist from Southern California. As Ashley Blue, she appeared in over 300 adult films, including the infamous *Girlvert* series (JM Productions), directed seventeen adult film features, co-hosted Playboy TV's *Night Calls Hotline*, and has won numerous adult film industry awards, including AVN's Female Performer of the Year in 2004 and Best Supporting Actress in 2005. She lives and works with her husband, photographer Dave Naz, and her cat and dog in the Hollywood Hills.